About the authors

Kenneth King is Professor of International and Comparative Education and Director of the Centre of African Studies, University of Edinburgh. He is the author or editor of several books , including *Aid and Education* and *Changing International Aid to Education* (edited with Lene Buchert).

Simon McGrath has been a research fellow at the Centre of African Studies, and became Research Director at the Human Sciences Research Council in Pretoria, South Africa in October 2002. Both authors have published extensively in African Studies and International Comparative Education and have been researching development cooperation for a number of years.

KENNETH KING | SIMON McGRATH

Knowledge for development?

Comparing British, Japanese, Swedish and World Bank aid

HSRC Press
CAPE TOWN

Zed Books
LONDON · NEW YORK

Knowledge for Development? Comparing British, Japanese, Swedish and World Bank aid was first published by Zed Books Ltd, 7 Cynthia Street, London N1 9JF, UK and Room 400, 175 Fifth Avenue, New York, NY 10010, USA in 2004.

www.zedbooks.co.uk

Published in South Africa by HSRC Press, Private Bag X9182, Cape Town, 8000, South Africa.

www.hsrcpublishers.ac.za

Cover designed by Andrew Corbett
Set in Monotype Dante and Gill Sans Heavy by Ewan Smith, London
Printed and bound in the United Kingdom by Biddles Ltd,
www.biddles.co.uk

Distributed in the USA exclusively by Palgrave Macmillan, a division of St Martin's Press, LLC, 175 Fifth Avenue, New York, NY 10010.

A catalogue record for this book is available from the British Library
Library of Congress cataloging-in-publication data: available

ISBN 1 84277 324 0 cased
ISBN 1 84277 325 9 limp
South Africa ISBN 0 7969 2058 3

Contents

Acknowledgements

This book arises out of a three-year research project funded under the British Economic and Social Research Council's Future Governance Programme between 1999 and 2002. Our gratitude goes to the ESRC and to Professor Ed Page, the Programme Director.

Our research could not have succeeded without the assistance of the large number of development co-operation agency staff who gave time to answer our questions. Particular thanks must go to a smaller number of staff who facilitated our visits to their organisations. In Sida, Ingemar Gustafsson supported visits to Stockholm and organised a one-day seminar to discuss our work and related issues. Ingemar also presented at our mid-term seminar. In the World Bank, Catherine Gwin organised a seminar at which we presented to a number of World Bank staff. Also in the Bank, Erik Johnson arranged for Kenneth King to attend the second Global Development Network Conference in Tokyo in 2000. Thanks go also to Steve Denning for attending our mid-term seminar and to David Ellerman for making the journey to Edinburgh for the annual African Studies Conference in 2002. David Court was one of our referees for the original application and also helped to arrange office space for us in the Bank on more than one occasion. In DFID, Charles Clift was an invaluable contact and another presenter at our mid-term seminar. In JICA, Keiichi Kato invited Kenneth King to Tokyo, and he himself came to Bonn to present in the mid-term seminar. Masaei Matsunsaga organised a seminar in JICA Headquarters at the end of the project and was a regular resource for knowledge and contacts.

The mid-term seminar was hosted in Bonn in April 2001 by Wolfgang Gmelin and the German Foundation for International Development (DSE). We benefited both from Wolfgang's intellectual rigour and from his magnificent hospitality. Thanks go to him and also DSE for their production and dissemination of a volume of proceedings arising from the seminar.

More generally, we profited from meetings arranged by the online community on Knowledge Management for International Development Organisations, in Brighton and in The Hague. Equally, Kenneth King gained from the Knowledge through Development conference organised by Michel Carton in Geneva in November 2002.

Our thanks go also to the graduate students of both the Centre of African Studies and the Faculty of Education, University of Edinburgh, several of whom commented on papers and draft chapters of this book, as well as to the large number of agency staff and academics who also commented on preliminary findings.

We owe, finally, a great debt to our families for tolerating our absences, for interacting critically with our endeavours, and for accommodating the seemingly endless streams of documentation that came back from Tokyo, Stockholm, London and Washington.

Kenneth King and Simon McGrath,
Edinburgh and Pretoria

Abbreviations and acronyms

AIDA	Accessible Information on Development Activities
AVU	African Virtual University (World Bank)
CDF	Comprehensive Development Framework (World Bank)
CIDA	Canadian International Development Agency
CSP	Country Strategy Paper (DFID)
DAC	Development Assistance Committee (OECD)
Danida	Danish International Development Agency (now part of the Ministry of Foreign Affairs)
DFID	Department for International Development (UK)
ECDPM	European Centre for Development Policy Management
EDI	Economic Development Institute (now WBI) (World Bank)
EGDI	Expert Group on Development Issues (Sweden)
ELDIS	Electronic Library for Development Information Services (UK)
EPA	Economic Planning Agency (Japan)
ESCOR	Economic and Social Committee on Research (DFID – now Committee for Social Science Research
ESRC	Economic and Social Research Council (UK)
ESW	Economic and Sector Work (World Bank)
FASID	Foundation for Advanced Studies on International Development (Japan)
GDLN	Global Development Learning Network (World Bank)
GDN	Global Development Network (World Bank)
GDNet	formerly the quasi-independent website of the GDN, funded by DFID – now more formally subsumed in the larger structure
GKP	Global Knowledge Partnership (World Bank)
GTZ	German agency for technical cooperation
id21	Information on Development for the 21st century (UK)
IDE	Institute for Developing Economies (Japan)
IDML	International Development Mark-up Language
IDRC	International Development Research Centre (Canada)
IDTs	International Development Targets (now called Millennium Development Goals
IFIC	Institute for International Cooperation (JICA)
IK	Indigenous Knowledge
ILO	International Labour Office
IMF	International Monetary Fund

InfoDev	Information for Development Programme (World Bank)
ISP	Institutional Strategy Paper (DFID)
JBIC	Japan Bank for International Cooperation
JICA	Japan International Cooperation Agency
J-Net	JICA Network (for e-learning)
JOCV	Japanese Overseas Cooperation Volunteers Programme (JICA)
KIS	Knowledge and Information Services Department (DFID)
KM	Knowledge management
KPU	Knowledge Policy Unit (DFID)
MAFF	Ministry of Agriculture, Forestry and Fisheries (Japan)
MENA	Middle East and North Africa Regional Vice Presidency (World Bank)
METI	Ministry of Economy, Trade and Industry (Japan)
MOF	Ministry of Finance (Japan)
MOFA	Ministry of Foreign Affairs (Japan)
NDS	New Development Strategy (Japan)
NIB	Agency for International Assistance (precursor to Sida)
NPO	National Programme Officer (Sida)
ODA	Official Development Assistance
ODA	Overseas Development Administration (precursor to DFID)
OECD	Organisation for Economic Cooperation and Development
OED	Operations Evaluation Division (World Bank)
PRA	Participatory Rural Appraisal/Participatory Rapid Appraisal
PRISM	Project Reporting and Information System Management (DFID)
PRSP	Poverty Reduction Strategy Paper
PTTC	Project-type technical cooperation (JICA)
RRV	National Audit Office (Sweden)
SAREC	Swedish Agency for Research Cooperation with Developing Countries (now part of Sida)
SIDA	Swedish International Development Agency (precursor to Sida)
Sida	Swedish International Development Cooperation Agency
SOVP	Senior Overseas Volunteer Programme (JICA)
SWAP	Sector-wide Approach
TICAD	Tokyo International Conference(s) on African Development
TSP	Target Strategy Paper (DFID)
UNDP	United Nations Development Programme
UNICEF	United Nations Children's Fund

UPE	Universal Primary Education
USAID	United States Agency for International Development
WBI	World Bank Institute
WDR	World Development Report (World Bank)
WID	Women in Development
WorLD	World Links for Development (World Bank)
WSSD	World Summit for Sustainable Development

ONE
Researching knowledge-based aid

Setting the scene

Since 1996 there has been a remarkable growth within development co-operation agencies of interest in knowledge-based aid. Most agencies have launched projects that seek to make their work better grounded in the knowledge that they already possess within their organisations and to explore more effective ways of acquiring external knowledge related to development. At the same time, there has also been a growth in emphasis on more effectively disseminating this knowledge – to other agencies, to their own civil societies, to their partners in the South, and to the billions of poor people who are the stated beneficiaries of the whole intertwined aid and development project. Equally, there has been a revisiting of old notions that the poor are poor in large part because of their lack of appropriate knowledge. To the old account, expressed in many colonial and missionary texts, are added the new dimensions of globalisation (as the force shaping the knowledge needed) and information and communications technologies (ICTs – as an important new set of tools in the dissemination of this knowledge).

This book is the first that seeks to examine this phenomenon as a result of academic research in a series of agencies.[1] It does so through a detailed analysis of what the new knowledge-based aid means at the level of discourse and practice in four leading development co-operation agencies.

In so doing, we are mindful that this knowledge-based aid contains a language that suggests that the lessons of past aid and development mistakes have been learned and that a new ethics of aid is an important aspect of the language of the new approach. However, we are also aware of both the continuing critiques of aid practices that suggest that there is much more business-as-usual than transformation, and the continued questioning of the theoretical underpinnings and practical impacts of aid and development.

In writing this book, we inevitably had to engage with the literatures on aid and development, and have sought to add to these. Accounts of agency policy and practice tend to polarise between 'official versions' (e.g. Kapur et al. 1997) and polemical attacks (e.g. Hancock 1989), and have been heavily focused on the multilateral agencies. Some, however, have more successfully attempted critical engagement, through an analysis that uses national case studies of the relationship between stated policy and its operationalisation (e.g. Mosley, Harrigan and Toye 1991), through a sensitive and reflective negotiation of access to a single agency in a single sector (e.g. Jones 1992), or through an analysis of the nature of development discourses and their playing out in a national context (e.g. Ferguson 1994). Whilst Crewe and Harrison (1998) talk of an ethnography of aid, even their work does little to get inside bilateral or multilateral agencies. Valuable though their approach is, their case studies are essentially of a large NGO (with real insider insights, as one of them worked for this NGO) and of a project of a multilateral agency. This present book is an unusual attempt (cf. King 1991) to look in depth across a group of bilateral and multilateral agencies in a way that allows for critical dialogue with the agencies. It is also an attempt to produce a sociological reading that moves between the realms of text and practice.

Agency accounts of aid are typically ahistorical. In their rush to develop new ideas and to gloss over past failures, agencies have tended to construct a collective amnesia about the past. It is inevitable, therefore, that current aid discourse recreates many elements of this past without recognising them. One of our concerns in this book will be to provide some historical depth. It is particularly important that we explore where knowledge-based aid has come from. We shall preview two strands of this context here before returning to them in some depth in the next two chapters.

Knowledge-based aid is only a small part of the broader changes that have taken place in development co-operation since the fall of the Berlin Wall. The World Conferences of the 1990s, the growing importance of the Development Assistance Committee (DAC) of the Organisation for Economic Co-operation and Development (OECD) and its promulgation of six International Development Targets, and a new architecture of donor co-ordination mechanisms have furthered a broader ideological convergence of agencies.[2]

The new aid agenda brings with it new knowledge needs. However, it also brings a new importance for knowledge as a major theme of development and co-operation. The new focus draws heavily on wider arguments about the centrality of knowledge to economic success and about the connective power of new ICTs. Through the interweaving of these accounts in a literature and practice of knowledge management, agencies have begun to look at internal patterns of knowledge use as a key response to the critique of their effectiveness. At the external level, the term 'knowledge sharing' has become attractive as a way of distancing agencies from the widespread critique of conditionalities, while at the same time seeking to ensure that agency positions have influence over Southern countries' policies. Concurrently, arguments about the importance of knowledge economies have been directly translated into the development context to argue that knowledge is the key determinant of development (World Bank 2002a).

Research questions

However, this agency fascination with knowledge is in need of careful questioning. What does the emergence of knowledge-based aid amount to in practice? What explains its emergence? Why do agency approaches differ and how significant is this? Whose knowledge and whose visions of development are prioritised and whose marginalised? Does knowledge-based aid make for more efficient and effective agencies? Does knowledge-based aid make for more efficient and effective aid? This book seeks to address these questions.

As knowledge-based aid develops further it will also be important to research its impacts on the supposed beneficiaries in the South who are to be helped out of poverty through its operations. However, this is beyond the scope of our study.

A new way of researching; a new way of working

Almost at the very moment that the 1998-99 World Development Report on *Knowledge for Development* (World Bank 1998a) (see chapters 3 and 4 of this book) was published, the British Economic and Social Research Council (ESRC) announced a new research programme, 'Future Governance', that would seek to develop new knowledge about policy processes internationally. One of its particular interests was in the way that policy ideas spread across national boundaries. In the Centre of African Studies at the University of Edinburgh we were coming to the end of a research grant and were thinking of new proposals. One of these was for a comparative study of a set of development co-operation agencies. The almost simultaneous appearance of the World Development Report and the ESRC programme led us to rework our idea somewhat. Not really yet aware of how the knowledge interests of the World Bank were beginning to spread across the bilateral community, we decided to include the knowledge-for-development focus within our overall proposal to examine what appeared to be the emergence of new ways of working amongst development co-operation agencies. It was thus, perhaps through serendipity, that we embarked on a research project that quickly became primarily focused on the discourse and practice of knowledge-based aid (King 2000).

Thus, from a very broad concern with changes in agency discourse and practice, it was through subsequent research on agencies that we came to a narrower focus on the ways in which knowledge had become an important element of this discourse and practice. In this sense, the focus of our theoretical and empirical explorations emerges primarily from its grounding in the data, although the importance of the focus could have been derived from an extrapolation of trends external to development co-operation agencies, given the emergence of accounts of knowledge economies and knowledge management.

For the purpose of the funding application, we had to select a set of agencies in order to explore in detail how the new ways of working were emerging, if that was indeed the case. Whilst both of us had knowledge of, and working relations with, a number of agencies,[3] we did not have the current and detailed knowledge to select those agencies that would be the most interesting case studies of the new approach to aid. Nonetheless, based on the knowledge that we did have, and the practicalities of running a research project, we selected four case-study agencies. From the multilaterals, we decided to select only the World Bank, although we were very aware of the growing importance of the European Union as a major provider of official development assistance (ODA). The Bank was not only the biggest player in development co-operation but also often the trendsetter, including in knowledge-for-development. We decided on the British Department for International Development (DFID), both as an agency with which we had good contacts and as one that was undergoing a process of rapid transformation (including a name change) under the new British government. We selected the Swedish International Development Co-operation Agency (Sida) as Sweden appeared to be a leader in thinking and practice about key trends in development co-operation such as sector-wide approaches and nationally led development partnerships. Our fourth case study was the Japan International Co-operation Agency (JICA). Japan had been the largest bilateral donor throughout the 1990s in absolute terms. More importantly, however, JICA was the one major agency that came from outside the West. Thus, it offered the possibility of examining practices and discourses that emerged from a radically different cultural context.

A first phase of interviews showed that issues about knowledge and development did have resonance for all four agencies. It also importantly indicated some major divergences as well as convergences of language and activities. Crucially, this phase of research began a process of dialogue with the agencies rather than traditional data-gathering. Thus we found ourselves invited to a number of agency-oriented fora to participate in discussions about knowledge and development, and to contribute to agency development of their policies and programmes in these areas. As a result, our research began to move early on from mere observation into active participation in the construction of the field we were studying.

Knowledge theory and knowledge research

It is important to consider the effect that immersion in the literature on knowledge had for our researching of knowledge practices and discourses. Coming from a comparative education perspective, much of the current knowledge debate serves to reinforce the central importance of context within that discipline. The British pioneer of comparative education, Michael Sadler, writing more than a century ago, emphasised the danger of decontextualising knowledge through careless borrowing from other experiences:

> We cannot wander at pleasure among the educational systems of the world, like a child strolling through a garden, and pick off a flower from one bush and some leaves from another, and then expect that if we stick what we have gathered into the soil at home, we shall have a living plant. (Sadler 1979 [1900]: 49)

At the end of the twentieth century, similar sentiments were to be expressed by Joe Stiglitz, then Chief Economist of the World Bank, two years prior to receiving a Nobel Prize for his work on knowledge and information: 'The overwhelming variety and complexity of human societies requires the localisation of knowledge' (Stiglitz 2000 [1999]: 7).

Thus, knowledge theory reinforced our professional training in stressing the importance of context. Comparative work faces the challenge of paying more than lip service to this notion. Of crucial importance here is the extent to which it is possible to understand multiple contexts, particularly within the constraints of a time-limited research project. In our other disciplinary home of African Studies, much of the debate in this regard centres on the issue of language. As Mbembe puts it: 'It should be noted, as far as fieldwork is concerned, that there is less and less. Knowledge of local languages, vital to any theoretical and philosophical understanding, is deemed unnecessary' (Mbembe 2001: 7). Our limitations in this regard must be noted. Whilst it can be argued that English is the language of development, particularly knowledge-for-development, it is clear that our lack of competence in Japanese or Swedish had a double impact on our research. First, it made inaccessible those parts of the 'archive' of Sida and JICA written in their national languages. Second, it limited the extent to which we could claim to understand the culturally embedded meanings behind texts and practices. None the less, the experiences of this project convince us of the worth of attempting such research. This points to the importance of acknowledging such limitations and seeking to address them honestly and openly. It became particularly important to check meanings with agency staff, academics and students from Japan and Sweden, to seek to understand perceptions of how discourses and practices were culturally embedded, and to explore with the assistance of colleagues some of what remained untranslated amongst agency documents.

There are a number of other elements of knowledge (and learning) theory that also have implications for research such as this. First, this theory emphasises the networked, social and distributed nature of knowledge. Second, work on the difference between tacit and codified knowledge points to both the importance of the former, and the difficulty of accessing it.[4] Third, Argyris and Schön's (1978) work on organisational learning has made the important distinction between 'espoused theory', that to which an organisation is officially committed, and 'theory-in-use', that which appears to be manifested in its practices.

These point to the need to get beyond the conventional case-study blend of analysing official documents and backing this up with a series of interviews with key informants within the organisations. Rather, it raises the challenge of focusing clearly on where knowledge is inscribed in policies and practices, and exploring this further through the virtual, team-based and networked nature of the contemporary organisation. Repeat interviews, many of them with more than one informant and with different combinations of informants, often reflected the ways in which staff chose to organise and present themselves for interactions, but also shed valuable light on the fragmented and sometimes contradictory nature of discourses and practices. Meeting some of the same agency staff in interviews, at workshops within their agency and at the inter-agency level, and more informally in conferences, corridors and canteens enriched this process.

Argyris and Schön's work also pointed to the importance of seeing large organisations such as these as having an internal architecture, which makes the bridge between a study of the organisation-as-monolith and the organisation-as-individuals. Grounded in organisational theory as well as learning theory, their account highlights the nature of organisations as a collection of departmental or divisional fiefdoms, increasingly overlaid by a series of cross-departmental structures that often operate with close reference back to the dominant departmental model. Thus it was imperative to examine agencies also at the level of some of these structures. This took us into a variety of departments and units and into mini case studies of particular knowledge projects. Foucault (1972) has already popularised the notion of an 'archaeology of knowledge' in his study of disciplinary discourses. However, we wish to re-use the notion in a somewhat different way, which relates our study of knowledge to some of the practices of the field archaeologist. Part of the challenge for the archaeologist is to understand how the site relates to its broader context, both spatially and theoretically. The site will often be excavated through identification of potentially significant locations within it, where a series of test pits and trenches will be dug; some of these will prove unrewarding and will be quickly abandoned. This is similar to our approach. The overall picture, significance and context were essential, but we also chose to explore each individual agency through a focus on what appeared to be significant projects, activities and departments. These were each specific to the agency in question. This was a comparative project at the level of overall methodology and research questions, not at the narrow level of common and rigid research tools and interview schedules.

Key social theory accounts of knowledge have highlighted the close relationship between knowledge and power. This was an issue for the research project. It was important to seek to maintain access to what are powerful agencies and to seek to understand their motivations and practices in a sensitive way. However, it would be impossible to ignore the depth and breadth of the critique of the World Bank in particular, and aid in general. The sheer scale of criticisms of the Bank over more than fifty years and the degree of anger and hurt it has caused did influence how the Bank's policies and practices were interpreted. Nonetheless, it was also important to avoid an approach in which the power of agencies was overstated and initiative denied to Southern actors. Moreover, this needed to be done within a project in which funding was for trips to agency headquarters not to the South.

Perhaps the most challenging aspect of the project was how to research the virtual life of the modern development co-operation agency. Much of the practice and theory-in-use of agencies is now positioned on intranets and in discussion groups and e-mails. Indeed, these processes have accelerated as our research has continued. Some of this was revealed to us, or was in the public domain, in the case of some discussion groups, but much of it is necessarily hidden. One strategy we used for accessing such virtual knowledge second-hand was a series of life history interviews with agency staff, in which we asked them to say how their everyday practices within their organisations had changed over time. This is necessarily a partial and problematic approach.

Researching documents in a digital world

Much of the data that has been collected and analysed is documentary. However, it is important to note some of the differences in the process of collecting and analysing such texts as compared to a decade earlier when Kenneth King (1991) was writing *Aid and Education in the Developing World*. First, the growth of desktop publishing and the internet have combined with agency concerns about greater transparency, or better public relations, to bring about a step change in the number of documents that are now produced by agencies.

Second, the internet has also led to the easier availability of much of this literature. What was once 'grey literature' that had to be physically acquired, often through the good offices of an agency colleague, and which not too long ago would simply not have been available for more than consultation, is now available in huge quantities without leaving one's own desk.

Third, this shifts the challenge of research much more from collection to selection and means that there is far more to be analysed than previously.

Fourth, the emergence of organisational intranets has led to decisions having to be taken about which documents should be in the public domain and which should not. This often appears to be done rather unsystematically but does force the researcher to seek the reasons behind such decisions. From the limited access that we did get to intranets it appeared that decisions were more likely to be based on innocent motivations rather than a desire to keep things hidden. Bilateral agency disclosure policies are largely determined outwith the agency by overall government policies. Thus, DFID's policies and practices reflect the partial acceptance of freedom of information by the current British government, and its fascination with electronic governance. During the project, JICA was forced to respond to a radical opening up of Japanese government documentation to public scrutiny. Sida has been subject to full public access to its documents since 1988. The requirement to disclose more could be expected to have had an impact on what is said in documents, but this is not amenable to easy analysis, although some interviews did point in this direction.

Fifth, researching agencies' websites has a greater fluidity than traditional archive or library work. Over the life of the project a number of documents disappeared from websites or had their addresses changed. The changing patterns of presence and absence of documents and topics on websites and of overall site architecture are themselves indicators of changes in both discourse and practice. A good example of this is the treatment of the theme of knowledge on the World Bank's site. This went through a number of phases as we studied the Bank. At times the Bank's concern with knowledge was evidenced by a clear link from the organisational home page. On other occasions, however, it was through having pages bookmarked that a long trawl through sub-menus across a series of pages was avoided. The range of 'knowledge projects' accessible through the main knowledge page also shifted over time. Some never featured whilst other established projects appeared or disappeared.

Naturally, the central methodological issues of textual analysis remain. In keeping with the emphasis on context earlier in this chapter, we favour a position in which text and context are both analysed in a critical way. Whilst there are merits in the post-modernist position that texts cannot be understood in an absolute sense, a careful reading of texts in conjunction with their contexts of production does permit a plausible account of the meaning of a text in which both the text and the reader are historically and culturally located. In talking of contexts, it is worth highlighting the historical dimension. As Watson (1998) has argued, comparative education has a duty to contest the atemporality of much of current culture and research. It was important for our research to keep in mind that knowledge had always been part of the business of agencies. Equally we needed to remember that many of the allegedly new ways of working (such as sectoral programmes) had been tried before. Moreover, we believed that individuals', organisations' and communities' perceptions of what was occurring with knowledge-based aid were deeply shaped by their conscious and unconscious readings of the past.

Interviewing agency staff

Knowledge-based aid both resides within certain projects and hence locations in an agency, and infuses (or fails to infuse) the whole range of agency activities and departments. This needed to be reflected in interviews, of which there were more than 250. Moreover, the challenge of researching four agencies meant that fieldwork was conducted in short bursts, with repeated visits to each agency over the three years of the project. Furthermore, in order to allow for additional visits off the project budget, short trips were often tied to other meetings to which the researchers had been invited. We shall return to this later.

Sampling was necessarily a mixture of the purposive and opportunistic. Whilst we had a small group of key informants who had agreed to assist the research within their own agency, other interviews had to depend on whether the particular individuals identified were available at the times we were visiting the agency. For each visit we had a list of people that we wished to interview, but this was revised as our interviews progressed. Here it is worth pointing out the importance, in research of this kind, of attempting a very rapid initial analysis of interview data. Comparative research across agencies makes fieldwork very intensive, and it is imperative to be able to abandon certain lines of inquiry and to embrace others based on an awareness of what has been said in the interviews during a visit.

Agency interests in knowledge were increasingly dynamic during the period of research. This meant that certain issues were important for agency staff at specific moments. Equally, the horizons of sectoral and country-focused staff were strongly shaped by new initiatives and by important deadlines. One knowledge-related example can give a flavour of this. In June 2001, World Bank staff working on knowledge projects were very aware of an internal evaluation of their work that was to lead to a new proposal to the Board about the future of knowledge activities. It was into this context that we entered when visiting the Bank. The point here is that in such a research context it is crucial that researchers be aware of what is uppermost in the minds of those they are seeking to interview. Having such an awareness had clear implications for the nature of interviews. Whilst they could be described as semi-structured, in the time-honoured way of much qualitative research, this would not do justice to the often dialogic nature of the intervention. Here was an area that was both new to the agency and of which few outsiders had any knowledge. We were thus unusual visitors who also could be sources of knowledge. Many, though by no means all, interviews had more of a sense of conversation and a sharing of knowledge. Given the critique that we were developing of much agency practice as knowledge extraction from the developing world, it was also desirable on ethical grounds that our work should avoid the same criticism as far as was possible. Moreover, this approach could also be justified epistemologically as part of a broader concern to make explicit the standpoints of researchers as well as researched.

Whilst it was crucial to reach those in charge of the major knowledge projects within the agencies – the 'knowledge champions', as some of the knowledge literature would term them – it was also important to explore the perception of these projects from elsewhere in the agencies – those agency staff termed by others as 'footsoldiers'. One approach to this was to interview members of staff involved in other major agency initiatives, in order to examine whether there had been any influence on these from the knowledge projects. Another way that we approached this was to go to staff in the sectoral and country departments of agencies involved in the everyday activities of development co-operation. The aim here was to see what, if any, of the knowledge discourses and practices had filtered down to the operational staff. In particular, we were concerned to see what difference, if any, had been made to their everyday practices.

From our interviewing, and some internal agency documents, it became clear to us that there was widespread concern about the exclusion of field-based agency staff from the knowledge revolution. There was no funding within our proposal to allow for field visits. Nonetheless, a number of field staff were contacted either when we were in the field ourselves through other activities or when we encountered them at non-project-related meetings.

As noted earlier, we were aware of the importance of understanding the longer history of agencies' knowledge discourses and practices (King 1986). These did not simply spring from the void in the late 1990s but existed in other forms and under other names previously. It was here that the small number of life history interviews with agency staff, mentioned previously, played an important role (King 2002).[5]

The recurrent nature of interviewing was very valuable. Some particularly valuable informants were interviewed six or more times. The multiplicity of interviews allowed for the expansion and clarification of points but, more crucially, allowed for some sense of temporal dynamics to be introduced into the interview data.

The value of joint interviews was not identified in our original proposal. However, given that about 40 of our 250 interviews were with two or more agency staff, it is worth reflecting a little on this type of interview. Such combinations were at the suggestion of agency staff. Sometimes the rationale was that it would be valuable for a more junior colleague to be present for the discussion, as a way of accessing the tacit knowledge of their colleague and the researcher(s). However, on a number of occasions such interviews were with staff from different units who found themselves having intersecting interests in knowledge-based aid. Thus it appeared that the joint interview was designed to allow for the exploration on the agency side of some of the dynamics of working together, including using the interview as a way of establishing certain positions. This was of value to the research as it opened up new dimensions for analysis, particularly when certain individuals appeared in more than one such interview, alongside different colleagues. Without attempting to organise focus groups of busy agency staff, such joint interviews did provide some insights into organisational architecture and the range of internal opinions and their interplay. This experience highlights the importance of flexible research design as opposed to the current fascination with over-specification before the research has begun.

Some interviews were joint in the different sense of both researchers being present. This accounted for about 50 interviews. In these cases, we informally divided up the areas we would cover and combined our notes after discussion. Having two interviewers present in the field was important in first visits to some agencies for securing access for the more junior researcher. However, it also proved valuable in allowing a greater coverage in one trip and permitting a dialogue at the time about what was being found and priorities for the rest of the trip. What impact the presence of two interviewers had on interviews is less apparent but also worth considering.

Some interviews were invaluable in assisting the documentary analysis. A number of interviewees were identified because of their key participation in the drafting of important agency documents, and these interviews allowed greater insight into the processes and rationales that lay behind reports such as the 1998–99 World Development Report.

Although we conducted more than 250 interviews, the texts of these are not immediately obvious in what follows. A small number of staff were reluctant to be 'on the record', and we have taken the decision, with almost no exceptions, not to quote directly from any of the interviews. Rather, what was said in the interviews strongly informs what we write, even though the majority of quotations are taken from documentary sources.

Virtual participant observation

The emergence of a knowledge focus in agencies is inextricably linked to the development of new information and communications technologies (ICTs), most notably e-mail and the world wide web. It is not surprising, therefore, that some of the debate about knowledge should have taken place through the medium of on-line discussion groups. The World Bank, sometimes with external partners such as Panos, has conducted a number of e-mail-based consultations, including on the 1998–99 World Development Report. Major knowledge projects, such as the Global Knowledge Partnership, the Global Development Network, the International Development Mark-up Language Initiative and the Development Gateway (see chapters 3 and 4) have also used this as an important part of their planning activities. DFID also had an electronic consultation for the information and knowledge sections of its 2000 White Paper, which we discuss in chapter 5.

Such discussions thus seemed a potentially rich source of data for our project, and both of us participated in a number of them. However, the overall benefits in research terms did not compensate for the time expended on this activity. None of the discussions we participated in had a heavy involvement of agency staff. Rather, discussions were dominated by NGO staff and consultants. Sometimes, interventions read more like advertising for the individual or the organisation rather than useful contributions to the discussion.[6] Thus, as a way of accessing agency thinking directly, many of the discussions were of little value. Nonetheless, some moderators did suggest that there were a number of agency staff members lurking in such discussions. This highlights one of the challenges of using such groups for data collection: that participation can be hidden. What emerges in data collection terms is the negative message that such groups are not seen as valuable by most agency staff. This was confirmed in a number of interviews. Staff did not see such groups as an efficient way of gathering knowledge. Instead, many saw such discussions as a public relations exercise designed to show that the agency was interested in outside opinions. However, staff had their own ways of accessing knowledge and opinions that they considered to be more effective.

This is not to say that on-line discussion groups are not a useful field for research. There has been valuable work done already on such groups at the sociological and methodological levels (Paccagnella 1997; Moran 1999). However, for this study of knowledge-based aid they were of surprisingly little relevance.

Research as participation

A little of what we did under the project could be seen as falling under the traditional notion of participant observation. In the World Bank, for instance, it was possible to get passes that allowed relatively unlimited access to buildings. We were given office space to work from and we were free to visit canteens unaccompanied. Thus it was possible to have a range of interactions with staff, including participation in elements of the social life of the organisation, such as the monthly Irish lunch or watching games from the World Cup finals. In this way a deeper sense of the organisation could be developed.

We have already noted that the practice of the research often moved into dialogue. This was also illustrated by a number of invitations to present our views about elements of knowledge-based aid in agency seminars and workshops, and requests to provide commentary on certain policy documents and initiatives, including one formal consultancy.

Participation in seminars on knowledge played an important dual role of providing a very rich source of data about agency thinking and internal interactions, as well as allowing for feedback on our provisional analyses.

However, it was through mainly non-project activities that the best ethnographic sense of agencies emerged and where we came closest to taking on the guise of participant observers. This is important to note, for discussions of methodology typically give the impression that the research project is the only point at which the researcher interacts with the field of study. This was not the case with us, and it was in our other work that much of importance emerged.

As members of the secretariat of the Working Group for International Co-operation in Skills Development, we both had the opportunity once a year during the project to spend time at meetings that brought together staff from a range of agencies, including those that we were researching. As participants in these meetings, we got a broader insight into trends in agency thinking. These meetings are a good example of inter-agency knowledge sharing and provided much food for reflection. However, it could be argued that the informal interactions with agency staff, particularly from our case-study agencies, were equally valuable. Although it was not commissioned by one of our four case-study agencies, our involvement in an evaluation of Danish assistance to skills development also gave valuable practical insights into the knowledge activities of agencies (Ministry of Foreign Affairs, Danida 2002).

This concern to link the research project to our broader practice was an important strength of our work, allowing multiple spaces for interaction with agency staff and varied insights into their worlds of work. We also made use of other points of potential connection with the project. Kenneth King is editor of the bi-annual newsletter, *Norrag News*,[7] which has for seventeen years provided commentary on development co-operation trends, and which offers a forum for researchers, practitioners and policymakers to interact in print. Two of the issues during the project's lifespan were focused on knowledge-based aid. These provided opportunities to publicise the research, to get further insights from staff of the case-study agencies, and to link these to broader debates about knowledge and development. We also focused one of the annual African Studies Conferences in Edinburgh on development co-operation more generally (Hayman *et al.* 2003). Under Kenneth King's convenorship, the 2001 Oxford Conference on Education and Development had a strong knowledge and development focus.[8] During the life of the project, Simon McGrath took over the editorship of the OneWorld think tank on aid policy and management, which also provided a useful point of connection with agencies and their critics.

Dissemination as research

The project highlighted the importance of a cyclical approach to the different phases of the research process. From early in the life of the project, we paid considerable attention to the dissemination of work in progress as a means of further data collection. This is evident in some of the comments above about agency workshops and publications such as *Norrag News*. Time was spent in placing project papers not only on the project website but also on other prominent development research websites, such as ELDIS and GDNet. These sixteen papers were widely advertised, particularly to agency staff. Several were presented at conferences. Through doing this, we received a number of comments from agency staff that enriched our understanding. We also developed contacts with other researchers in what is a very new and disparate field. A number of interviews were structured around responses to analyses of earlier visits to the particular agency. On some occasions, critiques of some of our analyses led to us being provided with documentation that had hitherto not been shown to us. Final drafts of agency chapters were shared with a small number of agency contacts and their comments were considered carefully, although not always acted upon.

One important element that had been written into the initial research design was a mid-term seminar to assist in the sharpening of research focus. We were fortunate in having the support of the German Foundation for International Development in this. They hosted a week-long seminar for 25 participants in Bonn in April 2001. This brought together staff from the four case-study agencies, plus German agencies, and researchers from both North and South. This was particularly valuable in allowing the space for lengthy discussions about knowledge-based aid in what was the first such forum for this topic. Moreover, the book that arose from this meeting (Gmelin, King and McGrath 2001) was yet another resource for our method of dissemination as research.

As with many other elements of the research practice, this focus on dissemination as research is in keeping with the nature of the topic being explored. Knowledge sharing as an iterative process became both a focus of study and a way of researching.

The structure of the book

In the next two chapters we will look in more detail at the current trends in development co-operation and the origins of knowledge-based aid. Neither chapter is designed to provide definitive accounts of the literatures on aid or knowledge for development. Rather, they are intended to provide both conceptual and historical contexts in which the whole of the book can be understood. Chapters 4–7 provide case studies of four agencies: the World Bank, DFID, Sida and JICA. They are all organised broadly around four elements of how knowledge-based aid can be understood. First, we look at what discourses of knowledge emerge from our research in the respective agencies. Second, we examine how knowledge and notions thereof are embedded in a series of what we shall term knowledge products: major agency documents. Third, we investigate what may be termed the knowledge projects of each agency: the range of projects and programmes designed to improve the agency's use of knowledge, whether internal or external. Fourth, we analyse knowledge as practices: the ways in which knowledge use is inscribed in the daily activities of staff and the organisations themselves. In each of these chapters, we also seek to go beyond the agencies' own discourses to raise broader issues about the desirability of knowledge-based aid. In the final chapter, we draw together these broader issues to provide an overview of the early years of knowledge-based aid and a set of issues that will be important as it continues to develop.

Notes

1. In Gmelin, King and McGrath (2001), agency staff and researchers produced a joint volume that provided a first book-length treatment of some of these issues. In that volume, however, much of the discussion was based on the reflections of agency staff and researchers on their professional experience rather than on specific research into agencies' knowledge practices.

2. This, of course, is not complete and never is likely to be. Some of the divergences will be apparent in chapters 4 to 7.

3. Kenneth King was already the author of *Aid and Education in the Developing World* (King 1991) and co-editor of *Changing international aid to education* (King and Buchert 1999); and both of us had experience of consultancy and consultations for agencies.

4. Essentially, tacit knowledge refers to that which is understood internally by an individual but which has not been systematically expressed, while codified knowledge is that which has been explicitly and systematically expressed.

5. In several cases, these interviews were with people whom Kenneth King had known for up to thirty years. The length of our own combined history of researching aid was important both for accessing agency staff and for keeping a sense of historical perspective in the study.

6. This is not true of the on-line community 'Knowledge management for International Development Organisations', which has been operating throughout much of the period of this research; this is a highly interactive network,

and its core members have also managed to meet face to face on a number of occasions.

7. For more information, see www.norrag.org

8. The Oxford Conference is convened by the United Kingdom Forum for International Education and Training (UKFIET); see www.ukfiet.fsnet.co.uk

TWO

The new aid agenda

This book is about the ways in which knowledge (both internally and externally oriented) has become a central element of aid and development discourse. In this chapter, we wish briefly to outline the broader picture of that discourse. This will inevitably be done in a highly summary, selective way, given the huge literature that could be consulted. Crucially, one of its main aims will be to show that this discourse has changed considerably over time, with many changes reflecting an often unconscious return to past development ideas.

The changing fashions of development co-operation
The continuously swinging pendulum of aid discourse

> The wheel has once again turned from an almost exclusive emphasis on economic growth to a more comprehensive set of economic and social objectives, including poverty reduction. It remains a source of amazement to observe this continuous swinging of the pendulum, with so little being learned from experience. (Emmerij 1996: 309)

Although Rist (1997) and others have seen the early origins of development and aid in the changes in human interaction and philosophy associated with industrialisation, modernity and the Enlightenment, it is conventional to date the beginning of the development era to January 1949 and President Truman's inaugural address to the American people (Sachs 1989; Rist 1997).[1]

Since 1949, notions of aid and development have followed a series of pendulum swings, to use Emmerij's metaphor.[2] Importantly, such swings appear to owe more to political and economic cycles of differing duration in the North than to changed Southern circumstances. The 1950s and 1960s saw the height of decolonisation as large numbers of countries in regions such as Africa and South and South-East Asia gained independence. The road from political independence to economic development was largely seen as short and unproblematic. This was the era of the long post-war boom in the developed economies, and the parallel 'modernisation' in the 'developing' economies was widely assumed to be feasible. There was considerable emphasis on the training of high-level personnel to replace expatriates, on infrastructural development, and on large capital projects as countries moved towards the assumed rapid economic take-off. Strikingly, the prescription differed little whether the necessary financial assistance was to come from Moscow, Tokyo or Washington.

By the end of the 1960s, the growing Northern pessimism about the end of its own post-war boom combined with a Latin American critique of the theoretical weaknesses of development, and with growing evidence of the practical failures of the overall development project. The two most prominent responses to the apparent crisis of development came from the World Bank.

First, in 1969, the Commission on International Development reported as requested by the World Bank. Led by former Canadian Prime Minister Lester Pearson, this Commission sought to address the growing complexity of aid and the increasing concerns that it was proving ineffective. Much of what was recommended, including a 'war against poverty' (Commission on International Development 1969: 8), sounds very familiar to those versed in current aid debates. Whilst it admitted that donors had a legitimate interest in seeing whether recipients were serious about development, the Commission argued that this new notion of donor–recipient partnerships had to be driven by governments in the recipient countries:

> It is natural, therefore, that aid-providers are particularly interested in whether recipients make sincere efforts to help themselves, or whether the resources put at their disposal are wasted. However, this interest, unless carefully limited and institutionalised, creates opportunities for friction, waste of energy, and mutual irritation. Any such relationship must involve advice, consultation, and persuasion, but there must be clear and accepted channels for this and an equally clear distinction between the responsibilities of the partners. The formation and execution of development policies must ultimately be the responsibility of the recipient alone, but the donors have a right to be heard and to be informed of major events and decisions. (Commission on International Development 1969: 127)

In support of this new partnership approach, there was a strong message that obligations must be mutual:

> Developing countries cannot reach for ambitious goals unless they know that serious programmes will find external support. They are entitled to ask what commitments aid-givers are ready to make and how these commitments will be lived up to. Performance is not a one-way street. (Commission on International Development 1969: 17)

This notion of donor responsibility led the Commission to call ambitiously for a commitment to an official development assistance target of 0.7 per cent of Gross National Product, to be reached by 1975 (Commission on International Development 1969: 18). In addition, the Commission recommended the streamlining of aid administration, joint project evaluation, better co-ordination amongst different agencies' strategies, the restructuring of technical co-operation, and debt relief. All of these themes are still part of the discourse of the current era, even where practice lags behind rhetoric. However, in stark contrast to the current discourse, the Commission argued against uniform policies and targets, concluding that the only possible universal target for the South might be an average GNP growth of 6 per cent per annum (Commission on International Development 1969: 124).

Some of the agencies we will study in this book, notably JICA and Sida, stress the importance of the attitudinal domain in the donor–recipient relationship. This was also stressed in the Commission's findings: 'Co-operation for development means more than a simple transfer of funds. It means a set of new relationships which must be founded on mutual understanding and self-respect' (Commission on International Development 1969: 6). The second significant shift in aid discourse and practice at the end of the 1960s and the beginning of the 1970s was represented most visibly by a change in leadership at the World Bank. In 1968, Robert McNamara, previously US Defense Secretary, became the Bank's new President. Under McNamara, the Bank became the leader of the 'war against poverty'. It was at the forefront of the new focus on meeting the 'basic needs' of the poor, especially the rural poor, that spread across many agencies in the early 1970s (McNamara 1981). This basic needs focus was seen in the concerns of several of the other multilateral agencies, such as the International Labour Office, with its concerns with employment and the urban informal sector, which the ILO placed on the policy agenda in the early 1970s. It was also evident in several bilateral programmes, such as that of the British Overseas Development Ministry (HMSO 1970). However, this trend was not universal. Japan, for instance, continued to build on its own development experiences (see chapter 7) to fund strategies for infrastructural development and economic growth in South-East Asia.

By the end of the 1970s, however, the basic needs approach began to be overtaken by a new ideological orthodoxy that was spreading from Britain and the USA. The elections of both Reagan and Thatcher in 1979–1980 saw the emerging ascendancy of neoliberal thinking in OECD countries. Quickly this became a powerful force in Northern thinking about development. Again, the World Bank (along with the International

Monetary Fund – IMF) was at the centre of the new fashion. Prominent Bank reports, such as *Accelerated Development in Sub-Saharan Africa* (World Bank 1981), began to construct the case for a new reading of the reasons for Southern underdevelopment and for future development strategies. It was argued that Southern countries largely had themselves to blame for their development failings and that they required a radical restructuring of their economic systems so as to make them more globally competitive. Increasingly, an essentially uniform set of policy reforms was presented to a large and diverse set of countries. The key elements were as follows:

- greater fiscal discipline
- tax reform
- liberalisation of the financial sector
- exchange rate reforms designed to promote non-traditional exports
- trade liberalisation
- encouragement of foreign direct investment
- privatisation of public services
- greater deregulation of production and services.

Through the new instrument of the Structural Adjustment Loan, the Bretton Woods Institutions (the Bank and the IMF) began to insist that a detailed set of such reforms had to be put in place as a condition for new loans.[3] For many countries that had seriously over-extended borrowing during the boom of oil-driven investment in the 1970s, and were now struggling to meet seriously increased import and debt-servicing costs in the early 1980s, loans from the Bank and the IMF appeared to be essential no matter how onerous their conditions appeared to be.

Later in the 1980s and into the 1990s, the vision of structural adjustment began to broaden. Criticism of their impact, such as reduced public spending on social sectors like health and education, led to an attempt to make programmes more comprehensive and to include 'safety nets'. But with this came a greater range of interventions into areas of national policy. At the same time, concerns within the World Bank and the IMF about the limited success of implementation of adjustment led to a growing emphasis on good governance, as political constraints were seen as the major factor behind poor adjustment implementation. By the mid-1990s, as we shall see below, the range of themes on which donors had convictions about what recipients should do had expanded greatly. Indeed, Carlsson and Wohlgemuth (2000b) liken the modern development co-operation agency to the old-fashioned department store, struggling to sell every product as the range of possible goods continues to expand. However, the overall discourse of aid was also showing profound signs of change as poverty once again moved centre stage.

External factors acting upon aid since the beginning of the 1990s

Since the late 1980s there have been a large number of changes in the overall nature and structure of development co-operation. Much of the change comes from forces external to the field itself. The end of the Cold War has altered both rationales for aid and the casts of donors and recipients (Forster 1998). Whilst strategic and diplomatic concerns remain important (especially in the Middle East), the old competition between East and West to provide aid has now gone. A number of important donors, including the Soviet Union and East Germany, have disappeared, whilst others have reduced their activities. In several cases, erstwhile donors have become recipients. Significantly, the Eastern and Central European countries, for the most part, appear to have entered a different relationship with donors, based on closer cultural ties, a perception of the shorter time frame of assistance and a greater sense of symmetry. Economic progress in some parts of the world has seen other countries cease to be recipients, or has seen them graduate from 'less developed' to 'middle income' status, with the ensuing change in their access to grants and loans. In some cases, these countries have begun to engage in their own development co-operation activities (e.g. Chile, Egypt, India, Thailand).[4]

The cast of aid actors has shifted at the multilateral level too. The decline in the influence of the United Nations, which began with the hostility to it of the Conservative regimes in the USA and Britain in the early 1980s, has continued. The pre-eminence of the Bretton Woods Institutions has been strengthened, and extended by the emergence of the World Trade Organisation as a multilateral organisation of the same kind. The OECD and the G8 have increased their influence over development (Mundy 1998). The 1990s also saw the acceleration of the European Union's role as a development actor above and beyond the individual national programmes of its members (Gmelin 1998). These combined changes in multilateralism are made more significant by the increasing proportion of national aid budgets that have been allocated for funding of multilateral programmes. The relative decline of the role of the more democratic and inclusive United Nations in favour of organisations solely for or dominated by the world's richest nations raises the question of whether development co-operation has shifted more explicitly under the control of the wealthiest and for their interests. When it is remembered that official development assistance is far smaller than foreign direct investment in the South (Heyneman 1997), and that the latter largely goes to the less poor, the asymmetrical nature of control of resources for development is made even starker.

Inevitably, some of this shift in power is masked. The most prominent element of the new architecture of aid is the series of International Development Targets (or Millennium Development Goals, as they have become). Part of the rhetoric surrounding these is that they are globally owned. Certainly it is true that they have been ratified retrospectively by the United Nations General Assembly. However, their origins are in need of some brief consideration for they point to two of the most important changes in the way that development co-operation has been organised since around 1990.

The 1990s could have been designated by the UN as 'the decade of the World Conference'. Beginning with education at Jomtien in early 1990 and continuing through children (New York 1990), environment (Rio de Janeiro 1992), human rights (Vienna 1993), population (Cairo 1994), social development (Copenhagen 1995), women (Beijing 1995), human settlements (Istanbul 1996), food security (Rome 1996), and climate change (Kyoto 1997), the decade saw a renewed interest in trying to solve the world's development challenges (North and South) through the means of large, showpiece events. Out of these conferences came a large number of resolutions. In some cases, such as for environmental and reproductive issues, the contestations were highly publicised and the compromises widely criticised. In other cases, a veneer of consensus overlay a depth of negotiation and disagreement. In some cases, such as environment and climate change, it was widely accepted that the recommendations were meant for all parts of the world. In others, such as education, there was a strong sense that the recommendations were really only meant for the less developed countries.

The impact and visibility of some of the conferences were greatly increased by the decision in 1996 by the Development Assistance Committee of the OECD to base its new development strategy, *Shaping the 21st Century* (OECD–DAC 1996), on a selection of themes from the conferences of the first half of the 1990s. This led to a series of six 'International Development Targets' (IDTs):

- a reduction by one-half in the proportion of people living in extreme poverty by 2015
- universal primary education in all countries by 2015
- demonstrated progress towards gender equality and the empowerment

of women by eliminating gender disparity in primary and secondary education by 2005

- a reduction by two-thirds in the mortality rates for infants and children under age 5 and a reduction by three-fourths in maternal mortality, all by 2015
- access through the primary health-care system to reproductive health services for all individuals of appropriate ages as soon as possible and no later than the year 2015
- the implementation of national strategies for sustainable development in all countries by 2005, so as to ensure that current trends in the loss of environmental resources are effectively reversed at both global and national levels by 2015. (OECD–DAC 1996: 6)

While the IDTs clearly were important elements of the world conferences and captured the new focus on poverty reduction, it is striking that other themes that emerged from the conferences were not taken up by the OECD. These include human rights, debt, labour and employment issues, and the arms trade. Many DAC members have subsequently placed the IDTs at the core of their national aid policies, although some see them as more central than others. For instance, as we shall see in subsequent chapters, DFID has built its aid strategy very explicitly around the IDTs, whilst Sweden has seen them as little more than confirmation of some of its own existing approach. The World Bank too has endorsed the IDTs, although they do not appear to dominate the Bank's strategy. Even where the IDTs do not explicitly receive prominence, it is now typical to find that agencies have developed a series of cross-cutting concerns that are intended to inform all their activities: poverty, gender, environment, HIV–AIDS, conflict, and governance.[5]

One of the strengths of the IDTs is that (environment excepted) they provide quantifiable targets for development. Moreover, the OECD has also sought to support these by a further series of indicators on sub-themes (Chang et al. 1999). However, the limited number of targets and the quantitative focus do raise issues about the narrowness of the conception of development that is contained within the IDTs and the way in which Southern people become objectified targets to be acted upon rather than subjects of their own development (Carton 1998).

Economic and technological changes have also had profound impacts on development co-operation. This is something that we shall consider in greater detail in the next chapter. However, it is important to note here that globalisation has profoundly reoriented development co-operation possibilities and challenges. The growth of new information and communication technologies and the rise of the knowledge economy discourse are also very important for the nature of development and aid, as the next chapter discusses in some detail.

Aid discourse at the start of the new millennium

The current discourse of development and aid seeks, at the overall level, to marry a faith in the globalisation of markets with an espoused commitment to poverty reduction. This discourse contains very many elements, three of which appear particularly pertinent to our discussions.

Delimiting development

First, as we have already noted, there is an issue of what constitutes development. Over time, structural adjustment became concerned with the sphere of politics as well as economics. However, in the past five years, there have been a number of prominent comments from within the World Bank's leadership about the need for an even broader conception of development. As current World Bank President, James Wolfensohn, argues: 'We cannot adopt a system in which the macroeconomic and financial is considered apart from the structural, social and human aspects' (Wolfensohn 1999: 7). Whilst far from unproblematic, this is indicative of new thinking in the Bank about the breadth of the development notion, which is reflected in the appointment of a growing number of employees with professional backgrounds in areas other than economics and engineering. At the same time, there is a growing acceptance within agencies that development is not simply a technical issue, but a highly politically and culturally sensitive one (Kifle, Olukoshi and Wohlgemuth 1997; Stiglitz 1998). Whilst this is clearly often honoured in the breach, there does appear to have been a genuine shift in agency discourse towards greater awareness of context and culture (e.g. Sida 1997c) (see chapter 6 of the present volume).

There remains considerable scepticism and mistrust about this expanded vision of development. Authors such as Crewe and Harrison (1998) argue that the growing agency interest in culture, context and the social realm is purely for their positive assumed impact on aid effectiveness. Certainly, there is much in the World Bank's arguments in favour of partnership, for instance, that stresses the pragmatic reasons for its adoption. In this view, it is the crisis of aid caused by the failings of the structural adjustment era that have led to the adoption of new concepts, rather than any fundamental change of ideology.

The rediscovery of partnership and participation

Second, there is an issue of what type of relationships are at the heart of aid. With the rise of good governance and concerns about the effectiveness of adjustment, there has re-emerged a discourse of partnership, ownership and participation first noted in the Pearson Commission. This discourse operates across the agency community at a series of levels. First, at the macro level of policy discussion, there has been a powerful shift in emphasis in agency documents away from conditionalities and towards a language of partnership, in which the erstwhile recipient country is the ultimate owner of development:

> We must accept that the projects we fund are not donor projects or World Bank projects – they are Costa Rican projects, or Bangladeshi projects, or Chinese projects. And development projects and programmes must be fully owned by local stakeholders if they are to succeed. (Wolfensohn 1999: 1)

> What we are talking about is a new approach to development partnership.It is a partnership led by governments and parliaments of the countries, influenced by the civil society of those countries, and joined by the domestic and international private sectors, and by bilateral and multilateral donors … Critically, it is a partnership where we in the donor community must learn to cooperate with each other, must learn to be better team players capable of letting go. (Wolfensohn 1998: 17–18)

Such a concern with ownership and partnership is reflected in new (or reinvented) tools for development co-operation. At the sectoral level, the late 1990s saw a number of agencies return to the old notion of sector-wide programmes. This has led in some cases to budgetary support, where a number of agencies subsume their support for a sector under a common basket of funding and a government-led sectoral strategy.[6] In 1999, Wolfensohn proposed the far more ambitious notion of a Comprehensive Development Framework (CDF) (Wolfensohn 1999), which sought to map all such sectoral initiatives within a country on to a single, coherent matrix. Though not formally abandoned by the World Bank, this initiative appears to have been largely overtaken by the Bank's current commitment to Poverty Reduction Strategy Papers (PRSPs) as the basis for successor loans to structural adjustment facilities. PRSPs, more than sector-wide programmes, place a heavy emphasis (at least rhetorically) on the role of civil society in policy development.

In the cases of Sida and JICA, this partnership language is not so new. What both agencies also bring to the discourse is an emphasis on the ethical and attitudinal dimensions of the partnership relationship (Karlsson 1997; Cedergren 1998):

> Partnership should be seen as an attitude, in a form of cooperation that is based on a shared basis of values and mutual trust ... The aspiration should be to bring about increased equality and mutual respect in the relationship, in awareness of the fundamental inequality represented by the donor's upper hand in terms of resources. (Ministry for Foreign Affairs, Sweden 1998: 99)

The language of partnership does not totally overcome the older talk of conditionalities, however. For some within the World Bank, for instance (World Bank 1998d; Devarajan, Dollar and Holmgren 1999), there is a need to remain strong on the issue of conditionalities. This has led to various formulations that seek to balance the forces of partnership and conditionality. In the British development White Paper of 1997 (DFID 1997) and the proposals for the Comprehensive Development Framework (Wolfensohn 1999), this balancing led to a distinction between full partners, suitable for sector-wide programmes or the CDF, and others suitable only for a more limited version of partnership:

> We should offer our assistance to all countries in need. But we must be selective in how we use our resources. There is no escaping the hard fact: more people will be lifted out of poverty if we concentrate our assistance on countries with good policies than if we allocate it irrespective of the policies pursued. Recent studies confirm what we already knew intuitively – that in a good policy environment, development assistance improves growth prospects and social conditions, but in a poor policy environment, it can actually retard progress by reducing the need for change and by creating dependency. (Wolfensohn 1997: 1)

> In countries with poor policies and no credible reform movement, assistance should assume the more modest and patient role of disseminating ideas, transmitting experiences of other countries, training future policymakers and leaders, and stimulating capacity for informed policy debate within civil society. (World Bank 1998d: 4–5)[7]

Moreover, the vision of development partnerships is heavily shaped by the IDTs and other elements of what donors consider 'sensible policies' (DFID 1997). Conditionalities are given further impetus by the growing subjection of development co-operation, like other elements of Northern public expenditure, to the pressure of accountability to national auditing agencies and their powerful emphasis on relatively narrow conceptions of efficiency (McGrath 1998).

At the micro level of communities, the language of ownership is presented in the form of participation. Here agencies have drawn heavily in recent years on the language and tools of participatory research. The participation homepage for the World Bank (http://worldbank.org/participation) leads visitors through several hundred documents, including the nearly 300-page *World Bank Participation Sourcebook* (World Bank 1996b).

At the community level and in countries deemed unsuitable for full partnership, the role of NGOs has been given strong support by development co-operation agencies in a continuation of the privatisation philosophy of the 1980s.

The language of partnership also has implications for the untying of aid. On the one hand, better coherence between trade and aid policies is seen as crucial to symmetrical relations between countries (e.g. DFID 1997); on the other, tying aid disbursements to the purchase of products and services from the specific donor country has increasingly been seen as contrary to notions of national ownership.

Partnership often stresses the importance of long-term relationships (e.g. Ministry for Foreign Affairs, Sweden 1998). However, the Nordic experience in particular has also shown that the downside of long-term relationships is dependency (Catterson and Lindahl 1999).

Part of the issue here is technical assistance: the provision of (largely) Northern staff to work in projects and organisations. As we shall see in subsequent chapters, technical assistance is supposed to support national capacity, but has too often acted to undermine it (Sidibé 1997). Concerns with technical assistance and capacity development are once again widespread in the agency community (King 2002).

What does the new partnership discourse amount to? Whilst Sweden and Japan in particular have stressed the ethical dimensions of partnership, it is argued that the underlying rationale for partnership is merely pragmatic (Woods 2000). Certainly, the aid effectiveness impact is a recurrent theme in many of the World Bank's documents that talk about partnership and ownership (e.g. Wolfensohn 1998, 1999).

It is also argued that attention to the processes and substance of partnership and ownership are undermined in practice by the continuing faith of both the World Bank and other agencies in certain other tenets of development ideology. Conditionality seems to be alive and well, even though it is ultimately contradictory to autonomous development (Hirschman 1971; Sen 1999; Kanbur 2000; Ellerman 2003). Partnership is also undermined by the pressure within agencies for speedy disbursement (German and Randel 1998). In such a climate, time spent in ensuring ownership or developing indigenous capacity is seen as wasteful.

Equally, it can be argued that the whole model of the development policy process is flawed (McGrath 2001a). Agencies have a strongly espoused theory of development as consensus, which leads to claims that PRSPs and participatory rural appraisals (PRA) are means towards ensuring ownership of development by all stakeholders. However, these assumptions are strongly contested by a number of authors (e.g. Cooke and Kothari 2001 [PRA]; Guttal 2000 [PRSP]). Moreover, the assumed nature of civil society also appears flawed. In Africa, for instance, strong autonomous stakeholders are hard to find (Mkandawire 2000; Mwiria 2001). Furthermore, the model of how policy is made seems far away from current accounts in African political theory (Bayart 1993; Chabal and Daloz 1999). The model also appears to assume the existence of autonomous NGOs, which ignores the very real tendency towards NGO co-option as they become increasingly dependent on agencies for funding and even legitimacy (Edwards 1998; Klees 1998; Tvedt 1999).

The genuineness of the ownership-for-development approach is also seriously undermined by the extent to which donors have balanced their increasing demands on the South with increases to development budgets. At present, only four major donors are meeting the Pearson Commission's recommendation of 0.7 per cent of GNP, and there are, in fact, downward pressures on development budgets even in these countries. Many commentators question how seriously donors are taking development when they seem prepared to spend so little (e.g. German and Randel 1998). This failure of commitment is made even starker when development budgets are compared to the amount expended on German reunification (King 1997) or the costs of EU expansion, not to mention the costs of the Common Agricultural Policy.

Knowledge for development and the agency as a learning organisation

Third, there has been the growth of discussion about the role of learning in development co-operation agencies, allied to a more fundamental debate about the way that knowledge is used in development. This will be the major focus of this book. However, it is worth anticipating a few aspects of these twinned debates at this point.

Agencies have become increasingly concerned about how they make use of their own existing knowledge and how they learn to develop better policies and practices. This is linked to a fascination with the range of new ICTs that are available to support such processes, but also to a growing awareness of the ways in which organisational management affects the use of learning and knowledge.

Several of the themes discussed in the previous section – ownership, partnership, participation, capacity development – clearly are also closely related to issues of learning and knowledge, particularly between different development actors.

However, the new discourses of learning and knowledge within agencies remain deeply problematic, as we shall see throughout this book. Agencies are state bureaucracies (or, in the case of the multilaterals, act like them). This leads to two important tendencies that are inimical to both national ownership and learning in the South. First, they are inevitably heavily influenced by political considerations, which can shape their policies far more effectively than notions of learning or knowledge. Second, they exhibit a bureaucratic tendency towards seeking routines and universal rules that makes them ill-fitted for the complex and contextual field of development (Forss, Cracknell and Stromquist 1997). The World Bank also shows a particular tendency towards new 'big ideas' driven by the need of each new President to build his own legacy.

One of the key tensions that will run through this book is between the growth of a new, more positive language of knowledge within agencies and a sense that old asymmetries of power remain largely in place. The relationship between power and knowledge is clearly as central to the new aid agenda as it was to its previous forms.

Notes

1. Much of the groundwork for notions of development took place in the 'age of empires'. However, it is argued that there is a distinct break with key elements of the language of colonial development in the period immediately after 1945.

2. Our treatment of the complexity of development theory will be short and oriented towards our broader aims in this book. For a comprehensive treatment, see Leys (1996).

3. Mosley, Harrigan and Toye (1991) point out that conditionalities were common even before 1980. However, there does appear to have been significant change at both the quantitative and qualitative levels at around this point. Mosley, Harrigan and Toye also show convincingly how conditionalities were not uniformly enforced in practice.

4. Japan has placed considerable emphasis on supporting the aid activities of such countries as the lead partners in South–South cooperation (see chapter 7).

5. Intriguingly, good governance, i.e. multi-party democracy, did not become one of the IDTs.

6. See Caddell (2002) for a detailed analysis of the operations of a sectoral programme for education in Nepal.

7. Interestingly, this policy priority is perhaps being reversed since 11 September 2001. Thus the *EFA Global Monitoring Report* (UNESCO 2002) argues 'instead of the countries with the weakest policy environments receiving the least attention from the international community, they actually must receive the most attention' (reported in *Financial Times* 14 November 2002: 5).

THREE
Knowledge for development

In the previous chapter we outlined how the language and practice of development co-operation have seen significant change (as well as much continuity) since the beginning of the 1990s. In this chapter we are concerned with exploring the way in which these changes have led to new knowledge needs in agencies and a new language about the centrality of knowledge for development and co-operation. We will stress in what follows the importance of understanding the genesis of development co-operation agencies' current strong interest in knowledge as a central element of development policy and practice. This interest relates both to the growth of internal knowledge management strategies designed to make aid more effective and efficient, and to an emphasis on the role of knowledge in promoting development in the South. This distinction, and tension, will be important for our analysis in subsequent chapters.

We will outline the origins of this interest in knowledge from its roots in political economy and management studies, showing how it has entered into agency discourses. We will then seek to outline some of the criticisms of this discourse that problematise its notions of both knowledge and development. However, this is not the place to go into the more than 2,500 years' worth of philosophical debates about knowledge.

The origins of knowledge-based aid
The knowledge economy

In traditional economic theory, wealth is created out of the three factors of production: labour, land and capital. The path to industrialisation, at least for Britain as the 'first industrial nation' (Mathias 1969) and for those following close on its heels, has widely been seen as lying through the exploitation of abundant natural resources. However, even from the earliest period of economic take-off into industrialisation, technological innovation was judged to be crucial to success. Such success was not built primarily on recourse to traditionally accepted forms of knowledge, but on learning from experimentation and reflection on practice. Nonetheless, a sense of the importance of knowledge for economic success can be seen in the Industrial Revolution. In 1826, British industrialists and scientists founded the Society for the Diffusion of Useful Knowledge, which produced a penny magazine that reached 200,000 subscribers at its peak (McGinn 2001). As the Industrial Revolution progressed, so the dominance of the practical technologist began to be challenged by the growing relationship between science and industry. Knowledge and progress were also closely related in the partnership between Christianity and civilisation in Victorian Britain and its empire. This again was given name in the Society for the Promotion of Christian Knowledge. At the same time, the Meiji period in Japan saw a conscious attempt to learn selectively from other countries in order to modernise. However, whilst the industrial economy was profoundly a knowledge economy, it was not named as such.

Some leading economists did write explicitly about the economic role of knowledge long before the notion of the knowledge economy achieved prominence. Marshall (1891) included a brief discussion of knowledge in his *Principles of Economics*. Schumpeter (1934) addressed knowledge in his *Theory of Economic Development*. Hayek wrote an article published in 1945 entitled, 'The use of knowledge in society' (Hayek 1945). Machlup (1962) had a book published with the title, *Production and Distribution of Knowledge*. He and others in the human capital school were to develop a clear account of the role that knowledge played in the economy and society.[1]

However, it was in the context of a perception of radical economic, political, social and technological transformation at the end of the 1960s that the critical importance of knowledge for economic success was to come to the fore. Although authors such as Drucker (1969) saw some of the key elements at the time, it was only from the mid-1980s that a detailed analysis emerged of a period of fundamental change in the advanced capitalist economies. A group of accounts suggested that a crisis occurred in these economics between 1968 and 1973 that shifted them from one mode of organisation to another (e.g. Piore and Sabel 1984; Hall and Jacques 1989; Boyer 1990). This crisis period corresponds to the time of the political challenge surrounding the Vietnam War from the youth and student protests in North America and Western Europe in 1968 to the first oil crisis of 1973. Political and cultural rebellion by significant sections of the youth were combined with a sharp economic downturn that decisively ended the Keynesian golden age of post-war high employment and low inflation. The new phenomenon of 'stagflation' emerged as unemployment and inflation both rose. The system of fixed exchange rates, agreed at the Bretton Woods conference at which the International Monetary Fund and the World Bank also were instituted, collapsed. Taken together, these major changes brought an end to the dominance of Fordism, which had been characterised by mass systems of production, mass consumption of standardised products, and mass-based modes of political and cultural organisation and identity. In its place emerged post-Fordism, characterised by more flexible production systems, new niche markets, and the greater individualisation of product and service. Allied to new debates surrounding postmodernism, the emphasis in cultural, political and social organisation shifted to individuals' multiple identities. The importance of class apparently declined and interest-group politics emerged as a powerful socio-political force (King and McGrath 2002).

As the 1990s developed, this account was expanded by accounts of globalisation (e.g. Giddens 1990). Although there is considerable contestation within globalisation accounts (King and McGrath 2002), there is some agreement over the centrality of the growth of global networks of production and of the speed and intensity of relationships within them. More importantly, a new infrastructural and technological architecture allows the almost instantaneous flow of capital and information between sites that form part of a global network. These financial flows lead to a new financial system, with the massive growth of markets in futures and other new financial tools to expand ways of extracting profit. The process of globalisation is fuelled by, and in turn fuels, the rapid development of new ICTs. Within a decade, social interactions in the North have been transformed by personal computing, the internet, e-mail, mobile phones, text messaging, video conferencing, and digital photography. Multi-faceted globalisation also brings with it its own new forms of global institutions, most notably the World Trade Organisation (Castells 1996; Held *et al.* 1999; King and McGrath 2002).

Post-Fordism, globalisation and the ICT revolution combine to bring about the argument for a knowledge economy. Together they lead to a massive increase in information flows and a new economic emphasis on turning information into knowledge. Early in the literature on globalisation, Robert Reich (1991) produced an account called *The Work of Nations*, designed to be the definitive account of the new model of economic organisation in the same way as Adam Smith's *Wealth of Nations* (1966 [1776]) had outlined the nature of the early Industrial Revolution. At the core of Reich's argument was the need to produce enough 'symbolic analysts', the core knowledge workers of the new knowledge economy.[2] Knowledge now was the only factor of production that mattered, 'the only source of long-run sustainable competitive advantage' (Thurow 1996: 74).

The knowledge economy account quickly captured the attention of political leaders. Reich was soon to move from Harvard to become Clinton's Labour Secretary. In Britain, the Blair Administration was to find its own 'knowledge guru' in the shape of Charles Leadbeater (2000), who was to be an influential adviser to the Department of Trade and Industry. A remarkable range of other countries also took the knowledge economy message to heart, as reflected in the following self-depictions: the 'clever country' (Australia); the 'information island' (Bermuda); and the 'intelligent island' (Singapore).[3] In 1996, coincidentally at the same time that it was setting out the International Development Targets, the OECD produced an influential report on the knowledge economy (OECD 1996).

Knowledge management

In parallel to the emergence of the language of the knowledge economy came a corporate discourse and practice of knowledge management. In the early 1990s in the United States, a growing awareness of a changed external environment for firms was coupled to the rapid spread of new ICTs to produce a sense that information needed to be better managed. From early on in the process, there was also a sense in many corporations of the knowledge and experience that had been lost during the often severe 'downsizing' of the 1980s. Increasingly, corporations sought to develop strategies for knowledge retention and management. From the mid-1990s, this widespread change in corporate practice began to generate a rapidly expanding literature in management studies.

As the literature of the knowledge firm developed, so two broad tendencies in theory and practice began to emerge. The first may be termed the technological approach. Here the emphasis was on the capture of the knowledge that already existed in the firm. As one book's title succinctly put it: *If Only We Knew What We Know* (O'Dell et al. 1998). This school of thought put the emphasis on codified knowledge, that which had been organised, synthesised and recorded. This process of capture was closely linked to the promise of new technologies. Databases rapidly became an important element of the knowledge firm. Moreover, the development of e-mail and corporate intranets meant that this captured, codified knowledge could quickly be transmitted around the corporation.

This model of knowledge seems at times to come close to being about information or even data. Moreover, it appears to have a largely unproblematised view that knowledge is universally applicable and can be captured in a set of synthesised notes on best practice that can be shared round an organisation. Knowledge is seen as being present in individual minds, and the challenge is in extracting this so that other individuals can learn through acquiring this knowledge. From the perspective of education, this appears very much like the banking model, so roundly criticised by Freire (1972).

The second broad tendency in the account of the knowledge firm may be termed the social. Here the emphasis is much more on tacit knowledge. Often drawing explicitly on the work of authors such as Polanyi (1967), the argument was that much of what was really useful knowledge was embedded in the experience of individuals and could not easily be captured and codified (Davenport and Prusak 1998). This led to an emphasis on how to connect people within organisations through the sharing of stories and through learning together in teams. The model of learning here was much more experiential, reflecting both Deweyan and Marxian traditions. There was more emphasis on the creation of new knowledge than on the dissemination of that which was already codified. Interestingly for our study, Nonaka and Takeuchi (1995) argued that Japanese economic success was built on its performance in knowledge creation through active learning. Their account of the social nature of such learning reinforced the accounts of American academics such as Lave and Wenger (1991), which had spread into the management literature. Lave and Wenger stressed the importance of 'communities of practice' as sites of learning, a concept that was to spread rapidly through corporate knowledge management schemes. The title of their book, *Situated Learning*, also points to the importance in this account of context and a rejection of the universalist position of the technological approach. Instead of small synthesised pieces of best practice, the emphasis here is on sharing stories (Davenport and Prusak 1998; Denning 2000).[4]

That two tendencies can be drawn out from the theory and practice of knowledge management of course does not mean that there is a simple polarity in this area. Indeed, authors increasingly are stressing the existence of different types of knowledge and a range of knowledge needs within firms (McGinn 2001). Thus, there has been the growth of a theory and practice in which a social account is at the core but elements of the technological approach are seen as useful. It has also been argued (e.g. Hall 2002) that knowledge management represents the latest phase in the development of methods of extracting surplus value from workers, through the exploitation of their knowledge, both tacit and explicit.

As positions on knowledge management have matured, so the language has begun to shift to knowledge sharing, which seems more reflective of a social rather than technological understanding. The emphasis on knowledge sharing has seen issues of trust and organisational culture come to the fore (Davenport and Prusak 1998; Leadbeater 2000). This emergent interest in organisational culture, and a borrowing from researchers of learning such as Lave, point to the potential intersection of the model of the knowledge firm with that of the learning organisation.

Organisational learning

An interest in the possibilities of and barriers to organisational learning has a long tradition in economics and management literature, although historically subsumed under the broader literature on the organisation of the firm (e.g. March and Simon 1958). It was the work of Argyris and Schön (1978) that was to develop the notion in a rigorous and sustained manner. Much of their attention was focused on the barriers to learning that existed within firms in terms of structures and cultures that prevented learning or discouraged sharing of information. They emphasised the need to move beyond reactive 'single loop learning' to develop a systemic and systematic approach to 'double loop learning'. Such learning requires not just that the problem is solved but that steps are taken to reorganise structure and culture as necessary. As the 1990s began, the notion of the learning organisation was to be popularised by Senge (1990). In keeping with the style of the popular management text, the argument was based firmly in brief case studies and positive thinking. It stressed the importance of teams and the ways in which the barriers to double loop learning could be overcome. Although this account is clearly influenced by the shifts in the corporate world linked to the emergence of post-Fordism, there is no sense of the emergence of ICTs or globalisation.[5]

Whilst there are clear intersections between the knowledge firm and the learning firm, Davenport and Prusak (1998) note that the two literatures have largely developed independently of each other. Senge's index has only one reference to the compartmentalisation of knowledge, whilst much of the knowledge literature does not seem to be concerned about learning, or has an implicit banking model that is far removed from Senge's dynamic sense of learning. Yet, as this brief outline of knowledge and learning firms shows, there is much overlap, now that more recent knowledge accounts have stressed culture, structures and incentives and have begun to draw on understandings from learning theory.

Knowledge-based aid
Knowledge for development

In a sense, knowledge has always been part of development, whether as the spread of Western knowledge and epistemologies across the globe or in the everyday practices of development actors as they draw upon knowledge for their work. As we noted in chapter 2, the development era is widely thought to have begun with the inaugural address of President Truman of the USA in January 1949 (Sachs 1989; Rist 1997). In this, the relationship between knowledge and development is clear:

> Fourth, we must embark on a bold new program for making the benefits of our scientific advances and industrial progress available for the improvement and growth of underdeveloped areas.
>
> More than half the people of the world are living in conditions approaching misery ...
>
> For the first time in history, humanity possess the knowledge and skill to relieve the suffering of these people. (Reproduced in Rist 1997: 249)

However, the notion of knowledge for development was to receive renewed and explicit attention in the late 1990s as the World Bank began to be influenced by a number of the trends and discourses outlined in the previous pages.

In the late summer of 1996, James Wolfensohn, the recently appointed president of the World Bank, was looking for a big idea for his speech to the annual meeting of the World Bank and IMF that September. This speech was likely to be of particular significance, as there was strong pressure on Wolfensohn to reform the Bank in order to reduce its perceived profligacy and to improve the effectiveness of its aid (e.g. Caufield 1996). For the Wolfensohn presidency not to be simply one of decline and defensiveness, it was vital that an original and persuasive account be developed of the need for radical change. It was suggested to him that the growing interest in knowledge in the corporate and political realms would be an area worth exploring. So it was that the annual meeting saw Wolfensohn declare that the World Bank should be the 'knowledge bank':

> We have been in the business of researching and disseminating the lessons of development for a long time. But the revolution in information technology increased the potential value of these efforts by vastly extending their reach. To capture this potential, we need to invest in the necessary systems, in Washington and worldwide, that will enhance our ability to gather development information and experience, and share it with our clients. We need to become, in effect, the Knowledge Bank. (Wolfensohn 1996: 7)

Knowledge management was made a core theme of the new 'strategic compact' between the Bank's management and staff, the strategy for organisational renewal (World Bank 1997). Within two months of Wolfensohn's speech, a high-level working group chaired by vice-president Jean-François Rischard[6] had produced a report outlining the new knowledge strategy of the Bank. One element of the programme that they recommended was a series of research studies into the economics of information and knowledge, with the possibility of this becoming a theme of a subsequent *World Development Report*, the Bank's highest-profile annual document (World Bank 1996).

This possibility was soon to become reality. The 1998–99 *World Development Report* was titled *Knowledge for Development* (World Bank 1998a). The Report started from the premise that the ICT revolution made developmentally useful knowledge potentially available for poor people more quickly and easily than ever before. However, through its links to globalisation, it also brought the possibility of an expanding 'digital divide'. The Report argued for investment in education, embracing of globalisation, and the liberalisation of the telecommunications sector as central to the narrowing of knowledge gaps. It also drew on the 'new institutional economics' (e.g. North 1990) to argue that informational failures must be addressed.[7]

Although strongly grounded in the economic paradigm of the Bank, with its technical and apparently value-free style (Meyer-Stamer 1999), the Report did catch some of the messianic fervour with which knowledge had been brought into the Bank's canon. Nowhere was this more apparent than in the first two paragraphs: 'Knowledge is like light. Weightless and intangible, it can easily travel the world, enlightening the lives of people everywhere. Yet billions still live in the darkness of poverty – unnecessarily'[8] (World Bank 1998a: 1). With this came a tendency to overstress the importance of knowledge to poverty and to portray the poor as being in a knowledge deficit: 'Poor countries – and poor people – differ from rich ones not only because they have less capital but because they have less knowledge' (World Bank 1998a: 1). The Report went on to argue that much of the reason for South Korea's better economic performance than that of Ghana was based on the former's superior use of knowledge (World Bank 1998a: 20).[9]

The Report suggested that much knowledge could be sourced from the North but that there would also be a role for national systems of research and development in the South. As well as the ability to generate new knowledge or acquire it from outside, the Report highlighted the importance of being able to absorb relevant knowledge. Such relevant knowledge was about correct policies and management systems, but it was also about health, agriculture and sanitation.

Development co-operation agencies had a clear role in this vision: 'Development institutions have three roles in reducing knowledge gaps: to provide international public goods, to act as intermediaries in the transfer of knowledge, and to manage the rapidly growing body of knowledge about development' (World Bank 1998a: 6). For the Bank to be a successful actor in knowledge for development, it must be successful at knowledge management:

> How well these institutions perform depends on their ability to manage vast amounts of information. For example, every World Bank staffer who works in a developing country accumulates knowledge about a particular sector or region or activity. Often this knowledge is used for the specific task requiring it, then shelved. Think how much more valuable it would be if that knowledge were made available to every other staff member working on similar issues and projects. Then add the much greater benefit to be had from sharing that knowledge with the rest of the world.
>
> The information revolution is making it easier to manage this wealth of knowledge. By 2000, the World Bank intends that relevant parts of its knowledge base will be made available to clients, partners, and stakeholders around the world. The objective is to develop a dynamic knowledge management system capable of distilling knowledge and making it available for further adaptation and use in new settings. To do that effectively, however, also requires building the capability in developing countries to assess and adapt relevant policy and technical knowledge to local situations, and when necessary to create new knowledge, which in turn may be relevant for other countries. (World Bank 1998a: 7)

The vision was one in which the Bank's greater internal focus on managing its own professional knowledge would inevitably lead to benefits for partners (or clients, in the Bank's language), as the Bank would be able to provide for them the best practices from a range of countries.

This vision, however, illustrates one of the central controversies that the World Bank's knowledge vision generates. The account is one in which the Bank has superior technical expertise and breadth of comparative development experience as compared with other agencies or clients. However, the Bank is willing to share its knowledge. This assumes and hides a number of things. First, the Bank's knowledge is portrayed as technical and value-free, notwithstanding the depth and breadth of the critique of the Bank's ideological biases. Second, it is assumed that there are clear-cut answers to development problems, regardless of the weakness of development in practice. Third, policy-making is seen as a rational and technical process in which the best knowledge is converted into the best policy, in spite of the range of evidence about the inevitably political and contested nature of typical policy processes.

Moreover, the stress on the externally focused aspects of knowledge for development needs to be placed alongside the reality that the bulk of the finance for the Bank's knowledge strategy was for internal activities. Although these were seen as being in the ultimate interest of the clients, it is still striking that the bulk of the resources would be directed at the knowledge needs of Bank staff rather than those of Southern countries. This tension between the internal and external dimensions of knowledge for development is at the core of our critique of knowledge-based aid, as we develop it in the following chapters.

Although there was some discussion of indigenous knowledge, and some reference to the role that agencies could play in South–South knowledge sharing, too much of the vision of the Report was on Southern deficits and Northern (particularly World Bank) transmission (Caddell 1999). Knowledge that is culturally, socially or spiritually valuable was not part of the vision, which remained resolutely in the economic sphere.

Knowledge-based aid activities

It should be clear from the discussion so far that knowledge is understood in a number of, often conflicting, ways. Rather than attempt to define it, it is more useful to look at the ways in which it has been used in practice in development co-operation. From this, the range of what constitutes knowledge-based aid may be seen.

Internal knowledge management and staff development

As was noted above, the bulk of funds in the World Bank knowledge programme were devoted to internal knowledge management, and this appears to be typical across agencies that have adopted knowledge approaches. Internal activities have included database development, such as at GTZ, and other more technological and informational initiatives. Intranets have been seen as crucial by some agencies, such as DFID (see chapter 5). However, agencies have increasingly focused more on the social aspects of knowledge sharing. Indeed, Steve Song, of the NGO Bellanet, suggests that communities of practice have emerged as the most popular element of internal knowledge activities across agencies (Song 2001). Increasingly, too, non-technological aspects such as meeting spaces have attracted attention, perhaps most notably in the new DFID headquarters (see chapter 5).

It is worth noting that communities of practice can be both internally and externally focused. However, it seems that the great majority of agency communities have internal participants only, though there is a marked shift towards sharing externally, for example at the Canadian International Development Agency.

Intranets and communities of practice are intended to develop staff capacity as a response to the new challenges faced by agencies. A number of other activities also take place in agencies towards the same ends. In some agencies, formal staff development programmes are well developed, but this varies considerably. Across a range of agencies there has been a growth in recent years of departmental and inter-departmental seminars designed to keep staff up to date with important development issues. Several donor countries have had long-term relationships with independent research organisations that are charged with improving knowledge flows from research to operational and policy staff (examples would include the Nordic area studies institutions and the Institute of Development Studies in the UK).

The frequent overlap and confusion between knowledge and information in agencies have also resulted in initiatives for e-working being included in knowledge programmes. Everyday practices of agency staff have been transformed in recent years by new technologies, and a number of agencies are engaged in ambitious programmes of digitisation of documents, and even libraries in the case of the DFID (see chapter 5). Often, however, these efforts are driven by cross-government programmes of 'modernisation' or by new freedom of information requirements rather than by any consideration of how such projects might affect the supposed partners in and beneficiaries of the agencies' work.

Inter-agency knowledge sharing

Inter-agency sharing has received relatively little attention in terms of the knowledge debate. This may be due to the previous growth of common reporting systems through the OECD and donor working groups. Although ICTs have clearly supported the work of these groupings, little has emerged in the way of new inter-agency communities of practice. One large initiative that has emerged is the Accessible Information on Development Activities project, which seeks to develop a common digitised database on aid activities (see chapter 4). This seems to be a classic example of the technological approach to knowledge sharing.

It is worth noting that the 1990s saw a major increase in the number and range of formal inter-agency consultations. Much of this was linked to the preparation and follow-up of the world conferences, but a number of standing agency working groups not linked to these processes also emerged in fields such as small enterprise development and skills development.

Research

Research on information and knowledge was one of the four strands of the World Bank's initial knowledge strategy. However, research more generally has always been, and continues to be, a crucial element of their knowledge activities. Research means different things to different agencies. For the World Bank, a lot of research is done in-house by its large staff of disciplinary specialists (see chapter 4). In Sida, research is primarily thought of in terms of support to Southern research (see chapter six). In DFID, research has traditionally been something funded by DFID but carried out by the British academic community, in increasingly genuine partnership with Southern researchers (see chapter 5). In JICA, much of the formal knowledge on which practice is based comes from 'development studies', 'basic design studies' and 'thematic and country studies', in which Japanese consultants play the primary role (see chapter 7). Research by and for the South has also been supported by a range of other Northern actors, including the International Development Research Centre (IDRC), Canada, and the Institute for Research on Development, France.

International public goods

The 1998–99 *World Development Report* highlights the issue of international public goods as one with which development co-operation agencies should be concerned:

> Just as there are national public goods, so there are international ones, and many types of knowledge fall into this category. No single country will invest enough in the creation of such goods, because the benefits would accrue to all countries without the creating country receiving full compensation. But international institutions, acting on behalf of everyone, can fill this gap. (World Bank 1998a: 6)

The Report goes on to cite the example of the Consultative Group for International Agricultural Research, a network with strong financial support from a number of agencies. Other examples would include the search for an AIDS vaccine and the attempt to eradicate malaria.

Infrastructural and institutional development

The importance of support to Southern ICT infrastructure is clearly present in both the World Bank's 1996 knowledge strategy and the

1998–99 *World Development Report*. This is reflected in a range of projects and programmes, including the infoDev programme of the World Bank and various telecentre and other community connectivity initiatives from a range of agencies and NGOs. This issue is at the heart of the language of the digital divide and the response to this of the G8 since the Okinawa Summit.[10]

From the World Bank and DFID in particular there is also a strong argument that ICT infrastructure in Southern countries will never develop successfully unless telecommunications markets are freed up. The influence of the new institutional economics is seen very clearly in the language used here, both in the *World Development Report* and the DFID White Paper of 2000 (DFID 2000l) (see chapter 5).

Knowledge transfer

Structural adjustment led to an increased agency focus on getting the right policy advice to Southern governments. However, this advice was intimately connected with the growth of conditionalities. Rather than attempting to engage in a process of contextually grounded learning with partners, agencies appeared to be engaged primarily in a process of prescriptive knowledge transfer based on their own universalising theories. This legacy of transfer with conditionality is an important barrier to the success of more recent agency attempts to move into a more symmetrical knowledge relationship with partners. Although the language of partnership has been accorded more importance, the language of conditionalities remains in new forms, such as the International Development Targets.

Away from the policy arena, there is little sense that agencies have made much impact in their avowed aspiration to transfer 'developmentally useful knowledge' to the poor. Whilst old extension approaches have largely lost favour, few new approaches to knowledge transfer to the poor have successfully emerged as yet, though there is the beginning of efforts to reconnect the older discourse of capacity building and development with the new language of knowledge acquisition and local ownership.[11]

e-learning

Agencies have long had a fascination with the possibilities of ICTs – including radio, television and video at different points in time – for supporting learning. The emergence of the internet and e-mail have served to strengthen this focus. It has also led to a sense of new possibilities for the short courses that agencies have offered to professionals and policy-makers in the South. A number of agencies and other Northern organisations, including the British Council, the World Bank (see chapter 4) and JICA (see chapter 7), are clearly excited about the vastly increased numbers that can be reached through e-learning. Questions can be raised, however, about the quality of this learning as opposed to traditional face-to-face methods, and the degree of contextualisation that is taking place. In talking of aid to e-learning, it is important to note that the same OECD governments that are promoting e-learning as part of their aid programmes are often also supporting it as a means of increasing the export earnings of their higher education institutions. Tensions between these two strategies are inevitable.

Technical co-operation and capacity development

Technical co-operation and capacity development have always been important elements of aid, and continue to be so. At its best, technical co-operation has had a rich view of knowledge, stressing the importance of culture, of face-to-face contact, and the tacit nature of much useful knowledge (Sida 1992; also see chapter 7 below, on JICA). Particularly in the Swedish model, there is a strong sense of the relationship as one of mutual knowledge construction and of the importance of capacity development for all partners, including Swedish ones, and at the systemic level (see chapter 6). Technical co-operation is currently receiving heightened critical attention from within agency circles. The UNDP, along with countries such as Canada, The Netherlands, Sweden and Britain, is pushing very strongly for a transformation in the conduct of technical co-operation, which both stresses the positive vision noted above and, crucially, seeks to untie its provision so that those involved do not have to come from the donor country. This is currently being resisted by other countries, including the USA and Japan. In the latter case, untying is seen as an undermining of the bilateral relationship that Japan sees as crucial to any genuine knowledge sharing (see chapter 7).

Capacity development has also found new favour in some agencies. For example, the Swiss Agency for Development and Co-operation has instituted a programme of 'human and institutional development' for itself and its partners. Significantly for our discussions, it has been explicitly linked to issues of knowledge (in the World Bank – see chapter 4) and learning (in Sida – see chapter 6). Here the language has seen a shift away from an emphasis on Southern deficits to a greater stress on mutuality, as is seen most clearly in the Swedish approach, as we show in chapter 6. Of course, such emphases are not entirely new for either technical co-operation or capacity development. As such, it is important to question how far a positive rhetoric is reflected in practice.

Short courses and scholarships

The period in which agencies have become so interested in knowledge is also, paradoxically, the period in which long-term scholarships for study in the North have fallen into deep decline. Whilst students continue to move North in large numbers, they are typically from the newly industrialised countries (most recently and dramatically China), often funded by their governments, or from the small elites of the poorer countries, through private funding. Thus, a significant agency source of knowledge and capacity development for the poorest countries has declined markedly and has not been replaced by the promised growth of in-country programmes.

Short courses have remained important for a number of agencies and continue to bring 'change agents' to the North. However, the knowledge and ICT revolutions have led to an apparent shift in the organisation and delivery of such programmes. There has been a move away from courses devised because the host country had expertise, for instance in hydroelectricity or forestry in the case of Sweden, to ones that reflect more of a sense of Southern needs. There has also been some shift away from a simple one-way transfer mode, in which the Northern instructors were assumed to have the knowledge, to a more democratic approach, in which the participants are assumed to be knowledgeable. This is linked crucially to a greater acceptance of the importance of context, a key message of the knowledge revolution. ICTs have allowed a new emphasis on networks (or communities of practice) of participants after the courses have ended (as can be seen in both Sida and the World Bank, but also in the programmes of the British Council and the German Foundation for International Development). However, the future of these programmes is brought into some question by the rapid expansion of e-learning provision by agencies. The relative merits of the different modalities remain inadequately addressed, though, as the new technologies capture the imaginations of agency staff. Lower unit costs have attracted far more attention than issues of quality.

Southern knowledge capacity

The university systems of much of the South have experienced two decades of decline. This has partly been due to the changing fashions of aid (World Bank 2000c).[12] The education-for-all orthodoxy led many donors to pull back from their support of higher education. Crucially, this came on top of the impact of structural adjustment in reducing Southern governments' ability to support higher education from their own funds.

The knowledge economy discourse has prompted many agencies to revisit this position. Most importantly, the World Bank developed a major new report on higher education (World Bank 2002a), directly influenced by knowledge economy arguments, some of which can be traced clearly to the 1998–99 *World Development Report*.

The tradition of Northern support to Southern higher education had been kept alive through the 1980s and 1990s by the large American foundations (e.g. Ford and Rockefeller) and the research-specific agencies and development research councils of a small number of donor countries, notably Canada, Sweden and The Netherlands. Of these bilateral initiatives, Canada's IDRC was, arguably, the most radical. In its early years, from the beginning of the 1970s, it pioneered making research grants directly to institutions and networks in the South, without requiring linkage or twinning to Canadian or Northern research institutes.

Whilst the World Bank does acknowledge the role of public higher education, it is also very interested in the role of both private providers and think tanks. It argues that the latter are important contributors to critical debate about policy and, hence, to good governance (Stone 2002). However, the rise of the think tank may in practice reinforce attempts to claim technocratic neutrality for development theory rather than further illustrate trends towards acknowledgement of subjectivity. Belief in the possibility of ideology-free research is clearly present, for example, in Stiglitz's keynote address to the first Global Development Network conference (Stiglitz 2000 [1999]).

The role of private sector research and development in the South is also a clear theme of both the *World Development Report 1998–99* and the 2000 UK Globalisation White Paper (DFID 2000l). These appear to have been influenced by endogenous growth theory (e.g. Romer 1986), which suggests that spin-offs from advances in firms' research and development plays an important role in overall economic growth. Indeed, it is argued that effective investment in research and development is more useful for growth than investment in physical capital (Kaplan 2000). Moreover, in keeping with knowledge economy arguments, this relative importance is seen as likely to grow over time. For countries in the South, this leads the World Bank and DFID to stress foreign direct investment as one important way of accessing developmentally useful knowledge. Thus, pro-globalisation policies are seen as promoting knowledge-led competitiveness.

Southern knowledge sharing

The World Bank's support for think tanks is most apparent in the evolution of the Global Development Network (Stone 2000, 2002; see also chapter 4). This is explicitly intended to be a forum for Southern knowledge sharing, through conferences, collaborative research and electronic activities. However, its structure and debates about its governance have highlighted a tension between an economistic and technocratic vision of development on the one hand, and a greater ideological and disciplinary pluralism on the other. Interestingly, this tension saw different elements of the World Bank supporting opposite positions.

A range of agency-supported websites, such as ELDIS and GDNet, are intended to be important sources for South–South sharing through the encouragement of the posting of research papers from the South.[13] However, the emergence of knowledge-based aid appears to have done little to focus agency support on Southern-based knowledge networking or the development of Southern institutional capacity for knowledge production (Johnson 2002). Indeed, it has been argued that the heavy investment in the Development Gateway potentially threatens existing Southern sites of knowledge sharing (Bissio 2001; Wilks 2002).

Japan has perhaps done more than other donors to support South–South knowledge sharing, in a tradition that predates the fascination with knowledge-based aid (see chapter 7). Elements of this concern include the series of Tokyo International Conferences on African Development and attempts to promote knowledge sharing among policy-makers and researchers from Africa and Asia.

Indigenous knowledge

Indigenous knowledge operates within very different paradigms from that of development knowledge as understood by agencies. Nevertheless, there has been a growth in agency interest in indigenous knowledge, perhaps most notably from The Netherlands. This has spread even to the World Bank, where its Africa Region has been behind a major initiative for codifying and sharing indigenous knowledge (see chapter 4). This is clearly a highly complex area, but issues obviously arise about the extent to which this is a privileging of indigenous knowledge on its own terms or an extraction from it of what is seen as developmentally useful (Arce and Long 1992; Long 1992; Apffel-Marglin 1996).

Knowledge-based aid or learning-led development?

The possibilities and limits of bridging the knowledge management and learning organisation literature have already been noted. This suggests that there is merit in thinking about learning-based accounts of aid as well as those based on knowledge. Of course, knowledge and learning are intimately related. However, there are also tensions between their meanings that are in need of exploration. In particular, a number of authors (e.g. Ellerman 2000a; King 2001; Tilak 2001) are concerned that the knowledge-based aid paradigm can too easily slip into a focus on what agencies know and want to disseminate rather than on what they and their partners do not know, and need or want to learn. Moreover, given that the discovery of knowledge-based aid is at least partially driven by aid effectiveness concerns, it is somewhat ironic that knowledge is being emphasised over learning when there is little evidence for answers to many perennial questions about aid.

A relatively positive vision of the possibilities of learning-based development is possible. This approach would draw together accounts of individual development through learning in communities (Lave and Wenger 1991) and national development through genuine and broad ownership (Sen 1999) in a way that revisits and updates some early and now widely neglected development thinking (e.g. Hirschman 1958, 1971; Ellerman 2000b). This suggests that the challenge for agencies and their Southern partners lies not so much in managing knowledge but in supporting social learning as a means of knowledge generation and sharing.

Closely related to these arguments about learning-based development are the concerns of some agencies with capacity development. In this view, widespread national ownership of development will become a reality only if there is considerable support for the development of individual and organisational capacities and wider systems and incentive regimes (Gustafsson 2001).

Alternative accounts of knowledge and development

The story so far has been that of the origins and nature of knowledge-based aid. However, to stop at this point would be to ignore the very extensive literature that is critical of the notion of knowledge for development, in both its most recent and its earlier forms. This section will therefore provide an overview of some of the key elements of such accounts, and their implications for an analysis of knowledge-based aid.

Behind these critical accounts of knowledge and development lies a far wider social theory tradition. Kuhn's (1962) work on paradigms and Foucault's (e.g. 1970, 1972) work on discourse and the 'archaeology of knowledge' laid much of the groundwork for current understandings of the contested and constructed nature of knowledge. Educationalists from Bernstein (1971), through Apple (1993), to Muller (2001) have sought to explore what is valued by pupils, schools, economies and societies as 'useful knowledge' and what is rejected. Through feminist critiques of patriarchal knowledge construction (e.g. Lorde 1984; Collins 1991) and

Southern critiques of Northern constructions of knowledge (e.g. Smith 1999; Mbembe 2001), scholars and activists have sought to lay bare the basis of power upon which knowledge is constructed and reclaim spaces for other forms of knowledge and knowing. These critiques taken together constitute a rejection of the way in which the Enlightenment tradition has seen rationality, truth and universality as unproblematic notions. Instead, they point to the embodied, interpretive, complex and contextual nature of knowledge.

Knowledge for development and the social theory of knowledge disagree in their views on the limits of knowledge. Critics of development rationality argue that it assumes that the world is knowable objectively. Instead, they point to the construction of knowledge out of a complex interaction between social, cultural, institutional and situational factors that builds upon existing concepts and practices (Gadamer 1975; Arce and Long 1992).

This intellectual tradition leads to a questioning of the way in which development emerged as a notion, and its existence as a particular discipline with its own special brand of knowledge. Leys (1996) and Rist (1997) have shown how it is based on particular assumptions about modernity and progress, as part of the larger Enlightenment project. Development is also materially located in the particular political economy of the 1950s and 1960s. This includes the Bretton Woods system, Keynesian corporatism (at least in Western Europe), the Cold War, and the primacy of the nation state (Leys 1996; McGrath 1999). Yet both these broader and narrower foundations have been largely undermined by major economic, political and intellectual trends of the last quarter of the twentieth century, broadly associated with globalisation, post-Fordism and postmodernism.

A number of authors have also highlighted the problematic nature of development's reliance on economics as its lead discipline (e.g. Apffel-Marglin 1996; Dore 1997; McNeill 2000; Denning 2001).[14] In spite of the trends in social theory noted above, economics has retained a powerful emphasis on theory as opposed to practice, and on truth as opposed to values. A limited regard for context, history and power serve to encourage a technocratic approach in which the intensely political nature of policy-making is ignored and non-economic arguments are rejected (McGrath 2001a).

In development thinking more generally, and particularly in elements of knowledge-based aid, there is an assumption that knowledge, policy and development outcomes are unproblematically related. This assumption is rejected by a large body of academic literature on the policy process (e.g. Hirschman and Lindblom 1969 [1962]; Lindblom 1968; Page

2000). The relationship between research and policy is highly complex (Stone 2002) and intensely political. Agency accounts tend to assume that policy-making is based on consensus. There appears to be a mental model operating in agencies in which it is assumed that stakeholders will come to rational decisions based on the available knowledge. Authors such as Kingdon (1995) have, however, suggested that research rarely gets translated into policy, whilst others point to the ways in which power and ideology shape the resolution of conflicts between different knowledges (Arce and Long 1992).

The move from policy to intended outcome is also problematic. Policy sociologists such as Ball (1990) have suggested that policy is often more about the creation of discourses that mobilise political, ideological or financial resources rather than planning for future practices. Given the asymmetries of power and the presence of conditionalities in the aid relationship, it may be that Northern policy sociology seriously under-plays the gap between policy and practice in Southern contexts (McGrath 2001a).[15]

Agency accounts of knowledge for development are also weak on context and complexity. Disciplines such as international and comparative education, however, stress the dangers of policy thinking that is devoid of historical and cultural contexts (Watson 1998; McGrath 2001b). In this tradition, policy transfer is seen as far less important than policy learning through adaptation, a notion that is clearly included in some agency thinking (Gustafsson 2000; Stiglitz 2000 [1999]), but is far from mainstream.[16]

Another set of accounts looks at the way in which agencies are poor at using knowledge. Carlsson and Wohlgemuth (2000b) highlight a number of ways in which agencies fail to learn. Agency learning is also undermined by the need to disburse, as a number of writers from within agencies acknowledge (Lintonen 2000; Bergmann 2001; Denning 2001).

However, other approaches point to the ways in which learning failures arise out of the nature of the development discourse. Post-development, anti-development and Foucauldian accounts have focused on the way in which development texts and practices construct the un(der)developed Other in ways that do more to legitimate development than to address the needs of those who become the objects of development (Ferguson 1994; Escobar 1995; Rahnema and Bawtree 1997). Roe (1991), Mearns and Leach (1996), Baumann (1999) and Ellerman (2001b) all argue that agencies often base their practices on received wisdoms or official doctrines that provide an incomplete or incorrect basis for policy and practice.

Agencies increasingly display a powerful tendency towards identifying quantifiable targets. These include not just the International Development Targets but the attempt to develop a set of secondary targets (Chang *et al.* 1999). This may reflect the political and bureaucratic contexts within which agencies are operating. However, it also sends powerful signals about which knowledge counts, and adds to the asymmetrical nature of development partnerships (Carton 1998; Crewe and Harrison 1998; Berg 2000). Social theory has become increasingly interested in complexity and the existence of multiple truths, but this remains far from the agency (and broader governmental) way of seeing the world (Uphoff 1996; Scott 1998).

The currently dominant poverty agenda among agencies can narrow conceptions of what counts as developmentally useful knowledge. This holds for the International Development Targets as an important manifestation of this agenda. The language of sector-wide approaches (SWAPs) and the Poverty Reduction Strategy Papers (PRSPs) seems to hold the promise of a partnership-based approach to development where Southern voices are paramount. This vision would seem to accord power to Southern knowledge about development priorities and practices, and reduce the dominance of 'universal' knowledge as constructed by the agencies. However, this positive outcome is highly contested. Crucially, it is far from evident that shifts in language about knowledge and partnership will be enough to effect a radical change in models of development co-operation, imbued as these are with power, bureaucratic norms and vested interests (Hayman *et al.* 2003).

At the same time, at the more micro level of projects (for projects are still alive and well in spite of SWAPs and PRSPs), the discourse of participatory development has spread from academia through NGOs and into agencies. This has led to an apparent prioritisation of local over expert knowledge (see e.g. Chambers 1995).[17] However, Mosse (2000) and Kothari (2001) both argue that this apparent reversal masks more complex webs of knowledge and power that retain considerable power for the expert (transformed now into facilitator) and for the organisations and ideas of development.

A concluding comment

Knowledge for development is clearly open to serious objections in spite of agency claims that it is about Southern ownership and development. This chapter has sought to explore where it comes from as a way of informing the critique of the theory and practice of both internal knowledge sharing activities of agencies and their approach to knowledge for development. Knowledge clearly is important to development (itself a problematic notion) but in a highly complex and contested way. Indeed, perhaps the greatest benefit of the 'discovery' of knowledge by agencies is its effect of opening up their activities to a new form of scrutiny, which challenges them to follow the fuller logic of what they profess to believe in and do as a result of their belief in knowledge for development.

This is the challenge we have set ourselves in writing this book. In the next four chapters, we shall explore it in more detail through an analysis of elements of the knowledge discourses and practices of four major development co-operation agencies.

Notes

1. It is worth noting in passing the importance of information to economic theory. Debates about the importance of asymmetries and imperfections of information have been central to debates between neoliberal and neo-Keynesian economists (see Leijonhufvud 1981). As our case studies of development co-operation agencies show, there is often a conflation of information and knowledge in current accounts. Indeed, one of the leading current analysts of what we would call the knowledge debate, Manuel Castells, writes of the Information Age (Castells 1996).

2. Reich's account was not simply about the need to compete in the emergent global knowledge economy. His analysis is also very concerned with the negative social impacts of globalisation.

3. The variety of epithets is striking. On one level, it can be seen as pointing to the conceptual confusion that exists in much of the thinking about knowledge and information. On another, however, it appears that the main purpose behind these epithets is the production of memorable 'sound bites'.

4. We shall come back in subsequent pages to the work of Steve Denning, in his role as Programme Manager for the World Bank's Knowledge Management Programme.

5. Of course, these were not widely discussed concepts at the time.

6. Rischard had been a senior supporter of an informal network of World Bank staff interested in knowledge management that was already meeting on a regular basis. Wolfensohn's speech allowed this network to become more visible and to take the lead in producing this new strategy very quickly. Their ability to respond quickly to Wolfensohn's speech naturally increased his support for their work.

7. The influence of this school of thought will be seen also in the chapters on DFID and Sida.

8. The imagery of darkness and ignorance was by no means new. Africa, after all, was stereotypically the 'dark continent' in popular European imagination. Moreover, in his September speech of 1972, World Bank president Robert McNamara talked of 'a developing world darkened by illiteracy' (McNamara 1981: 210).

9. What the Report actually said was that most of the gap between the two countries' performance could not be explained by conventional analyses,

implying by the context that knowledge was likely to be the explanatory factor. It is interesting to note that this rather cautious and implicit statement had given way to a far bolder and cruder statement by 2000: 'Forty years ago, Ghana and the Republic of Korea had virtually the same income per capita, but by the 1990s Korea's income per capita was six times Ghana's. More than half of that difference can be attributed to Korea's success in acquiring and using knowledge' (World Bank 2000a: 1).

10. For instance in the Canadian-led initiative termed the Centre for Connectivity in Africa.

11. An inter-agency meeting in Manila in January 2003 sought to bring together the discourses of capacity and knowledge under the umbrella of aid effectiveness. See report on the International Symposium on Capacity Development and Aid Effectiveness (2003). http://www.undp.org/capacity/symposium

12. However, Mkandawire (2000) and Mwiria (2001), in an African context, point to the role that Southern governments have played in contributing to the problems of academia.

13. Inevitably, however, these sites are also heavily used by Northern researchers, both to access materials and to post their own.

14. Denning's is perhaps the most significant of such critiques, given his background in the World Bank.

15. Caddell (2002) provides a valuable exception to this tendency in the case of education and development in Nepal.

16. Sida is unusual among development co-operation agencies for the number of senior staff (past and present) with degrees in international and comparative education. Whether this has encouraged the organisation as a whole to be more suspicious of simple policy transfer and more interested in learning is a matter for speculation.

17. This appears somewhat analogous and contemporaneous to populist attempts by neoliberal politicians in the North to reduce the professional autonomy of teachers, doctors, nurses and other public sector professionals.

FOUR

The World Bank or the knowledge bank?

The discovery of knowledge-based aid in the World Bank

Knowledge-based aid exists primarily because the World Bank embraced it. This is not to say that the Bank has been the sole influence on its introduction into other agencies, or on the reluctance of some others to adopt the approach. But it does serve to highlight the key role that the World Bank has played in this new approach to aid, a role that is typical of much of the World Bank's history. Since its origins in the Bretton Woods Conference, which sought to provide a 'new international economic order' for the post-Second World War period, the World Bank has been at the leading edge of much of what takes place in development.

It is not surprising, therefore, that the World Bank is also (probably even more than its Bretton Woods sister, the International Monetary Fund) the most frequent target of development and aid critics.[1] With its disproportionate voting rights for the wealthiest countries, the World Bank has been seen as too often serving the interests of its principal shareholders, especially the United States of America (Chossudovsky 1997; Centros de Estudios Internacionales 2000; Woods 2000).[2] Through the 1980s and into the first half of the 1990s, the international reputation of the World Bank reached a new low as widespread criticism of both the content and processes of its central policy of structural adjustment combined with growing critiques from both left and right of the amounts spent on salaries, benefits and buildings (Hancock 1989; Bandow and Vásquez 1994; Caufield 1996). Perceptions of the Bank's market fundamentalism led to disagreement within the aid community, with UNICEF's *Adjustment with a Human Face* (Cornia, Jolly and Stewart 1987) and Japanese criticisms of the Bank's *East Asian Miracle* (World Bank 1993; Caufield 1996; Wade 1996) as often-cited examples. Dissent within the Bank also appeared to be on the increase, with high-level resignations and leaked memos (Caufield 1996; Bond 2000). Most famously, in 1991, a memo from the chief economist's office was leaked that appeared to call for the dumping of toxic waste in Africa (Bond 2000).[3] It was into this climate that James Wolfensohn came when he took over the presidency of the World Bank in 1995.

Wolfensohn needed urgently to be seen to be addressing the expenditure of the World Bank. For this reason, a new Strategic Compact between staff and the organisation became the central tool for reform, developed in the first two years of his presidency (World Bank 1997). There was also a pressing need to address the effectiveness and efficiency of the Bank's operational work. In 1992, a team chaired by vice-president Willi Wapenhans had reported unacceptable levels of project failure. Moreover, it identified an inability to learn from others as an important element in this failure (World Bank 1992).

Although the Wolfensohn presidency has been about a number of things, this conjunction of the need to become a leaner organisation, criticism of the effectiveness of the Bank's operations, and a growing need to think beyond adjustment opened up a space for the notion of the knowledge bank to emerge.

In chapter 3, we noted how Wolfensohn's annual meeting speech of September 1996 took up the theme of knowledge as a core element of his strategy for reforming the World Bank. It is worth repeating the key paragraph from this speech:

> We have been in the business of researching and disseminating the lessons of development for a long time. But the revolution in information technology increased the potential value of these efforts by vastly extending their reach. To capture this potential, we need to invest in the necessary systems, in Washington and worldwide, that will enhance our ability to gather development information and experience, and share it with our clients. We need to become, in effect, the Knowledge Bank. (Wolfensohn 1996: 7)

This commitment was to lead to the introduction of knowledge management as one of the themes of *The Strategic Compact* (World Bank 1997) and to the 1998–99 *World Development Report, Knowledge for Development* (World Bank 1998a). As we shall see subsequently, it is a commitment that is still important to the Bank's overall strategy. However, before turning to look in detail at what being 'the knowledge bank' might mean, it is worth remembering that the World Bank had 'knowledge activities' long before James Wolfensohn appeared on the scene.

The World Bank's older knowledge strategies

Before it became commonplace to attach the word 'knowledge' to many different aspects of society and the economy, several of the World Bank's traditional activities had been responsible for building its knowledge base. Amongst what we may term these older 'knowledge projects', is the Bank's research group in development economics, which has been responsible for academic policy papers. However, it is also worth noting that criticisms of the work of this unit have often been at the heart of external and internal attacks on the World Bank's workings. A series of authors from Mosley, Harrigan and Toye (1991) to Denning (2001) argue that the power of this group of economists has prevented the emergence of other disciplinary traditions within the World Bank and that they have operated far more as defenders of ideological orthodoxy than as promoters of a vigorous, empirically based debate about development theory and practice. Thus, the development economics group has been an important source for knowledge generation and dissemination, but a controversial one.[4]

A much larger source of what Wolfensohn termed 'development knowledge' is derived from what the Bank calls economic and sector work (ESW): the pre-investment analytical work carried out by the Bank for its client countries. This is intended to cover in considerable detail the majority of countries in the world. However, it has also come under internal and external criticism for the quality of its analysis and for its failure to engage sufficiently with issues of participation and capacity development (World Bank/Harvard 2001; Wilks and Lefrancois 2002), a point we shall return to later.

Equally, there has been a long series of *World Development Reports* (*WDRs*), going back to the late 1970s, which has sought to establish the state of the development art on particular themes, including, as we have seen, on knowledge. However, here too the standing of these reports has been damaged by the events surrounding the resignation of the lead author of the *WDR* 2000–1, Ravi Kanbur (see p. 98).

In most sectors, the World Bank has sought also to develop and synthesise its own policy knowledge, often in ways that have been highly influential in other agencies, even if sometimes contentious for national governments, academic analysts and NGOs. One of the most topical of these is a major paper on tertiary education, already referred to, and titled, significantly, *Constructing Knowledge Societies* (World Bank 2002a). Another of the Bank's long-standing knowledge functions could be said to be the Operations Evaluation Department (OED), which, as in other agencies, has sought to report independently to the Board on aid effectiveness. Significantly, the OED chose the Bank's knowledge activities to be the focus of a major evaluation in 2002.[5] Lastly, amongst several of these older knowledge resources of the Bank, would be the World Bank Institute (WBI – in part a continuation of the former Economic Development Institute) which has a very wide-ranging mandate for client learning. As we shall see as this chapter unfolds, the WBI has become the principal nexus or portal for World Bank activities in co-ordinating and facilitating knowledge-based aid.

All in all, the sheer scale of these existing sources of economic analysis, sector policy review, evaluation, documentation and capacity building would have qualified the institution to regard itself as a knowledge bank long before it decided to become *the* Knowledge Bank. Indeed, it is an interesting question to what extent the Bank's formal decision to restructure itself to become more of a learning organisation and to take a lead role in managing knowledge for development has affected these older knowledge activities and these different sections of the World Bank. We shall bear some of these in mind in examining some of the more recent knowledge projects. However, we shall now turn to some of the overall language about the relationship between knowledge and development that has emerged from the World Bank under Wolfensohn.

The World Bank's vision of knowledge for development

Primary education is the largest single contributor to the economic growth rates of the high-performing Asian economies.

... the major difference between East Asia and Sub-Saharan Africa is due to variations in primary school enrolment rates.

If in 1960 the Republic of Korea had had the same low school enrol-ment rate as Pakistan, its GDP per capita by 1985 would have been 40 per cent lower than it actually was. (World Bank 1995: 23)

Forty years ago, Ghana and the Republic of Korea had virtually the same income per capita, but by the 1990s Korea's income per capita was six times Ghana's. More than half of that difference can be at-tributed to Korea's success in acquiring and using knowledge. (World Bank 2000a: 1)

It may seem strange to start an analysis of the relationship between knowledge and development under Wolfensohn's presidency with a quotation from an education paper that appeared just as he was about to assume his post. However, in the context of the further quotations its significance becomes clearer. Back in 1995, the primary school was alleged by the World Bank policy review on education to be the main factor in explaining the difference between the high- and low-income economies of Asia or between the high-income countries of Asia and those in sub-Saharan Africa. Now, since the World Bank embraced 'knowledge' in the autumn of 1996, and set out to become 'the Knowledge Bank' by the year 2000, it would seem that knowledge is the factor that really makes the difference. The World Bank would be the first to admit that sorting out the complex of relationships between knowledge and economic growth is highly problematic (World Bank 1998a: 18–22); nevertheless, there is a tendency to generalise about the role of knowledge in quotations such as the first above and others that we noted in chapter 3.

The World Development Report 1998–99

In terms of policy influence, the Bank's most public contribution to this new set of assumptions about the role of knowledge in development was its *World Development Report, Knowledge for Development*. In many ways, coming just two years after the Bank had decided to put knowledge on its masthead, it carried forward many of the aspirations that were in Wolfensohn's 'Knowledge Bank' speech, but it also betrayed some of the inherent tensions. In this chapter, we shall use it as a valuable starting point for a number of the Bank-related debates about knowledge. For one thing, it is a new testament to the power of knowledge, and is almost New Testament-like in some of its purple passages about enlightenment, most famously in the very first paragraph, which we quoted earlier: 'Knowledge is like light. Weightless and intangible, it can easily travel the world, enlightening the lives of people everywhere. Yet billions of people still live in the darkness of poverty – unnecessarily' (World Bank 1998a: 1). But in some ways, as the very detailed bibliographical note on its external and internal literature sources makes clear, the *WDR* also draws heavily on the older faith about the role of science and technology in development, and on what has been learnt about technology transfer and adaptation over thirty years.[6] Arguably, the word 'knowledge' has to some extent replaced what was written about 'technology' and technological capability in earlier decades, but the information and communication technology (ICT) revolution is what now makes the difference in terms of outreach, potential and impact of this now globally accessible knowledge.

The acknowledgement of the importance of technology is still there in the sense that one of the two great themes of the *WDR* is knowledge about technology or, rather, in many countries, the lack of or gaps in such knowledge. The other great theme is information problems or knowledge about attributes, that is to say knowledge about, for example, the qualities of firms, workers, or products. Thus one whole part of the *WDR* is about acquiring and absorbing knowledge, and has many parallels with the older literature on technological borrowing and adaptation. What makes it different is the seriousness with which education is taken as the key factor in technological creation, adaptation and communication.[7] The other difference is the enormous potential of applying the new ICTs to these processes of knowledge creation and absorption.

We shall look briefly at just a few of the elements in the *WDR*, and most especially those that relate to other key elements of the Bank as a 'knowledge agency', including the crucial role of education, the global–local knowledge tension, and the Bank's own role in knowledge management and sharing, both internally and externally.

The key role of education in knowledge for development

What is important about the treatment of education in this broader context of technological change and of information gaps is that the WDR not only affirmed the central role of basic education, with all the usual claims about its impact on agricultural innovation, enterprise, child health, nutrition and contraception, which had been commonplace in World Bank documents back into the 1980s, but it put clearly back on the agenda the crucial requirements of tertiary education and technical training, which had arguably been undervalued in many Bank papers over the previous decade.[8] Under the sub-heading 'Tertiary education: building knowledge for an information-based society' the WDR made it absolutely clear that basic education could only be a partial response to the challenge of globalisation. Again, the link to the demands of technological borrowing and adaptation, especially through the new ICTs, was useful in making the case for substantial investment in these sub-sectors of education: 'Besides teaching new and better skills, tertiary education and technical training produce people who can monitor technological trends, assess their relevance to the country's prospects, and help develop an appropriate national technological strategy' (World Bank 1998a: 42). The same link to the requirements of technology creation and adaptation led the WDR to underline the need for research degrees and the development of research capacity.

A third area of concern was facilitated by the wider interest in the ICTs and their implication for education. The WDR revisited the much older literature on the potential of distance education, and applied to it the extraordinary potential of ICTs for breaking through the barriers of traditional classroom learning, in virtual and other new forms of open learning. From this angle comes the vision of Wolfensohn's WDR introduction, which sees distance education as extending learning opportunities to millions otherwise denied a good education. This fascination with distance and especially e-learning was to spawn a number of Bank knowledge projects, as we shall see later in this chapter, as well as inspiring smaller but significant initiatives in other agencies such as DFID and JICA, as we shall see in later chapters.

Whether linked directly to the WDR or independently, we can see that this Bank-wide rethinking of education via the lens of knowledge and particularly new information technology leads into the new sector reviews by the Bank on vocational training and distance education (for example, in Africa [Johanson 2001, 2002]), the regional reviews (which again emphasise the role of knowledge[9]) and the 2000–2002 review of higher education. The last-named puts even more strongly than the *WDR* the absolute centrality of education in economic growth: 'The role of education in general, and of tertiary education in particular, is now more influential than ever in the construction of knowledge economies and democratic societies' (World Bank 2002a: 1). It is also the higher education paper which, significantly, takes furthest the direct challenge to institutions of the ICT revolution and the global knowledge economy. It is a brave new world that is envisioned, with dramatic examples of higher education taking advantage of the information and communication revolution, but also one in which it can be seen that the internationalisation of higher education is by no means a level playing field.[10]

The new knowledge-sharing World Bank

If one of the strands that the logic of the knowledge economy had begun to question was an education policy that prioritised primary education, another dimension that was picked up and given prominence in the *WDR* was the knowledge revolution within the World Bank itself (World Bank 1998a: 138–43). This is the most significant high-profile source that we have for the thinking in any agency about the implementation of knowledge-based aid.

As we have suggested in chapter 3, Wolfensohn did not discover knowledge management for the World Bank, but effectively publicised and promoted what was already a relatively large underground movement within the Bank. It was this pre-existing interest in knowledge management that allowed staff to respond quickly to Wolfensohn's speech with a report, *The Knowledge Partnership* (World Bank 1996a), that outlined in some detail the vision for a new knowledge strategy for the World Bank.

A group of Bank staff were well aware of the rapidly expanding knowledge management literature, and had already made the first informal links with some of the leading thinkers and 'knowledge corporations'.[11] They shared the conviction that in large organisations that carried out vast quantities of analytical work, such as the World Bank, the knowledge relevant to a particular challenge probably already existed, but was inaccessible. It was either locked in the heads and experiences of different individuals, but was 'tacit' (not out in the open and explicit), or it was embedded in key reports that were in the public domain but not known to those who needed them. Two things were vital to allow the organisation to profit from the knowledge that in some sense it already possessed. First, 'knowledge-based communities' had to be encouraged across a whole series of thematic areas, allowing members with a common interest – for example, in higher education, early childhood or in small enterprise – to share knowledge in a relatively informal way. Second, ICTs could dramatically assist the speed with which members of such groups could access data on critical problems, just in time, and frequently with the assistance of group-specific help desks.

Thus, the initial focus of the World Bank's new knowledge activities was largely on improving internal learning and efficiency. As we have suggested already, this was intimately connected with a larger reform agenda. Nonetheless, that reform also required that the Bank should become more effective in its operational work. Indeed, it was impossible that knowledge management for the Bank's own staff could ever be enough. Instead, knowledge sharing with clients, and with the broader development community, would need to be a central aim of the project, as Wolfensohn's initial speech, the knowledge strategy and the *WDR* all make clear. This is what the *WDR* has to say: 'Its objective is to make know-how and experience accessible not only internally, to World Bank staff, but externally to clients, partners and stakeholders around the world – and in the process to reach many who now have little or no access to its expertise' (World Bank 1998a: 139). This could be read in a critical vein as suggesting that the knowledge sharing is about getting the World Bank's knowledge more effectively into the hands (or, rather, minds) of this wide range of development actors. Such a reading could give rise to the suspicion that knowledge sharing is simply a more sanitised and effective way of carrying on with operational business as usual. Using the power of the Bank's knowledge more effectively to convince other actors of the merits of the Bank's positions would be preferable to having to use the naked force of conditionalities.[12]

A more positive, though not unproblematic, vision also can be seen in the writings of the first director of the Knowledge Management Programme of the World Bank, Steve Denning. What is intriguing here is the emphasis on the imperative to share knowledge within communities, since it is within communities, he argues (following authors such as Lave and Wenger 1991), and not within individuals that knowledge mainly resides. Such community-based knowledge is also highly context-specific. This latter insight is particularly important for the larger vision of the knowledge-sharing World Bank with its 'unique reservoir of development experience across sectors and countries' and its president's intention that it should be the 'first port of call for the world's best development expertise' (World Bank 1998c: 4). In a paper written after he had relinquished formal leadership of the programme, Denning made a comment that goes to the very heart of the ambition of the Bank to become a knowledge agency:

> Ironically, at the very moment that it becomes technologically possible to move information instantaneously around the world, comes the recognition that the context in which knowledge arose is often crucial to understanding or exploiting it. Knowledge without context is not knowledge at all. (Denning 2001: 135)

This is a potentially crucially important assertion, given the Bank's intention increasingly to share its knowledge worldwide. It is as if there are two fundamentally different interpretations of knowledge management and sharing in the World Bank. One, which is captured in the WDR 1998–99 in a box on 'Knowledge Management at the World Bank', presents a vision of the Bank's knowledge management system seeking to make the Bank a clearing house, a 'memory bank' of its own best practices, as well as a collector and disseminator of the best development practice from outside the Bank. The other interpretation, as we have just seen, is of a development knowledge that is intimately embedded in specific contexts, and where presumably the help desks and advisory services which support the various thematic groups would need to be very cautious about their ability to respond with certainty within their agreed time limit of 48 hours.

This tension between embedded knowledge-in-context and authenticated and approved 'best practice' is a theme we shall return to in our discussion of other knowledge projects of the Bank, as well as in subsequent chapters. However, if we are to believe Denning's own account, the initial decision to support the Bank's knowledge initiative was in part taken because of powerful examples of how specific local needs could be met by relevant local experience elsewhere.[13]

A reason for stressing that knowledge sharing in the World Bank was 'explicitly external from the outset', as Denning argues, was surely in part derived from the view that unlike a large competitive private sector company, the Bank should seek to accommodate, as an integral part of its shared knowledge base, the knowledge and insights of its 'clients' (the governments) and in turn the ultimate recipient communities for which governments are mandated to act. This would have been a very tall order, but is a powerful example of the apparently transformative thinking that the knowledge sharing discourse threw up. It is worth quoting at some length because, as we shall see in other knowledge projects of the Bank, the treatment of the 'local' as opposed to the allegedly 'global' becomes one of the more contentious issues in Bank knowledge:

> Also part of the challenge is the authentication of content. Since human beings often fully trust only the knowledge they themselves have helped create, development knowledge bases will reach their full potential only if practitioners in developing countries take part in building them. For explicit know-how, participation can be facilitated by opening knowledge bases for comment and review and by providing the means to register alternative views. For know-how that remains tacit, active participation by developing countries is needed in all phases of knowledge creation – for example, in project design and in building new knowledge bases. (World Bank 1998a: 140)

Here the language of authentication, that the Bank should be seeking to validate the knowledge that it will facilitate the sharing of, appears to run up against the strong concerns within the more progressive elements of the knowledge literature about encouraging free debate and allowing diverse opinions. Such a debate is of central relevance to the attempts by the World Bank to support the sharing of development knowledge in a brokerage or facilitatory role. This is at the heart of some of the biggest World Bank knowledge projects, such as the (Global) Development Gateway and the Global Development Network.

The quotation from the *WDR* above may sound strangely idealistic, but it is a telling illustration of what the 'New Knowledge Partnership' of Wolfensohn could have entailed. If what had been learnt about the crucial value of tacit knowledge and the role of like-minded communities in knowledge sharing had any salience, then the partnership could have meant a genuinely different relationship with 'clients' and with what came to be called 'external members of communities' (Denning 2001: 142). What the *WDR* captured as a real possibility for the World Bank and the development community more generally was the option that the advent of knowledge management could actually mean something very different from the World Bank or other agencies continuing as 'the repository of knowledge'. Aided by the extraordinary advances in ICTs, there could be stimulated 'true exchanges of knowledge, not just one-way transfers'. The *WDR*'s account of the potential of symmetrical knowledge sharing ended on an upbeat note: 'And as developing countries begin to put their own knowledge management systems in place, the opportunities for creating and exchanging knowledge about all aspects of development will soar' (World Bank 1998a: 142). The WDR thus contained elements in its language that could suggest that the Wolfensohnian reforms were genuine and were designed to make the World Bank a more open partner in development. They highlighted how the notion of knowledge for development could make internal knowledge sharing more effective and move the balance away from ideology and universalism to pragmatism and context. They suggested that a new relationship with partners could develop in which two-way knowledge sharing would be a central element. They pointed to a new concern with supporting Southern knowledge generation and the free flow of development knowledge, in which the World Bank could play a more facilitatory role.

However, the WDR also retained a heavy imprint of older Bank certainties about liberalisation and privatisation. It failed seriously to address the ways in which ideology and power had shaped development knowledge. It continued the longstanding World Bank self-portrayal as the leading technical expert in a predominantly technical field. It overstressed the positive development potential of ICTs and globalisation and underplayed many other elements of poverty and underdevelopment. Thus the Knowledge WDR (World Bank 1998a) takes us to the heart of the debate about the 'new World Bank' and the extent to which knowledge-based aid is about genuine transformation, window-dressing or even greater power over development. These themes will loom large in our discussion of some of the most prominent projects that have emerged out of the 'knowledge bank' and 'knowledge for development' discourses and the attempts since the middle of 2001 to develop an overall architecture and vision for what began as disparate initiatives.

Revising the strategy: the Ramphele review and a shifting focus for the knowledge bank

Early in 2001, the World Bank issued the review of the Strategic Compact (World Bank 2001a) and a new *Strategic Framework* (World Bank 2001b), designed to be the guiding document for Wolfensohn's second presidential term. In most respects, the official view of both documents was that the Strategic Compact had been correctly targeted, that some obstacles had been faced, that progress was satisfactory, and that the Bank should continue basically along the same path. As for the knowledge bank vision, this was largely affirmed although it was suggested that the task was far from completed. Particular challenges for the future were identified as the need for knowledge work to have more operational impact and a concern that the knowledge activities were not exploiting sufficient synergies.

Table 4.1 Objectives, activities and challenges for the revised knowledge bank

Level	Central objective	Key activities/instruments	Key challenges
External Helping clients benefit from global knowledge	Enhancing *client capacity* to access and make effective use of knowledge whatever the source	• Knowledge economy work • Much of the education and information and communica tionstechnology sectors • Technical assistance • GDN; infoDev; AVU; WorLD	• Responding to client demand for knowledge economy work • Making client capacity-enhancement core to our operational work • Systematically replicate good practices where they exist
Interface Products and services that share knowledge with clients	Enhancing the *sharing of knowledge* with our clients and partners	• Knowledge embedded in lending • ESW, technical assistance • Client training • Gateway and GDLN • Research • Bank website • Some thematic groups	• Move beyond 'letting 1,000 flowers bloom' to realising synergies between activities • Standardising and improving websites • Improving measurement and performance • Financing model for unbundled knowledge work

Internal

Knowledge sharing and staff learning

Improving the Bank's opera-
tional quality and effectiveness
through enhancing our own
capacity

Knowledge management/
sharing infrastructure, primarily:
- Thematic groups
- Advisory services
- Data services, live data bases,
  etc.
- Intranet and global IT systems
- Staff learning programmes

Consolidate progress through:
- Better integration with client and
  operational needs
- Reinforcing accountabilities and
  strengthening governance
- Introducing stronger
  measurement
- Making good practices
  commonplace

Source: World Bank (2001c: 16)

Parallel to this revision of the World Bank's overall strategy, one of the managing directors, Mamphela Ramphele, was given the task of leading a review of the range of knowledge bank activities. Her remit included these issues of articulation with operations and the relationships between the various initiatives. The challenge to the Bank of a relative decline in lending opportunities in some regions was also clearly identified as a pertinent issue. This indeed is one of the most salient issues for the knowledge bank notion. Regions such as East Asia, the Middle East and North Africa are increasingly able to access loans at more favourable rates than from the World Bank. Thus, the relevant regional vice-presidencies are seeking to transform themselves into consultancy providers rather than project managers. We shall return to this point later.

The Ramphele team produced a paper that went to the World Bank Board in October 2001 (World Bank 2001c), where it was treated primarily as information rather than something that required ratification as policy. Nonetheless, the broad strategic vision of the document was accepted and became effectively the knowledge bank strategy. The summary can be seen in Table 4.1.

This paper marks a significant watershed in the Bank's knowledge activities. Although an external dimension does seem to have been present from early on in the work of Denning and others, approval of this paper is indicative of high-level acceptance of the need to shift more to an external orientation. As the paper puts it, 'The emphasis in our knowledge work is moving from a heavy focus on better capturing and sharing knowledge within the Bank to client-related knowledge sharing and capacity enhancement' (World Bank 2001c: 13). This is not to say that the internal dimension has lost importance. Indeed, there are clear concerns throughout the paper about the extent to which knowledge sharing is improving internal efficiency and about the continuing failure to share effectively between Bank units. The transition from knowledge work to operations is particularly emphasised. The problem of cultural and incentive barriers to knowledge sharing is discussed. Moreover, the paper breaks new ground in the World Bank in trying to promote better integration of the knowledge function with the training, now renamed 'staff learning', function. As we shall see subsequently in the other agency chapters, new thinking about knowledge and innovations in learning has largely resided in different units and has seen limited articulation.

The paper acknowledges that better internal knowledge management can bring only limited benefits to a development bank. Rather, there is a strong imperative to address the sharing of knowledge with others. Here the relationship between knowledge and lending is considered anew.

A crucial part of this is economic and sector work (ESW). Indeed, the paper acknowledges the weaknesses in ESW identified by internal quality assurance mechanisms and the important issue of partnership in such work. The paper raises the question of whether training for clients is adequate. As we shall see below, this is partly the mandate of the Global Development Learning Network, one of the knowledge initiatives identified by the paper. Another such initiative, the Development Gateway, is also identified as a key site for knowledge sharing. Whilst much of the language of Wolfensohn has been about disseminating what the World Bank knows, the Board paper makes it clear that there is 'a two way street with learning from clients and partners' (World Bank 2001c: 7).

The return to the issue of capacity is a striking element of the Board paper. It marks a revisiting of a principal theme of the immediately previous presidency, one that had fallen out of favour as knowledge became the latest great idea. As with several other agencies, this revisiting of the notion of capacity is intrinsically connected with requestioning the role of technical assistance. As we shall see in chapter 6, when we look at Sida, there has been a long-standing critique of the effects of technical assistance on capacity. However, the beginning of the twenty-first century has seen a UNDP initiative to reform technical assistance, including the radical suggestion that it should be untied (Fukuda-Parr *et al.* 2002). The Board paper acknowledges that still not enough technical assistance is capacity enhancing. However, its particular twist is to link this fact explicitly to key elements of the emerging knowledge agenda within the Bank. Arguments first rehearsed in *WDR* 1998–99 about the knowledge economy are used to suggest that capacity enhancement is crucial to development. At the same time, the decline in Bank lending to middle-income countries has led to the growth of other non-lending activities, such as reimbursable technical assistance in the Middle East and North African region. The Board paper argues that this is another route through which the agendas of national ownership, capacity enhancement and knowledge-based aid can be combined. Whilst the knowledge bank started off with little explicit consideration of issues of capacity, the Board paper stresses that all the knowledge activities of the World Bank should be considered in the light of their role in capacity enhancement. In the words of an internal briefing paper produced during the consultation process, this is nothing short of a paradigm shift:

Changing the way we think about development to integrate knowledge as a central driver of growth, security and empowerment; update our view of the Bank's business and the way we measure and value our outputs and impact – from transferring knowledge and resources, to enabling learning and building capacity … We need to move beyond the idea of the Bank as the repository of finance and knowledge that is transferred to clients, and towards the idea of the Bank as a facilitator and enabler of client learning – the crux of capacity building, and the best way to create sustainable policy shifts and development. (World Bank 2001e: 3–4)

The Board paper does appear to mark a significant shift in the Bank's official position on knowledge sharing, although we have noted that there were strong hints of such a vision in the *WDR* and elsewhere. This is not to say that the new official vision is now dominant or even widely accepted, even though its arguments were largely reiterated in a follow-up paper to the Board for June 2002 (World Bank 2002c). We shall return later in this chapter to consider the debates about how far the knowledge bank vision is supported within the Bank and wider issues about its desirability. Our focus for the moment, owever, will be on the architecture of the knowledge bank as recognised by the 2001 Board paper.

The new architecture of the knowledge bank
Improving the Bank's operational quality and effectiveness through enhancing its own capacity
This is the internally oriented strand of the knowledge bank. It is seen as having five elements:

- Thematic groups
- Advisory services
- Data services
- Intranet and IT infrastructure
- Staff learning (World Bank 2001c: 16)

Thematic groups
One of the most important elements of the architecture of the knowledge bank has been the establishment of what are called either thematic groups or communities of practice. In tune with much of the corporate and academic thinking about knowledge management (e.g. Wenger 1998), Denning pushed strongly for support to an informal network of groups of staff who came together both virtually and face to face to discuss specific areas of professional practice and knowledge. In the current 'Knowledge Bank Vision', thematic groups are clearly seen as 'making effective use of knowledge to support the quality of our operations' (World Bank 2002b). The hundred or more communities of

practice were, understandably, formed initially amongst Bank employees, sometimes in cross-cutting thematic groups, but more commonly in the sectors or subsectors that reflected the existing interests of staff. For example, in Education in the Human Development Network, there were groups such as adult education, tertiary, secondary, early child development and economics of education, although interestingly enough not basic education. Not all parts of the Bank necessarily became part of the knowledge sharing system, nor did all staff become believers. For instance, the Development Economics research group appears to have taken little direct interest in knowledge sharing, possibly because it saw its mandate as 'universal' knowledge creation rather than anything governed by the more contextualised view of knowledge that Denning was promoting, although, as we shall see, a separate knowledge project emerged from there in 1999.

Although, at the time of writing, a little over half the groups are said to offer external access, it appears that the primary focus of the thematic groups has been on internal knowledge management, which then can form the basis for better external dissemination. This certainly is the sense to be got from the Roads and Highways group's statement:

> The mission is to build identity and cohesiveness among staff; promote communications between staff to facilitate team building, professionalism and sharing of experience; make staff aware of good practice through training courses and study tours; support training for borrowers in key areas identified by staff; and provide a world-class knowledge base. (http//www.worldbank.org/html/fpd/transport/r&h_over.htm, accessed on 24 July 2002)

Despite the strong World Bank staff focus of this group, the overall policy of the Transport Sector Knowledge Management System makes it clear that their target audience is very much more diversified, and includes government officials in client countries and partner institutions supporting the Bank's knowledge management system. (We should enter here a health warning on the extent to which the life and dynamic of a thematic group can be read off their web-site. A good deal of the life of active groups will now consist of e-mail traffic that is almost entirely invisible.)[14]

Nevertheless, in other cases, the website of the thematic group makes perfectly clear who are the World Bank members and who are the external partners. Thus the Tertiary Education thematic group (as of July 2002) was composed of ten World Bank task managers, representing different regions, and had an information partnership with the

OECD, and, to judge from its home-page, also with the Boston College Centre for International Higher Education, and with the Private Higher Education Studies department at the University of Albany. By contrast, the Early Child Development group has a directory of eighteen major external international partners including many of the major players in early childhood development such as Bernard Van Leer, Aga Khan Foundation, UNICEF and the Consultative Group on Early Childhood Care and Development, as well as a much smaller number of regional partners. Such sites provide information and extensive linkages to an enormous amount of external information, and it is possible that there is in these groupings or networks a fundamentally different relationship between the Bank contact points or animator(s) and the external partners than in those groups where there is a larger and more tightly knit set of Bank staff with common concerns and an agreed work programme but only a handful of external partners.

In some groups the situation may be that the Bank members are not even 'first among equals'; each of the international partners may have a similar set of linkages to each others' facilities and resources, or conceivably one or two of the external partners may even have a much longer tradition of networking or expertise in the thematic area than the Bank itself.[15] In a very small number of groups, it seems that there has been success in spinning off regional communities. Most notable of these is a Latin American community, Ayuda Urbana (http://www.ayudaurbana.com), which is a spin-off of the Urban Services to the Poor group and which brings together the administrations of the biggest Ibero-American cities.

It would also be intriguing to analyse a select number of these thematic groups in terms of their balance between knowledge creation through R&D and knowledge dissemination.[16] Jo Ritzen, former vice-president for development policy, has suggested that there may well have been a Bank-wide shift 'from a strong emphasis on creation to an overwhelming emphasis on dissemination' and that this balance may not maximise the Bank's effectiveness (Ritzen 2000).

This is an interesting comment, and in respect of thematic groups it is almost certainly the case that the overall emphasis of many has been on connectivity and on dissemination. Indeed the assumptions in the knowledge management and knowledge sharing movement are primarily to do with bringing into use knowledge which is already in the organisation somewhere but is not known (in the jargon, a firm 'getting to know explicitly what it already knows'). The frequently quoted examples of getting urgent requests for assistance from around the organisation answered just in time re-emphasise this priority of knowledge dissemination. This is the role of the advisory services.

Advisory services

Along with the thematic groups, advisory services are owned by sectors but are also overseen by the central knowledge sharing team in the WBI. The whole very impressive apparatus of help desks and twenty advisory services (each serving a series of associated thematic groups and now forming a community of their own) is organised around the premise that knowledge does exist (much of it within the organisation) and just needs to be effectively captured, organised into a data base of 'knowledge nuggets' and then networked.

Even a brief glance at the way in which a few of these advisory services work closely with their networks and thematic groups, how they handle requests, and how they provide up-to-date sectoral news not only from inside but also from outside the organisation renders it unsurprising that the World Bank continues to be rated in industry surveys as comparable with the 'best' of corporate America.

Data services and IT systems

Of course, one of the crucial developments that has helped to make this extraordinary interactivity possible has been the integration of a whole series of once separate databases, the putting of the Bank library on-line, and the connecting of all the main offices of the Bank so that there can be video-conferencing and immediate access around the world to the knowledge and information resources of the organisation. Some regions, such as Africa, have placed significant resources into large and diverse data sets for their region and countries, including an interest in indigenous knowledge.

Staff learning

The new knowledge bank strategy stresses the need to achieve better articulation between the knowledge work of the Bank and its erstwhile staff training programmes. These too have been undergoing considerable redevelopment since the Strategic Compact. This emphasised equipping staff with cutting-edge knowledge and skills to help build client capacity. Originally the human resources programme had been responsible for what might be termed 'non-development related' staff learning, including at senior executive levels. However, increasingly it would seem that in the new framework for staff learning (World Bank 2001f) the aim of the programme is to move into supporting the development of the core operational knowledge needed by front-line staff, including 'both global and local know-how'. Even though the focus is primarily on Bank staff learning, there is here, too, a new emphasis on 'joint learning by clients and staff'. Hence, the human resources programme, to an extent, aspires now to provide the very development-oriented learning which in more specialised forms is the subject of the thematic groups: 'This means expanding training in policy analysis, community-driven development, governance, public sector management, and social and institutional analysis' (World Bank 2001f). Such a focus will require greater articulation with the work of the World Bank Institute, already the lead player both in client learning and in the knowledge bank.

All in all, these learning resources, primarily for investing in Bank staff learning and operational effectiveness, have been running at double their earlier levels since the Strategic Compact, although Bank-wide budget cuts reduced this in 2001. Over US$70 million per annum have been going into the support of these 'cutting-edge skills' for Bank staff.

Some concluding comments on the internally-oriented elements of the knowledge bank

The World Bank's internal knowledge sharing programme has been consistently highly rated in industry surveys, and the Bank has played a key role in the corporate knowledge management community. In much of its work it has been towards the leading edge of practices. Moreover, it can be argued that it has put considerable thought into the ways in which this corporate set of best practice tools can be adapted for the different context of development co-operation. Equally, it is clear that the World Bank is pre-eminent amongst development co-operation agencies for both the scale and the quality of its knowledge sharing systems.

Nonetheless, without asking questions beyond the theme of good knowledge management practice and its operational effects, there are a few continuing concerns worth noting in this knowledge initiative that would appear so rapidly to have created an environment of knowledge sharing in the Bank. First, its original director, Denning, would be the first to admit that there is a long way to go in turning a large bureaucracy into an 'agile knowledge sharing organisation' (Denning 2001). Only half of the staff are members of the Bank's 'communities of practice', and his estimate is that it may take a decade or more to complete the transition.

Second, in the view of several senior managers, there remains a serious and even growing gap between what people are describing as 'best practice' and the extent to which this can be built into operations. Increasingly, the notion of 'best practice' seems to mean an ideal that is not put into practice precisely because of the pressure of reality. Staff in projects do not perceive that they have the time to use these knowledge resources. This is partly because of the sheer pressure of project development, and therefore the lack of time to take advantage of the knowledge structures which are there. Significantly, one senior manager we interviewed distinguished between the 'real work and the knowledge side', and spoke of 'the reality that there is no time to distil and make meaningful one's experience or knowledge'. In addition, the increasing tendency to use Trust Funds to hire shorter-term staff and consultants means that long-standing institutional memory within the Bank is more at risk. This tension between knowledge resources and work overload is confirmed by a recent study of, among other things, 'conditions for the effective use of knowledge' (World Bank/Harvard 2001: 19–22). This is a very real issue for the Bank, as the 2001 Board paper makes clear. There is a strong sense that the knowledge bank will have to make operational work smarter if it is to continue in something like its current form and with similar resourcing.

Third, in a December 2000 review of staff learning, carried out by the Society for Organisational Learning and involving a team that included Peter Senge, there is very powerful confirmation from a small series of interviews across the Bank that Denning is correct in saying the transition is far from complete. The review's 'overriding concern ... is that elements of Bank culture inhibit learning, which in turn diminishes effectiveness to deliver in the new global environment' (Humphries et al. 2000: 1).

Fourth, it is not clear whether the movement of the knowledge sharing programme out of its original home in operational and core services and into the WBI, takes it further away from the operational exigencies to which we have already referred. In one sense, the WBI, with its mandate to create 'learning opportunities for countries, Bank staff and clients, and people committed to poverty reduction and sustainable development' (World Bank Institute 2000), is the obvious home for the knowledge sharing programme, as it has a substantial knowledge agenda of its own. It would also seem to be able naturally to handle the internal–external dimension of thematic groups, as it was explicitly created to bring together client and staff learning. Indeed, as the WBI is much more oriented to client than to Bank staff learning, the new location could possibly encourage a greater focus on non-Bank members.

We shall return to some of these issues in the concluding sections of this chapter, and examine how they relate to broader issues. Our focus now, however, will shift to the growing external dimension of the knowledge bank.

Enhancing the sharing of knowledge with clients and partners

The second element of the World Bank's knowledge-sharing vision is a better relationship between the Bank and other development players. This includes a major focus on the work that the Bank has traditionally done for (and sometimes with) its clients, and its client training. However, there is an additional concern with new knowledge initiatives that are supposed to bring new ways of sharing knowledge.

Knowledge, research and lending

We have already noted that there are concerns within the World Bank about the quality of economic and sector work (ESW), and that one such concern is about the degree to which national actors and their knowledge are part of the process. The 2001 Board paper, other documents and several of our interviews highlight a strategic concern with 'fixing ESW' (this, indeed, is the name of one internal project). However, it is apparent that the disbursement culture of the World Bank mitigates against any such reform. At present, the culture and incentive structure of the organisation means that there is more merit in quick analysis that leads to speedy disbursement than in careful analysis that both increases the likelihood of project success and ensures that local analytical capacity is drawn upon and enhanced.

Changing the Bank's culture of research is also difficult. The main research unit remains the development economics group, and the dominant discipline and discourse remains that of economics (Denning 2001). In contrast to the growing emphasis on context and experience that Denning and others have been spreading through the Bank's thinking via the knowledge-sharing programme, the rationality of development economics has remained far more strongly grounded in universalist theory. 'Correct' technical analysis has remained more important than using research to develop partner capacity. This is in striking contrast to the trend within DFID, as we shall see in the next chapter.

We have also already noted the growing interest in 'unbundling lending and knowledge'. For some World Bank regional vice-presidencies, such as East Asia and the Middle East and North Africa (MENA), there are serious problems in disbursing funds. This is due to the middle-income status of many countries in both regions, which makes these countries ineligible for concessional rates of interest and makes the Bank an uncompetitive lender. This has led to a growing focus on alternative sources of business. MENA Region in particular has been developing a 'new knowledge-based business model'. In this, the intention is to make three- to five-year agreements with countries to supply them with a package of training, tailored briefing notes, technical assistance, and workshops. This has begun to be piloted both at a country level (in Morocco) and at a sectoral level (in Iran and Jordan).

The WBI and client training

The WBI, and its predecessor, the EDI, was traditionally a core means by which the World Bank's knowledge was disseminated through a series of client-oriented courses. Now it is seeking to respond to the challenge of greater operational impact for its work by tailoring courses more closely to programme and project support, particularly around PRSPs. It is also developing a stronger focus on targeted courses for narrower geographical regions, having identified a series of target countries in its latest business plan. As part of this refocusing, the language of training has largely been replaced by that of capacity building. Nonetheless, it is clear that the WBI still faces considerable challenges in linking more closely to operational work and in shifting from teaching to facilitating learning.

The Global Development Learning Network (GDLN)

Part of Wolfensohn's vision for the EDI was that it could harness ICTs to expand massively the sharing of the World Bank's knowledge 'by expanding the role of our Economic Development Institute, which already reaches thousands through its learning programmes – and is well on its way to reaching millions by harnessing teleconferencing, television and the internet' (Wolfensohn 1996: 7). The GDLN is the result of this vision. Through a series of distance learning centres internationally, participants are able to access WBI programmes from within their own countries using video conferencing and web-based learning. The GDLN seeks to be more than this, however, with a policy of carrying other organisations' content in addition to the Bank's own, and with a strategy of alliances with other actors in the field of development e-learning, such as the British Council and JICA (see chapter 7), in addition to its own expanding numbers of GDLN centres. There are clear benefits to the WBI and the World Bank in terms of the numbers that can be reached by distance methods. Whereas face-to-face approaches were resulting in about 30,000 trainees per annum, the GDLN reached 145,000 participants in its first two years and is likely to continue to expand its numbers rapidly for the next few years. However, there is need for some caution about whether quality is being sacrificed to quantity in this rapid expansion.

The Development Gateway

Most controversial of all the World Bank knowledge initiatives has been the Development Gateway (see, for example, Fidler 2001; Wilks 2002). For some outside analysts, this is *the* knowledge project of the knowledge bank. It is not difficult to see why, but arguably one or two of the other knowledge initiatives of the Bank have had much more impact on the Bank's way of working and on its employees than has the Gateway, at least so far.

Nonetheless, the attraction of the Gateway concept to its promoters when it was announced in 1999 was that it promised to provide on a single site 'a common platform for shared material, dialogue and problem solving that is easier to access than the current wealth of information on the Internet' (World Bank 2000b). Like *the* knowledge bank, it was *the* Gateway, and there was the expectation that this could become, through the application of ICT, the one-stop shop for development knowledge and development partnership. The vision of the Gateway had been present, in one sense, ever since knowledge was identified as one of the key foci of the Strategic Compact, and ever since the knowledge bank was first mentioned. It was associated with the notion of the World Bank's potential to play a leading role in a new knowledge partnership, precisely because of its relationships with governments and other institutions across the world, and because of its 'unique reservoir of development experience across sectors and countries' (Wolfensohn 1996: 7). This concept was initially concerned both with the Bank's view of its own unique position in development expertise, and with its assumed capacity to capture and share global knowledge with others. These two strains, of the Bank's own knowledge deposits and its desire to host the best development knowledge of others, have run through the debates about the Development Gateway. One of the key ways of the Bank becoming the knowledge bank emphasised these two dimensions, the internal and external, 'By networking – pooling our wealth of cross-country experience, capturing the best global thinking and expertise on a given issue, and making it easily accessible to our clients and partners' (Wolfensohn 1996: 7).

There is little doubt that the Development Gateway was soon seen as just this, one of the most public faces of the knowledge bank, 'an organisation that would be the first port of call for the world's best development expertise' (World Bank 1998b: 4). But what would distinguish it from all the other knowledge sharing we have been discussing in particular communities of practice, or knowledge partnerships, is that it would cover all development constituencies, including developing countries, the donor community, civil society, the private sector and other key partners. It was this very globalisation of development knowledge on to a single supersite that was perceived as a threat by many others dealing with knowledge for development.

The idea that the Bank would make relevant parts of its own knowledge base available to clients, partners and stakeholders around the world had been in vogue for several years and was simply reinforced by the *WDR* (World Bank 1998a: 7). Indeed, more than sixty attempts at doing just that had been represented by the websites of the various Thematic Groups already discussed, though these differ a great deal in terms of range and quality. However, by far the most comprehensive provision of the World Bank's development data has so far been its own website. As early as October 1996, when Wolfensohn announced the knowledge bank, the Bank's website was being accessed 1.5 million times per month, a figure that has since increased to 5.5 million (Wilks 2002).

However, compared to the provision of some topic-specific data from a thematic group, or to the possibility of accessing from the Bank website an existing report from the Bank's regular work and publications, the ambition of the Gateway was altogether greater. It set out deliberately to provide a service that would be valuable to NGOs, private investors, donors, researchers and developing country governments. Not just information and documentation posted like so many websites, but judgement and analysis about what works best, along with scope for interactivity and matchmaking. This, of course, is what distinguishes it from many of the regular development agency websites.

The sheer scale of the project is difficult to exaggerate:

> Gateway services will include online training modules, research findings, best practices and ideas, case studies, procurement services, information on development projects, funding, commercial opportunities, product reviews, news, jobs, and directories ... all tailored to the needs of specific audiences such as community leaders, private investors, policymakers, local government officials, and academics ... The Gateway will draw on a team of content managers and subject specialists, editors, writers, and other contributors from the development community, to evaluate, process, and present content. (World Bank 2001i)

The site is conceived of as being able not only to meet the information and knowledge needs of this extraordinary range of clients, from a very local NGO looking for funding possibilities or an investor looking for joint venture partners to a donor wishing to know the latest on aid flows, but to provide global or world-wide state-of-the-art knowledge as well as more country-specific data.

Why should such an effort even be necessary in an age of unparalleled abundance of information? That is itself part of the Bank's answer: that there is a huge amount of unsorted and fragmented development knowledge. The other crucial part of the Gateway's rationale is that most of the key constituencies it seeks to support are very far from realising the extent to which ICTs and the internet can dramatically extend the development scope and reach of all these different actors. Though most of the other knowledge projects of the World Bank have also used the potential of ICT as one of the ways they have changed their mode of operation or increased their clientele, this is the only initiative where the almost unimaginable reach and connectivity of the internet is absolutely central.

There are four large domains: aid effectiveness and coordination, civil society networks, private sector development, and government services. The scale of what is to be attempted differs a little across these domains but the formula has certain common characteristics. What it is not intended to be is merely a set of URL linkages to other agency, civil society and private enterprise websites. The stated intention is to seek to add value as well as offer connectivity. Thus in the aid domain, the ambition is to 'harmonise' the multiple databases on development activity, to provide critical guidance and tools for distilling and sharing this extremely diverse material, and to facilitate access to and interaction with the knowledge bases and databases on aid. Nor will it just be a case of contributing to and consulting these, but there will be scope for directly accessing debates and roundtables. Beyond this, there will be links to procurement opportunities, to possibilities for matching donor funds with development proposals, and to openings for exploring new communities of practice around specific themes or activities.

Already there has been some rapid progress in the integration of development project databases under the project called Accessible Information on Development Activities (AIDA). This pulls together into a single access point a series of comprehensive sources of data on aid-financed development projects by country and sector.

This is just a single example of the kind of added value that the Gateway seeks to bring to the globalisation of development knowledge. In the other domains, there are other kinds of data integration and data provision contemplated, which will be adjusted to the funding and information needs of these very different constituencies.

The sheer scale of what the Gateway is proposing to cover is such that it has until now been easier and more common to comment upon and critique the basic idea of a development hypermarket or super-site than any of its specific holdings. But as the 25 major topic areas are developed, it is going to be essential to examine both the particular coverage of a topic or sub-topic and the overall impact of this centralisation of sources of development knowledge. This is going to be a very different task from the tradition of external analysis of key policy documents by members of the research and advocacy communities. For one thing, as was mentioned in chapter 1, it is peculiarly difficult when the number of major topic areas and the specialised sub-topics are rapidly changing on the external website.

But a look at just one topic, aid effectiveness, would suggest that the topic site (http://www.developmentgateway.org/node/130604) cannot really be criticised for promoting a predominantly World Bank view of aid effectiveness. Less than 10 per cent of the 455 topics on this site (at the end of July 2002) are from the Bank.

For the purpose of this review of the Bank's knowledge projects, it may be worth emphasising the enormity of the task involved in critiquing what may be described as a rather rapidly moving target, even if just one of the Gateway's major themes, for example, aid effectiveness, were examined. Unlike reviewing a *World Development Report*, which is a particular length, analysing a Gateway topic area is a constantly changing task, with new content appearing every week. Most of this content is in the form of links to useful websites, articles, news sources, aid organisations, programmes and projects, official documents, aid directories and databases. Importantly, this is not just a useful sign-posting to official development aid. A number of key NGO sites, such as Jubilee 2000, the Reality of Aid project, Debtchannel.org, Panos, Euforic, ECDPM, the Bretton Woods project, OneWorld, and ELDIS, are all tagged. One or two of these, for example the Bretton Woods Project, provide critical commentary on the Gateway project itself.

Membership and access to the Gateway and its topic communities In our discussions of the mainstream knowledge-sharing programme of the Bank we spent quite some time discussing the membership, external and internal, of its hundred or so thematic groups, and we judged that there was considerable variety in their approach to membership. By contrast, it would appear that access to the different topics of the Gateway is wide open to external members. There is a strong encouragement on every page to make the Gateway 'my gateway', to identify a topic and to contribute as a member of one or more communities in sharing knowledge, entering content and asking questions:

The Gateway allows you to exchange information with other users around the world. To make this exchange as fruitful as possible, we encourage you to contribute knowledge you believe is relevant and useful about topics where you have professional or personal interest. The information can be in the form of case studies, articles, reports, favourite websites, tool kits etc. – anything on the web that is particularly helpful in your work. If it is publicly available on the web, or in an electronic file for which you have publishing rights, you can add it to the site.

... Other Gateway community members will have immediate access to what you have placed on the site. You can also comment on any item others have offered to a topic page by clicking on comment next to that item. (http://www.developmentgateway.org/Share, accessed on 24 July 2002)

This open encouragement to become a member of one of the Gateway communities and to contribute to the content or commentaries on each of its major topics is certainly very clearly laid out, and the encouragement towards interactivity and 'feedback' is reinforced on every single page of the Gateway, although largely not responded to by members as yet. The question must be: how on earth could any topic guide and its advisory group (most of them are doing this task part-time) deal with the potentially enormous flow of information, sorting out the wheat from the chaff?

It is almost certainly too early to make a judgement about even the single topic area that we have briefly looked at, let alone at the Gateway as a whole. For one thing, as the current Gateway director, Carlos Braga, admits, it is 'literally a portal under construction'; so it should not be surprising that some things seem to have disappeared after a very fleeting appearance on the Gateway stage, or that coverage changed dramatically in the first year after its formal launch. However, over time it will still be important to identify who is contributing to the Gateway, and why, and who is consulting it, for what. Our initial speculation would be that very few of these will be World Bank staff, an issue we shall return to for the knowledge bank more generally: 'I have just opened [your] recommended Gateway reference for the first and probably last time. It cannot help me with information relevant to what I am doing at the moment and if the information were theoretically there the search might be too time consuming' (electronic communication to Kenneth King from a Bank staff member, 8 September 2001).

From global gateway to country gateways Part of the initial vision of the Gateway was that it should spawn a series of country gateways. This had much to do with the initial timing of the Gateway idea alongside Wolfensohn's big idea of that year (1999), the Comprehensive Development Framework (CDF). Although not officially abandoned, the CDF has largely disappeared from sight in the Bank with 2000's big idea: the Poverty Reduction Strategy Paper, still going strong after two years. What the CDF had was a sense of support to national ownership of a comprehensive development strategy. The country gateways were seen as an important tool in catalysing national debates around such strategies. A series of country gateways have emerged (several with infoDev funding, see p. 87). However, in most of these, content and interactivity remain extremely weak. Indeed, there can be little optimism about the future of these gateways as viable sites for civil society discussion. Not that this is at all surprising in countries such as the Ukraine, one of the pilots, where press freedom is notoriously curtailed.

The accumulation of information versus the globalisation of development knowledge One of the more general issues that arises in the analysis of the Gateway is whether, on the basis of what little we have examined, it should really be feared to the extent that it has been by certain 'knowledge NGOs' and World Bank critics in both the North and the South.

What is conspicuously absent, at least so far, on those parts of the Gateway that we have examined is the kind of strong analytical work that has been associated with many of the World Bank's policy papers and WDRs in different sectors over the last twenty and more years. These have frequently been controversial and biased in favour of a particular viewpoint, but it has been possible to discuss them critically since they were available in both draft and final form in hard copy. But the aid effectiveness site on the Gateway, for instance, is not an obvious location for rapidly accessing the Bank's views on the most pressing aid debates of the day, on the Comprehensive Development Framework, or Poverty Reduction Strategy Papers or on Sector-Wide Approaches. It gives, rather, the sense of a smorgasbord, with a series of possibly tasty dishes, but without a menu or any coherent guide to its contents. There is just a brief paragraph of introduction to the Page Focus which claims that the aid effectiveness site will improve the effect of development assistance 'through systematic, coherent and timely provision of information' to a very wide constituency.

For those organisations that were very worried about the possible World Bank domination of the global development discourse via the Gateway, this is probably good news. This site may well turn out to be more concerned with information than with knowledge. It will provide access to many of the key locations in their topic areas, many of them outside the Bank, but the people who are entering the bulk of the material as members of the core Gateway team do not appear, with few exceptions, to be individuals who have been professionally committed to a single sector or thematic area for any length of time. Indeed, some of those entering content are clearly doing so over a very large number of what are termed their 'favourite communities', often as interns on the Gateway. These topic areas, therefore, are currently light years away from the concentrated, often long-term analytical work that has marked some of the key policy papers of the World Bank over the last two decades. The fact that there is advertised as one of the leading items on the home page of the Gateway 'detailed information about more than 300,000 development activities around the world' and another offering 'Facts and Figures: data and statistics across regions, countries and sectors' is some confirmation of this emphasis on development information rather than development knowledge or development policy.

Illustrative of this trend towards the information focus of the Gateway is its emphasis on the provision of toolkits, and its discussion of the technologies that allow shared access to this common work space. The Gateway's technology framework sees itself as providing a 'common platform' or 'a common space' on which information from many different sources can be accommodated (World Bank 2001h).

Arguably, however, the creative sharing of a technologically sophisticated work space with a very diverse community of interested outsiders is not something on which the Bank has any track record. Nor has it been a long tradition of the Bank to engage in on-line discussions of development topics or to foster 'a strong network of development communities on the web' (World Bank 2001i). Thus the constant encouragement to 'ask the community' or to comment or provide feedback or enter content on all manner of issues has not been the trademark of the World Bank. As we said earlier, it must be doubted if many regular Bank staff will really have the time and space to become the friendly topic guide, the ready answerer of questions, or the catalyst of a sizeable external community of practice.

This is not to doubt the genuineness of this apparent openness of the Gateway or to suggest that it is a demagogic response to the extended recent criticism of the Gateway concept. There is a sense that internal criticism of the Gateway has subsided since Braga took over its leadership. There must be some serious doubt that the smorgasbord or dictionary approach to development information will fulfil the original ambition of the Bank president, which was to link the 'unique reservoir' of the Bank's own policy knowledge with the best global knowledge from outside the Bank.

A lot depends on whether the Gateway can routinely expect to be able to draw upon the very best sectoral expertise in the Bank for timely analytical work. If not, it will risk ending up more a secondhand shop for material that has appeared elsewhere than 'the first port of call for the world's best development expertise' (World Bank 1998b: 4).

Sharing knowledge: concluding comments

Throughout these initiatives, and indeed through much of the official documentation of the knowledge bank, there is a tension between a language of symmetrical knowledge sharing and an older sense that the World Bank is the repository of much, if not all, that is best in development knowledge. The latter sense is also compounded by the feeling of operational urgency that we noted in the previous section. If projects have to be pushed forward and the Bank appears so knowledgeable, then it can be difficult for staff to see the merits in approaches that highlight divergent opinions or that seek to foster national capacity and ownership. In the competitive culture of the World Bank, product is far more important than process. This is not to deny, however, that there is a growing official emphasis on the need to shift towards greater sharing. The appearance of an emphasis on mutual learning appears to be more than simply rhetoric, although it is also far from an organisation-wide reality. Its significance is heightened by the return to a language of capacity development.[17]

Enhancing client capacity to access and make effective use of knowledge whatever the source

Whereas the above initiatives are seen as not having a primary focus on capacity enhancement, there is another set of knowledge initiatives that do have this as their explicit aim.

Knowledge economy work

Since the publication of the WDR 1998–99, its lead author, Carl Dahlman, has sought to take the Bank's concern with supporting knowledge economies further, through the 'Knowledge for Development' initiative. The programme seeks to support analytical capacity in middle- and low-income countries to understand their potential responses to the challenge of becoming knowledge economies. This focuses on four core areas:

- economic and institutional regimes
- education and training systems

- ICT infrastructure
- national innovation systems

This appears to be a popular programme with East Asian countries, such as the Republic of Korea and the People's Republic of China, as well as with the potential accession countries to the European Union; work is also starting in selected African countries.

Global Development Network (GDN)

This has been the most visible knowledge initiative of the development economics group in the Bank, although the WBI was originally a significant partner. Whilst its origins and some of its funding from the Bank go back earlier, the GDN was launched in Bonn in December 1999 under the banner 'Bridging Knowledge and Policy'. What made it especially unusual, when so many of these knowledge initiatives (whether Bank or non-Bank) have had strong Northern partners, was that the set of networks and think tanks represented initially in Bonn were exclusively from non-OECD countries, and the emphasis was firmly on capacity building and knowledge generation in the South (and East), drawing on a range of research grant mechanisms funded by the Bank.[18] But the representativeness of the single institutions picked by the Bank to be the think tank for a particular region was soon questioned, as was the almost exclusive disciplinary focus on economics. In other words the GDN was not seen to have the openness and inclusiveness of some of the other knowledge partnerships just discussed for the WBI.

In a very interesting illustration of different approaches within the Bank to the encouragement of knowledge development and networking in the South, the WBI encouraged the creation of a GDNet, a prototype website, hosted by the Institute of Development Studies at the University of Sussex in Brighton. This deliberately set out to encourage the visibility of a very much wider range of Southern institutions than the original seven that had been at the Bonn launch. In effect, this meant posting the research profiles and publications of several hundred Southern centres, as well as some Northern, on this GDNet site, which was mainly supported by DFID (see chapter 5). Unlike the central institutes of the GDN, this covered many more disciplines than economics. But the impression that the open-access structure of GDNet was an implicit criticism of the core GDN concept eventually resulted in the withdrawal of WBI support to GDNet, and the reconsolidation of the GDNet and GDN into a single entity. This was spun off from the Bank in July 2001, but with continuity in Bank funding and at least one or two Bank personnel. These included the initial project manager from development economics, Lyn Squire, who will remain in post till some time after the GDN relocates to New Delhi in July 2004.

It is intriguing that the GDN's third conference (in December 2001) was titled 'Blending local and global knowledge', since a tension between the global and local has been associated with the GDN from the outset. At the original launch meeting, the key speech given by the then chief economist of the Bank, Joe Stiglitz, was titled 'Scan globally; re-invent locally' (Stiglitz 2000 [1999]), very much a continuation of the message of the WDR on knowledge published that same year. One of the WDR's key recommendations for narrowing knowledge gaps was precisely to 'tap global knowledge and create local knowledge' (World Bank 1998a: 145). Perhaps aware of the implication that the global was the superior, world class knowledge, the GDN had significantly shifted its axiom by the time of its governing board in May 2001, and the motto had become: 'world class local knowledge for world class local solutions'.

It is still far too early to say whether the GDN will play a substantial role in implementing the vision of the knowledge WDR to which we referred earlier, in particular the involvement of developing countries in all phases of knowledge creation. However, it is clear that this is the intention and that there is a growing sense within the GDN of sensitivity both about the relationship between knowledge and policy and about the dominant role of economics and economic rationality.

InfoDev

The Information for Development programme predates the declaration of the knowledge bank, having been launched in September 1995. It is a global grant programme managed by the World Bank, but with more than twenty other funders. Essentially, it is designed to fund innovative projects in the field of ICT for development. This includes support to ICT pilot projects, such as e-commerce for small and medium enterprises; policy workshops, websites and conferences to share knowledge about ICTs; and support to several of the country gateways.

African Virtual University (AVU)

The AVU began as a project of the Africa region in 1997. After a funding hiatus in 2000–2001, the project has now secured further funding from the World Bank and a number of bilaterals, including DFID. The AVU is formally independent of the Bank and is headquartered in Nairobi. It has a series of thirty centres in fifteen African countries, which deliver a series of short additional courses to science and technology students through one-way video from Northern universities supported by on-site tutors. The AVU is also supported by web-based materials, including a large digital library. The AVU remains a rather low-technology version of e-learning, with a lack of connectivity amongst its African sites. Nonetheless, it does provide one of the largest schemes of support to knowledge and ICT capacity in Africa.

Indigenous knowledge

A very different angle from the GDN motto of world class local knowledge is the initiative of the Africa Region that has for the last four years been promoting the crucial role of indigenous knowledge (IK). In one way the conception of IK comes closest to the vision of the *WDR* to which we referred earlier, even though it is not on the official list of knowledge initiatives that are seen as having followed the *WDR* and the Strategic Compact. The argument of those most closely associated with promoting this version of knowledge for development are very clear about the relationship between local knowledge awareness and knowledge sharing at any global level: 'The vision of a truly global knowledge partnership will be realised only when the people of the developing countries participate as both contributors and users of knowledge' (World Bank 1998c: iv). The document *Indigenous Knowledge for Development: A Framework for Action* (World Bank 1998c) makes absolutely clear the requirement that the 'recipients' of development programmes be involved as 'donors' of knowledge, if there is to be a genuine attempt to adapt modern techniques to the local practices.

Of course, the IK programme is in some sense more restrictive than some of the uses of the term 'local knowledge'. The latter may well be used of the knowledge held by local modern firms, or by local (that is, national) universities, or by the decentralised offices of the donors; whereas more often IK is used to refer to the uniquely contextualised knowledge of a local (usually rural) community. It is usually argued that IK is dynamic in character, changing to reflect the needs of local communities as well as by contact with external systems, but also that IK is predominantly tacit knowledge, and therefore is likely to be resistant to the codification, transfer and exchange that are parts of the IK for Development programme.

This is almost certainly the case with a great deal of the knowledge that is embedded in craftspeople, herbalists, and other groupings that we might call local 'communities of practice'. However, before making too sharp a dichotomy between this knowledge and that which is the currency of the Bank's thematic groups, it should be remembered that Denning himself argued that most of what we know is tacit and that understanding the context in which knowledge arises is often crucial. So perhaps the gulf between the knowledge being traded amongst communities of practice in the World Bank and communities of craft workers in Ghana is not as enormous as might be thought.

What the IK initiative stands for, in wider terms, in the Bank is the challenge to Bank staff to be aware not just of 'best practice' globally – the state of the art in their field – but the means of adapting that to the local context. In the eyes of those responsible for the IK programme, this suggests much more knowledge by the Bank of local practices (Gorjestani 1999). Arguably, the IK programme has highlighted just one dimension of this knowledge and research in the South, and has done so primarily for one region of the Bank, Africa, although this application was extended in 2001 to all regions of the Bank, and there is now an element of South–South knowledge sharing. To an extent, therefore, it has sought to grapple with a challenge thrown down by the WDR: to expand the World Bank's knowledge management system to incorporate local knowledge from countries and sectors in which the Bank is active (World Bank 1998a: 140). That really has not happened. As we saw when we looked at the external members of the Bank's thematic groups, they were, with some notable exceptions, more likely to include a major institutional partner in the North than in the South, let alone incorporate local knowledge communities of the sort IK has pointed to in Africa.

Global Knowledge Partnership (GKP)

The GKP illustrates perfectly the role that the World Bank can play in facilitating knowledge sharing globally. With the general aim of sharing knowledge about the ways in which the information revolution can support and empower the poor, the Bank provided a light secretariat from June 1997 till July 2001, when this function moved, significantly, to Malaysia, the joint host of the second Global Knowledge conference on building knowledge societies. Here then is a powerful example of the light facilitation of a relatively symmetrical knowledge partnership, followed by the spinning off of the responsibility outside the World Bank.

Supporting capacity enhancement: concluding comments

Although there is a new emphasis in the Bank's internal discourse about the need to support capacity, and notwithstanding the investment in these projects, the extent of the capacity element of the knowledge bank remains far more modest than those elements that relate more directly to the Bank's own internal knowledge management needs and its more effective knowledge sharing with partners and clients.

The knowledge bank in practice: assessing the extent of transformation

Certainly the World Bank has progressed further in introducing knowledge-based aid than any other development agency. Clearly, there is a significant change in emphasis in recent documents towards notions of mutual learning and capacity enhancement that seem to indicate a shift away from the old Bank tendency to see itself as the source of all knowledge. Furthermore, the language used by some of the staff most active in the knowledge bank project points to a vision of a transformed organisation that is more open to internal and external criticism and which can genuinely work as a facilitator of knowledge sharing. The following is typical of the new, more modest Bank vision: 'Just as importantly, the World Bank – through a variety of consultative mechanisms – recognises that it does not possess a monopoly on knowledge and is learning from the insights and experiences of clients and others in the development community' (World Bank 2002d: 1)

Many activists and radical researchers, however, continue to see the World Bank as an important instrument of American and capitalist domination. In this light, the reforms are seen as either public relations exercises or as a way of increasing the power of the World Bank through a greater control of the distribution of knowledge. At the same time, a series of internal and external critics take the view that the reforms are supported by some in the Bank but bitterly resisted by others, and are obstructed by the way that the organisation operates.

In this section, we shall try to engage with this debate and provide our own analysis of what the knowledge bank is likely to mean. In particular, we shall seek to show that there need to be multiple levels to such an analysis. We will consider questions at four levels. First, how does the World Bank's approach to knowledge sharing compare with 'good practices' in this area and their likely relevance for the context of a development agency? Second, does the adoption of knowledge-based aid make the World Bank work more effectively? Third, has the knowledge bank transformed the World Bank or, if not, is this possible over time? Fourth, do the experiences of the World Bank in pursuing knowledge-based aid offer new possibilities for positively transformed aid and development paradigms?

Is the World Bank a good knowledge-sharing organisation?

The World Bank has been on the American Productivity and Quality Center's list of 'most admired knowledge enterprises' for the past three years. World Bank staff are regular presenters at industry seminars. Steve Denning's book on the role of storytelling in knowledge sharing (Denning 2000) has been well received within the knowledge community. Whilst the Bank was clearly influenced by various stages in corporate best practice, such as databases and communities of practice, it has also been a leader in making knowledge sharing more externally oriented, and has developed a capacity to draw selectively and strategically on others' experience. Compared to other development agencies, the Bank is clearly the leader in the field. Not only has it done more than other agencies, but it has shown a strong capacity to reflect on this and a willingness to be self-critical. Even on the web pages of the knowledge sharing group (http://www.worldbank.org/ks), there is more than simple description or celebration. The Bank has avoided being too technologically oriented, and has increased the external focus of its knowledge work over time.

There has been a serious growth in electronic working within the Bank, and this has facilitated both greater decentralisation and better cross-sectoral and cross-regional collaboration. Approximately half of the Bank's staff are members of thematic groups, and the advisory services are saving staff time (and, hence, money) in information searching. Inter-departmental seminars have grown exponentially in the Wolfensohn era.

Operational departments are becoming more interested in elements of knowledge work, such as the knowledge economy diagnostic. Moreover, the downward pressure on disbursement in several regions is likely to further this. Articulation between learning and knowledge activities is increasing, and there is a far better sense of informality, mutuality and teams in learning activities than previously. A number of the knowledge initiatives have been incubated in the Bank before leaving the institution, and are surviving as independent entities.

However, the success of the knowledge-sharing initiative should not be overstated. If half the staff are involved in thematic groups, the other half are not. Many groups are not functioning well and many staff are passive rather than active participants. There is still too little learning from outside, and many of the new knowledge initiatives have had little or no impact on how staff learn. The organisational culture remains inimical to knowledge sharing in significant ways. Research and knowledge activities are poorly articulated, with the principal research unit appearing very sceptical of the knowledge theory on which the knowledge bank concept has been built. The expert identity of Bank staff has not really been changed, and a tendency towards telling and away from capacity building is still apparent. There are concerns that training is often being repackaged as capacity development and that distance learning approaches may favour quantity over quality.

Some of the knowledge initiatives have clearly been too grandiose and too linked to Wolfensohn to allow for rigorous analysis. Some have made inappropriate technological choices or have been too unconcerned about governance issues. Wolfensohn's own love of technology and his tendency to launch initiative after initiative have obstructed the full operationalisation of the knowledge bank vision. The Bank's paymasters on Capitol Hill and elsewhere remain sceptical about the benefits of the experiment and conscious of its costs. Many senior managers appear to regard it as simply another of the management fads that the Bank is constantly adopting.

Has knowledge-based aid made the World Bank work more effectively?

This is one of the central questions in the current internal evaluation of the knowledge bank. There is as yet a lack of strong evidence on the fundamental issue of how the knowledge bank assists in the meeting of the International Development Targets. Inevitably, such evidence will be hard to produce and the question could be asked about other elements of development practice. Nonetheless, it is clear that the cost of the knowledge bank makes it susceptible to such questions.

The knowledge bank notion does in fact contribute a theory of how the World Bank can be more effective. The Bank has quickly moved beyond a perception that it simply needed to capture its own knowledge in databases that could then provide easy resources for staff in the field. Instead, it is beginning to develop a position in which it seeks to accept the 'contextual, contingent and complex' (McNamara 2002) nature of development and tries to shift from an emphasis on universal theory to a stress on how to share contextualised experiences more effectively and how to learn from them in new contexts (World Bank 2001g; Gorjestani 2002):

> The link between knowledge, learning and quality has to be explored in the light of the prior question; whose 'knowledge' gets learned and adapted, and how do we assure that our operational work is based on the most appropriate and locally relevant knowledge, not on abstract best practice. This in turn calls forth a prior question; is 'best practice'

really the key to operational effectiveness, or is operational effectiveness the result of successfully adapting general principles to a specific context in a way that is sustainable in the light of local capacity? (McNamara 2002: 2)

However, this transition in the World Bank's theory-in-use (cf. Argyris and Schön 1978) is far from complete. There is a strong sense from operational staff that knowledge work means more work rather than smarter working. Thus, the overall evidence on whether the Bank has become a more effective aid agency remains inconclusive.

Has the knowledge bank transformed the World Bank?

Other external commentaries on the knowledge bank have seen it as making the World Bank more certain and arrogant rather than less (Mehta 2000; Samoff and Stromquist 2001; Wilks 2002). However, the official line from the Bank, as seen in a range of speeches by Wolfensohn and, for a while, Stiglitz, is that the knowledge bank marks a shift away from old ways of working. Our analysis in this chapter has shown that the reality is somewhere in between the two extremes. Clearly, some elements within the Bank have seen the knowledge bank as simply a way of getting better public relations. Others have seen the new tools provided by ICTs and knowledge management as an opportunity for greater internal certainty and greater external preaching. However, from the internal and external criticism from the right, and from the wealth of interviews and documents from those involved in knowledge sharing, it is clear to us that a genuine attempt to change the World Bank's culture is under way.

The knowledge bank has changed the Bank in certain ways, but the more pertinent question becomes whether the greater project of transformation is likely to succeed. To explore this, we shall consider the views of two of the key players in the Bank's internal debates on knowledge since 1996, Steve Denning and David Ellerman. Both have a vision of how knowledge and/or learning could radically transform the nature of aid and the World Bank as the leader in this field.

Steve Denning, erstwhile co-ordinator of the core knowledge bank activities, is optimistic about the radical potential of the knowledge bank. He argues that the technological and economic changes that we outlined in the first part of chapter 3 will inevitably transform the nature of development agencies, aid and agency use of knowledge. He contrasts the new with a picture of the old certainty of the World Bank in its use of knowledge:

For the first 50 years of its existence, the World Bank was devoted to lending for development projects. There was a widespread perception that the World Bank itself was the place in which most development knowledge was located. World Bank staff did their best within the constraints to maximise client ownership of development projects, but in reality, as in science, there was practically no possibility of pursuing a project that did not comply with the existing World Bank paradigms. (Denning 2001: 139)

This position led to projects being designed because of what the Bank's overall ideology decreed, even where staff and clients thought they knew better. This was reinforced by the organisational tendency within the Bank towards an authoritarian and bureaucratic style that was common across the American corporate sector.

However, Denning argues that this model is no longer tenable in either the World Bank or corporate America. He argues that the new economic and technological rationality leads to a model of knowledge use internal to the organisation that is characterised by greater plurality and openness. This translates into a more reflexive and open external role as a knowledge broker.

Denning is open about the limits to transformation of the World Bank five years on from Wolfensohn's 'conversion', the different outlooks of certain units, the negative developments of some of the high profile projects such as the Gateway, and the challenge of managing the tension between lending and learning. Nonetheless, his account suggests that the organisation will be transformed and that many of the changes are already in place (Denning 2001).

A far more pessimistic account comes from the various writings of David Ellerman, who left the World Bank in late 2002, relinquishing the post of senior economist in development economics. His intellectual fingerprints can be seen on portions of the *World Development Report 1998–99* and on Stiglitz's Bonn speech launching the GDN. Since Stiglitz's resignation, Ellerman wrote a number of widely circulated memos that sought to question, *inter alia*, the way that the knowledge bank was being operationalised. Ellerman himself uses the term 'knowledge-based development assistance' in a number of his writings. He argues that the chances of the emergence of a successful knowledge bank are less likely. Instead, he suggests that the rhetoric on knowledge is likely to remain as hollow as that on national ownership of development:

In accordance with the principle of people owning the fruits of their labour, the doers will have ownership when they are in the driver's seat (indeed, the description as 'doers' would not be accurate if they had a passive role). But in the standard view of knowledge-based assistance, the helpers are teachers or trainers taking the active role to transmit 'knowledge for development' to the passive but grateful clients. 'Development' is seen almost as a technical process like building an airport or dam with the agency having the 'technical knowledge' to be transmitted to the clients. (Ellerman 2001a: 1)

He argues that the World Bank remains a bureaucracy in which loyalty and right-thinking are valued both from staff and clients (Ellerman 2000a, 2001b). In spite of the language of external transparency and internal trust, disloyalty[19] still appears to be punished (Ellerman 2001b). In spite of the language of national ownership, staff learn that they will be held personally responsible for projects and will be judged on product not process; and clients learn that what is valued is replication of what the World Bank has already pronounced (Ellerman 2001b). In such a situation, aid dependence and a lack of autonomous and effective development are inevitable. Moreover, the knowledge bank means what the name implies: a storehouse of validated wisdom.

Although he is highly sceptical about the possibilities of the World Bank radically changing, Ellerman does have a vision for what it could do as part of a transformed approach to development co-operation. Rather than acting as a storehouse and a protector and promoter of developmental orthodoxy, Ellerman argues that the Bank should become a facilitator of context-specific learning from comparative experience (Ellerman 2000a, 2000b). This model assumes that learning comes from the internalisation of knowledge built in active processes, not from the passive receipt of what others define as knowledge. Moreover, it assumes that context and tacitness are crucial. For Ellerman, where the Bank can play a role is in facilitating cross-country sharing of experiences and learning needs. Rather than knowledge bankers, staff would be knowledge brokers. This, as Ellerman is aware, would require a fundamentally different relationship between knowledge and power than is present in the existing World Bank. Another crucial element of this changed power–knowledge dynamic is the centrality of ownership. Ellerman argues that both the current agency rhetoric of partnership–ownership and the possibility of genuine development require an approach in which autonomy is enhanced. This suggests that genuine attention to capacity development is far more important than knowledge dissemination. However, it also highlights the difficulty of autonomy and development becoming realities when there is a donor–recipient relationship (Ellerman 2003).

Whilst it does seem reasonable to argue that there are tendencies towards some of the positive changes that Denning is highlighting, we find it difficult to share his optimism about the transformatory potential of knowledge-based aid. Instead, we favour Ellerman's argument that the fundamental nature of aid bureaucracies and the aid mentality make radical transformation unlikely. In spite of its free-market rhetoric and often intense internal competition for promotion, the World Bank does operate in a number of ways like a large state bureaucracy, and continues to 'see like a state' (Scott 1998) and to be as highly resistant to change as are most large organisations (Schön 1971). Moreover, the likelihood of the achievement of the positive vision of the knowledge bank is threatened not only by internal obstruction. From the perspective of 2003, it is far from clear whether the knowledge bank will survive the Wolfensohn presidency. New Bank presidents tend to come with new big ideas, rejecting or downgrading those of their predecessors. Moreover, there is considerable scepticism towards the project, as we have noted already, from the Bank's masters.

Do the experiences of the World Bank in pursuing knowledge-based aid offer new possibilities for positively transformed aid and development paradigms?

Denning's and Ellerman's differing accounts also provide useful insights for the debate about how aid can be changed. Denning points to the positive impact that new ways of knowledge use can have within an agency and, hence, in relationships with others. Ellerman usefully extends this by further emphasising the importance of learning over knowledge transfer and, more importantly, by making the issue of autonomy enhancement and, hence, capacity development central to the issue. The current knowledge strategy points in a positive direction with its talk of capacity and learning. This is in keeping with the broader language shift in the Bank towards ownership and participation. Moreover, there is a growing discourse amongst those active in the knowledge projects that mirrors social theory accounts of knowledge. Thus, it is possible to find a range of statements from within the World Bank that do talk in a plausible manner about a very different approach to development and to aid.

However, this is running far ahead of the main stream of Bank thinking. Moreover, in spite of the scale of activist criticism, the Bank is already seen by important elements of the Bush administration as having strayed too far from its mandate. At best, there is scope for the World Bank to promote a more open and symmetrical aid relationship and a less narrow definition of development. Efforts to open up development and aid in these ways will be subject to considerable contestation, however, and there will be tendencies to use new approaches such as knowledge sharing (as with participatory methods) to reinforce the old paradigm.

Notes

1. The work of a number of NGOs has been devoted to criticism of the Bretton Woods institutions. Probably the most exhaustive and timely analysis of the World Bank is to be found on the Bretton Woods Project's website: http://www.brettonwoodsproject.org.

2. Such a critique has even been presented by the World Bank's former chief economist, Joe Stiglitz, in numerous interviews and newspaper columns.

3. One Bank staff member told us that the memo was intended to be satirical and was not, as is usually thought, written by the chief economist himself. Whatever the true origin and intention, the memo was a public relations disaster for the Bank.

4. Indeed, it is likely that the work of this group will continue to have far more influence on policy internationally than new initiatives such as the Global Development Network and the Development Gateway, notwithstanding their aspirations to bridge policy and research.

5. This evaluation was still in the early stages when this chapter was completed. However, we were able to discuss this review at an early stage with many of those involved in it from OED and the staff they were beginning to interview. Independent of this, an external consultancy was also engaged to review the range of knowledge activities during May and June 2002. This largely concurred with the official internal view that the knowledge bank was progressing well but that there was a need to be more coherent and strategic in its future development.

6. Indeed the principal author of the WDR on Knowledge, Carl Dahlman, was known for his work on indigenous techological capability (ITC) in the 1980s. Contrast his conditions for the creation of ITC with the conditions for creating a knowledge economy in his unit of the World Bank now (Dahlman 1984).

7. The science policy and technology policy literature has seldom sought to integrate education as centrally as does the WDR. For a much earlier attempt to do so, see Fransman and King (1984).

8. There had been a higher education policy paper in 1994, and a paper on vocational and technical education in 1991, but in the Jomtien decade the Bank was more associated with support for basic primary education, especially in the poorer countries.

9. See the title of the Africa Region review: *A Chance to Learn: Knowledge and Finance for Education in Sub-Saharan Africa* (World Bank 2001d) with its stern challenge to education for a 'knowledge-based global economy'.

10. Virtual, franchise and corporate universities, for example, are much more evident in the richer countries of the world. See also *Norrag News 27*.

11. In the knowledge management (KM) profile of the Bank, Bruno Laporte,

Knowledge and Learning Services Manager in the WBI and Ron Kim, KM Officer, explain the key sources of the Bank's knowledge management strategy as follows: 'The key inspiration has been constant interchange and benchmarking with outside corporations and organisations such as the American Productivity and Quality Centre, and IKO (IBM's Institute of Knowledge-based Organisations), among others.' Bellanet, July 2002.

12. There was also a growing sense of the relative bluntness and ineffectiveness of the conditionality approach. Mosley, Harrigan and Toye (1990) had provided considerable case study evidence about the failure of conditionalities to produce the policies that were intended, whilst a number of World Bank economists began in the late 1990s to argue for a more effective way of ensuring compliance.

13. Denning has frequently used to great effect 'stories' of how local Bank officials in country X were able, in 48 hours, through the thematic groups/communities of practice, to provide their clients in government with highly relevant solutions to their problems, drawn from other local contexts.

14. For the range of thematic group activities, see World Bank 2002b.

15. In the case of the Early Child Group, for instance, external partners such as Bernard Van Leer and the Consultative Group on Early Childhood Care and Development have had much longer continuous preoccupations with the thematic area than the Bank.

16. An internal survey of the thematic groups has suggested that a third are doing very well, a third middling, and a third underperforming.

17. 'The knowledge agenda at the Bank, which started as more internally focused, is becoming increasingly externally focused, linked to the business of capacity building' (Bellanet, 2002: 2).

18. For the genesis of the GDN, see Stone (2000). A European hub of the GDN was added in 2000 in time for the second GDN conference in Tokyo. The European group was predominantly composed of economists. A Japanese hub was added in 2001 in the Japan Bank for International Cooperation (JBIC – see chapter 7). GDN-North America began operations in May 2002.

19. Here Ellerman has cited at least four cases. First, that of Joe Stiglitz, whose criticism of the Bank's own economic analysis when he was chief economist led to US Treasury pressure for him to be removed by Wolfensohn, which proved successful. Second, the case of Ravi Kanbur, who resigned as lead author of the 2000–2001 World Development Report after pressure both from within the Bank and from the US Treasury. Third, the case of William Easterly, a far more orthodox economist than Stiglitz or Kanbur, who was disciplined for writing an article in the Financial Times that was implicitly critical of the Bank's record on promoting growth, and who resigned as a result of pressure. Fourth, Ashraf Ghani, a senior Afghan researcher at the Bank who also ran into disciplinary problems for writing an article for the Financial Times, and who subsequently was seconded to the UN's Afghanistan crisis team on the intervention of Kofi Annan. Ellerman's own decision to leave the Bank also appears to have been precipitated by the costs of being seen as a heretical thinker.

FIVE

From information management to knowledge sharing: DFID's unfinished revolution

In common with many other agencies, and following the lead of the World Bank, the British Department for International Development (DFID) has been developing its own policy for better internal knowledge management. At the same time, through its research strategy and its support for the Global Development Network, DFID is developing its own approach to supporting Southern knowledge generation and dissemination.

It is important to note that DFID, in its current form, is a new agency. Its return to full departmental status in 1997, coinciding with the first Labour administration for eighteen years, was the catalyst for a flurry of policy documents and new initiatives, as we shall outline in the next few pages. The history of DFID can be traced back to the colonial period and, in particular, the Colonial Development Act of 1929. In 1961, a Department of Technical Co-operation was established as decolonisation gathered pace. Since then, the status of Britain's development agency has depended upon the party in power. From 1964 to 1970, a Labour government had a separate Overseas Development Ministry. Conservative rule from 1970 to 1974 saw the Ministry downgraded to the Overseas Development Administration, under the Foreign and Commonwealth Office. The return to Labour rule between 1974 and 1979 saw a return to a separate Ministry, which was overturned when the Conservative Party regained power. The current period of rapid expansion and major policy activity can be seen, therefore, in part as a reaction to the regaining of a separate identity.

DFID's knowledge discourses

Our first focus in this chapter will be on the extent to which knowledge appears in the discourse generated by the major policy documents that have arisen in the post-1997 phase of DFID expansion and independence.

The White Papers

There had been no White Paper on development in the eighteen years of Conservative rule. The promise to rectify this was one small part of the New Labour election campaign of 1997, as a token of its greater internationalist credentials. Indeed, this promise was met swiftly with the first White Paper, *Eliminating World Poverty* (DFID 1997), published within six months of the election. Released in late 1997, it predates the majority of agency thinking about knowledge. Where it does talk of knowledge, it largely conflates it with research and technology. One is left with the impression that knowledge is primarily embedded in science and technology. Of course, this is not so very different from the sense that one gets from much of the *WDR* 1998–99, as we noted in the previous chapter.

A notion of knowledge for development more in keeping with wider agency trends did appear in a portion of draft text for the second White Paper (DFID 2000a), but did not find its way into the final text. The draft text had stressed the importance of reorienting higher education links and research strategies to focus more on Southern capacity to generate, use and apply knowledge; on supporting Southern research networks; and on facilitating South–South knowledge sharing. Such proposals mirror some of the more externally oriented elements of the *WDR* 1998–99 and subsequent World Bank initiatives (see the previous chapter), and some elements of the Swedish approach to research co-operation (see the next chapter). However, in the final text these emphases were lost.

Rather, it appears that ICTs were more important than knowledge in the second White Paper, which has a strong sense of the 'digital divide' and the need to overcome it. In keeping with the influence of the new institutional economics[1] on much of the paper, it is argued that 'the constraints on access to ICT for developing countries are in the first instance regulatory' (DFID 2000l: 42).

This, coupled with a very limited emphasis on higher education (see below) or other forms of knowledge generation in the South, could be read as implying that there is knowledge available in the North and that improving Southern access to it is the key to development. If this is the case, then it is a far less sophisticated and democratic account of knowledge than that which can be found in key documents of other agencies, such as Sida and the World Bank, notwithstanding the weaknesses in those agencies' own formulations, which we explore elsewhere in this book.

The Target Strategy Papers (TSP)

In 1999, it was decided that DFID's strong policy commitment to the International Development Targets (IDTs), as expressed in the first White Paper, was in need of clearer articulation and operationalistion in sectoral and country work. The chosen modality to achieve this was the development of a series of Target Strategy Papers.[2] Even though there were only six IDTs, nine TSPs were decided upon:

1. Halving world poverty by 2015
2. Better health for poor people
3. Poverty elimination and the empowerment of women
4. Realising human rights for poor people
5. The challenge of universal primary education
6. Addressing the water crisis.
7. Achieving sustainability
8. Making government work for poor people.
9. Meeting the challenge of poverty in urban areas

It is clear that organisation of the task reflected much about the nature of the departmental structure of DFID at the time and the need to justify the roles of these departments in the light of the IDT commitment. All TSPs were intended to be cross-departmental in their focus, and collaboration between departments was encouraged. However, in several cases, such as education or economic growth, there was a very obvious lead department for the TSP, and the extent of actual cross-sectoral collaboration was often limited.

As regards their use of knowledge as a concept, the TSPs are very uneven, notwithstanding the strong common structure that was imposed upon them. It appears that this unevenness has much to do with the particularities of the different disciplinary and sectoral traditions and concerns that shaped the individual papers. The pressure for the Education TSP (DFID 2000j) to take a sharp line on the importance of primary education seems to have led what little emphasis there had been on higher education as an important contributor to development to be removed between the consultation document (DFID 2000e) and the final version.

This maintenance of an orthodox position on primary education and the linked failure to address the potential contributions of education to debates about knowledge and development stands in stark contrast to the World Bank's own sectoral paper of a year earlier (World Bank 1999) or the more recent World Bank report on higher education (World Bank 2002).[3] It also diverges radically from the Swedish and Japanese traditions that we discuss in the next two chapters. Here the key factor appears to be the then Minister's very clear position that any return to an emphasis on higher education risks diluting the message on primary schooling and, hence, the achievement of the relevant IDT. For her, it appeared that higher education was far more a site of elite formation than a necessary element of a national response to globalisation. It is ironic that this position seems based largely on World Bank research (for example, Psacharopoulos 1981, 1982) that the Bank has now begun to distance itself from, and which JICA and Sida were little influenced by at the time.

However, some of the TSPs do contain a broader, more complex notion of the role of knowledge in development. This includes some sense of the importance of supporting Southern capacity to generate knowledge, as in the Water TSP's acknowledgement that 'to generate knowledge more effectively, we must support the institutions that generate and share that knowledge, particularly those in developing countries' (DFID 2001a: 37).

The Urban TSP, for instance, acknowledges multidirectional knowledge sharing: 'Our research programme already supports much internal lesson-learning and lesson-sharing between our partners in the South. Indeed, many of the ideas for our research programme are generated by our partners' (DFID 2001b: 39). In some TSPs, there is also an awareness of poor people's own existing knowledge and knowledge needs. Nonetheless, it is apparent across the TSPs as a whole that knowledge primarily means research, and that this is largely Northern and scientific. The Education TSP's notion of the role of knowledge is significant in this respect: 'Promoting the sharing of research findings and knowledge on important strategic issues (for example effective schools, financial trade-offs, decentralisation) strengthens international action in support of UPE [universal primary education] and gender equality' (DFID 2000j: 31). Here the notion appears to be very much one of telling Southern governments what 'international best practice' says on issues that DFID has already identified as central to the education policy debate. There is no place in this vision for Southern knowledge or for issues of context. Across the TSPs, Southern knowledge deficits are far more in evidence than concerns about the development of Southern knowledge economies or societies.

Moreover, the TSPs are often stronger on DFID's own knowledge needs. While DFID is regularly depicted as a leader in research and analysis, there is a recurrent theme of the need for this to be further strengthened. Across the TSPs there is also a strong sense of knowledge sharing meaning the more efficient dissemination of DFID's position to donors. This reading is reinforced by the nature of many of the Institutional Strategy Papers, which are clearly about the 'influencing agenda' that is at the heart of DFID's strategy for co-ordination with other donors.[4]

Some further comments on knowledge and development in the major DFID texts

Taken as a whole, these major policy documents of DFID are strikingly silent on the relationship between knowledge and development. In neither White Paper, nor most of the TSPs, is there much sense of the debates about knowledge that are taking place elsewhere, within and beyond development circles. Why is this? The most obvious answer is that there is a tension between a strong focus on the knowledge agenda and one on the poverty agenda. We have heard this stated explicitly by DFID staff. Certainly, there appear to be some merits in such an argument, and there is a danger that the knowledge fascination of some agencies may take them far away from the realities of the poor (a point to which we will return). However, the World Bank would also claim that its primary focus is poverty eradication, and that knowledge is an increasingly vital tool in addressing this overall goal, notwithstanding the questions we have raised about what evidence the World Bank has for this tool's effectiveness.

It is insufficient to judge any agency simply by its key documents. These documents were written for multiple purposes and audiences and, though the absence is noteworthy, knowledge and development was not a priority in their construction. A more complex picture of DFID discourses on knowledge and development may be constructed through a reflection on more explicitly knowledge-oriented interviews, documents and discussions.

Knowledge and development in internal texts

We shall turn first to a series of internal documents that have been developed since 2000. Until recently, DFID's focus has predominantly been on information rather than knowledge; the 'information management framework' of 2000 (DFID 2000d) illustrates the point. Its primary focus is on the information needs of DFID: how to access and manage internal and external information. Where the exchange of information with outsiders is considered, it is usually couched in a language of customers and business that appears to reflect a wider British civil service discourse. There is a sense that DFID needs to acquire and disseminate information, not that it needs to share knowledge. This placing of the information strategy of DFID within a greater cross-governmental initiative is made clearer by the 'e-business strategy' of 2001, a requirement of all departments of state as part of the 'modernising government' initiative (DFID 2001e). Whilst this talks of a vision of DFID as a 'knowledge management organisation' (DFID 2001e: 4), the overall emphasis is very much on ICTs and the construction of information databases. Unfortunately, there is little sense in this of the special needs and challenges of DFID as a development agency that mark it out as different from typical, domestically oriented government departments. More recent internal texts are becoming much more concerned with how DFID can build itself as a 'learning organisation' (DFID 2002d).

The Knowledge Policy Unit and the case of the disappearing 'we wills'

The period since 2000 has also seen the growth of an internal knowledge agenda through three routes. First, the Knowledge Policy Unit (KPU) began to do more than simply think about research across DFID, its official task. As part of the work for the second White Paper, a number of draft policy commitments, 'knowledge we wills', were written from the KPU (DFID 2000a). Although these were not reflected in the final White Paper, as we have seen, they are nevertheless indicative of a strand of thinking about knowledge and development within DFID. Although only a page long, these represented at the time the clearest sense on paper of an awareness of the language of knowledge for development. There was a clear importance given to the need to reorient higher education links and research strategies to support Southern capacity to generate, use and apply knowledge. There was an understanding of the role of both local and global knowledge. DFID's role in supporting multidirectional knowledge sharing was affirmed, including via support to Southern research networks. These notions, and the danger of focusing too intently on internal knowledge management, were later expanded upon in a paper by the then head of the KPU (Clift 2001). We shall see later in this chapter how some of this vision has been acted upon, notwithstanding its omission from the second White Paper.[5]

The Information and Civil Society Department and the discovery of knowledge management

Second, what appears to have been the independent initiative of one field officer led to a process in which the Information and Civil Society Department began a small knowledge management project in mid-2001. The internal paper that started this process, '"Getting the knowledge" in DFID' (DFID 2000c) and a follow-up, 'Doing the knowledge' (DFID 2000m), link explicitly with the modernising government initiative,[6,7] the corporate trends in knowledge management[8] and the learning organisation literature. They argue strongly that DFID needed to manage its own knowledge better and learn more effectively than previously. This was largely couched in the language of organisational efficiency, which would lead inevitably to better aid effectiveness, a clear element of the World Bank's knowledge strategy, as we saw in the previous chapter.

At this time, a number of our interviewees were arguing that there were no real knowledge champions at senior levels. It was striking, therefore, that a joint paper emerged in March 2001 from the two deputy director-generals, Richard Manning and Barry Ireton, titled 'Working together more effectively and knowledge management' (DFID 2001d). This joint paper committed DFID to setting up a small knowledge management unit:

> Knowledge is a key resource for DFID and is increasingly one of our products. DFID has several activities in train to manage knowledge but we can improve our performance by building on current good practice in sharing knowledge and learning. A culture of sharing information and learning must be developed as a core value of the organisation, not as an 'add-on'. It is essential to joined up working.[9] One key benefit is improved individual performance, skills and competences, which improves organisational effectiveness. (DFID 2000d: 2)

The paper reiterated the need to make the best use of staff knowledge and to instigate cultural change in DFID in so far as this was necessary to increase knowledge sharing and improve knowledge use. Moreover, it argued that DFID's concern with influencing the overall development debate was clearly knowledge-based and, indeed, required a rich contextual understanding as well as more traditional theoretical and analytical strengths. DFID's role as a policy advocate and the role of contextual knowledge are issues to which we will return later in this chapter.

However, what is perhaps most significant about this initiative at the discursive level is that DFID's internal reorganisation of February 2002 saw a new area of competence for one of these two deputy director-generals (Barry Ireton): knowledge sharing and special initiatives. Nonetheless, from our interviews with those involved in senior positions in this new directorate, and from others, it appears that, at first, there was little attempt to develop a radically new agenda for knowledge. Rather, the emphasis was on cautious development of what was already in hand, though we shall note below the beginnings of a much more active attempt to build DFID into a learning organisation as well as one that is concerned with 'outward-facing knowledge sharing' (DFID 2000c: 1).

The advisory groups' review

Part of this caution may result from the emergence of a third process within DFID that could seriously impact on the future modalities for knowledge sharing and management. Almost at the same time as the February 2002 internal reorganisation, the new Permanent Secretary, Suma Chakrabati, began a review of the way that the advisory groups in DFID operate. This inevitably raised questions about support to research and external knowledge sharing, as in the KPU approach, and about internal knowledge management and external influencing, as in the Information and Civil Society Department's model.

In the February 2002 restructuring of DFID, the organisation was divided into four directorates: programmes, policies, knowledge, and human resources. Whilst the third and fourth of these have functions of relevance to our study,[10] it is the relationship between the first two that is crucial to the restructuring. At present, programme departments are concerned with the relationship between DFID and its recipient and donor partners. They are responsible for the Country Strategy Papers on how to work with the former, and the Institutional Strategy Papers on how to work with the latter. However, the responsibility for sectoral knowledge lay with the policy departments. Until mid-2002 these were:

- economics, business and statistics
- rural livelihoods and environment[11]
- education
- social development
- health and population
- infrastructure and urban development
- governance

From later in 2002 the entire Policy Division was broken out of these seven separate professional groups, and reconstituted into some 25 cross-cutting policy teams. Their names indicate just how different their focus now is from most of the former groups: Millennium Development Goals; Extractive Industries Transparency Initiative; Conflict; Urban and Rural Change; and so on. A few of these policy teams have a clear resonance with the former groupings. Many of the advisers find themselves working part-time in two groups, though there is still a link to their old departments through the Office of Chief Advisers. At the time of writing, it was unclear what the impact of these changes would be. Nevertheless, along with a parallel reviewing of the impact of DFID's research, this reorganisation has the potential to change radically the way that professional advisory staff work in DFID and the role that they play in the overall knowledge system.

Whilst this review is concerned with the sectoral expertise of DFID, some staff argue that there is a greater challenge regarding its knowledge of the national contexts in which it is working. Whereas the advisory groups, as currently constituted, are organised around the challenge of understanding issues in the relationship between, for instance, education and development, the country teams are primarily short-term implementers of already determined programmes. Thus, it could be argued that there are no comparable groups of staff with detailed country knowledge to advise on new work in specific contexts. Moreover, there appear to be weaknesses both in the recruiting of national staff into the advisory service (AMTEC 2001) and in linking with national research institutions in partner countries. Thus, it can be suggested that DFID is far stronger on the global knowledge, which the advisory service is already providing, than on the local knowledge that should be the basis for partnership-based policy making.

Although the specifics of the organisations are different across our four agencies, this issue of the changing role of professional staff in knowledge systems, and the relative power of universal over contextual knowledge, is repeated in all four cases, as we shall see. Any major transformation of the role and organisation of professional staff is likely to have very serious reverberations throughout the knowledge work of the agency in question.

Reviewing knowledge and development discourses across internal and external documents

Overall, it appears that the relationship between knowledge and development is more present at the level of internal documents than it is within the perspective of the White Papers and TSPs. However, even here one can detect a tendency towards prioritising internally focused knowledge management over broader notions of knowledge-based aid. Nonetheless, there is a distinction to be made between the external knowledge work that is being done by the advisory groups (and the KPU as a support unit for these) and the much more explicit strategy for internal knowledge management of the Information and Civil Society Department. The internal orientation of the official knowledge management project is largely confirmed by our interviews. Moreover, these suggest that the initial bias of DFID in favour of information over knowledge continues to be pervasive at the level of general understanding. Across our interviews there is less sense of strong advocacy for, or cynicism against, knowledge-based aid as there is in the widespread debate within the World Bank. Whilst a number of staff are clearly catching up with thinking about knowledge sharing practice, there is little of the wider thinking about other aspects of knowledge that is evident in our interviews with Bank staff.

Broadly speaking, three tensions appear to sit at the heart of DFID discourses of knowledge, if judged within their own frame of reference. First, there is a tension between the language of knowledge and that of information. DFID has generally been more comfortable with the latter, and this preference is interesting. Information is generally seen as a lower-order concept than knowledge. Whilst possessing information is seen as strategically important in economic terms, the literature generally points to the real competitive edge lying in the ability to turn it into new forms of knowledge. Information is conventionally linked to notions of management and technology. Knowledge, on the other hand, although it can be linked narrowly to management, also widens the gaze to issues of power, partnership, economic structure and development vision. Thus, the notion appears more amenable to social and critical readings alongside the technical.

Second, there is a tendency within DFID to talk of knowledge and research as a single construct. Research programmes are all described as 'knowledge and research', which seems to point to an unresolved tension about the meanings of both words. This tends towards an emphasis on the formal and theoretical aspects of knowledge. Hence, a frequent concern in DFID documents is to talk about dissemination of research rather than knowledge generation. This leads to a language of knowledge that does not reflect the concerns with informality, tacitness and embeddedness that are commonplace in the knowledge literature that we discussed in chapter 3.[12]

Third, there is also a regular conflation of knowledge with research and development, and with science and technology. In the former conflation, this leads to a view of knowledge that only considers market value, and to an emphasis on providing market incentives for knowledge generation and dissemination. In the latter conflation, it renders knowledge as technical and excludes social, cultural and spiritual concerns. Implicitly, it also downplays local, contextual or indigenous conceptions of knowledge in favour of the 'universal' and Northern-dominated.

Overall, Southern knowledge is not strongly stressed in DFID discourse when compared to the other agencies in our study. Whilst there clearly is support from a number of staff for a focus on knowledge capacity building, and acknowledgement both of academic and indigenous knowledge production in the South, these have not appeared as elements of an official discourse, although this began to be flagged in late 2002 by the review of DFID's research strategy.[13] In part, the apparent official suspicion of higher education as elitist may be responsible for this failure sufficiently to recognise Southern knowledge and the need to support its production and dissemination. Equally, DFID's strong official vision of itself as a policy advocate (its 'influencing agenda'), can run the risk of giving the impression that DFID comes to knowledge sharing with a mindset of telling rather than listening. This may have helped to shape the current primary emphasis in DFID's knowledge thinking on internal knowledge management rather than more externally focused knowledge activities. The full potential of any attempt to broaden knowledge management into knowledge sharing seems threatened by the legacy of the conflation of information and management and a related tendency by some elements within DFID to stress technological solutions. However, as we shall see in the next section, this largely negative picture does need to be somewhat offset by a set of projects that have emerged from within parts of DFID that pay more attention to external elements of knowledge sharing, and that seem far less concerned about transmitting development certainties.

DFID's knowledge projects

DFID as an honest broker of development knowledge

Emerging from the research activities of the advisory groups, and the related work of the Knowledge Policy Unit, have come a series of small initiatives that point to a model in which DFID seeks to be a facilitator of better sharing of 'developmentally useful knowledge' among academics, practitioners and policy-makers globally.

The Knowledge Policy Unit

The most explicit advocate of an external knowledge sharing agenda has probably been the Knowledge Policy Unit (KPU). Established in 1998, the KPU is primarily a mechanism for encouraging co-ordination between the knowledge and research activities of the various sectoral departments and the promotion of trans-sectoral research.

Through an application to DFID's 'Challenge Fund', the KPU has also been able to support two external attempts to promote knowledge sharing and research capacity development. These projects are the GDNet, an element of the World Bank's Global Development Network (see the previous chapter for more on this), which is built largely around a website for the sharing of development-oriented research (http://www.gdnet.org), and a science for development information network in collaboration with the science journal *Nature* (http://www.scidev.net). It has also supported some other small activities, including a workshop in Chennai during 2001 on knowledge management in international development.[14]

The latter is interesting as it indicates that the KPU, under its original leadership, was in a sense a second site of activity regarding the notion of the knowledge agency. Whilst the Information and Civil Society Department initiative appears often to have been a reactive strategy by the department that saw itself as the natural locus for knowledge work, the KPU was where there was a real awareness of the cross-agency emergence of knowledge-based aid. Hence, the Chennai meeting came out of a KPU concern that previous meetings of agencies on knowledge management (where it had represented DFID) had been too insular. Moreover, as we saw earlier, it was through the KPU that a knowledge and development strand was developed for the second White Paper, albeit unsuccessfully. It is unclear whether the original capturing of the official knowledge management mandate by the Information and Civil Society Department has locked DFID into a more internally oriented vision than might otherwise have been the case.[15] However, now that Policy Division and the Advisory Services have been rethought into flexible interdisciplinary teams, a strong case has been made for a 'knowledge and culture team' to be located also in close relation to the new structure (DFID 2002e).

Knowledge and research

The other major set of knowledge projects of DFID that also show the emergence of an external knowledge-sharing agenda are the various 'knowledge and research' strategies of the different sectoral departments. What vision of knowledge informs these? Crucially, it is important to note varied sectoral and disciplinary traditions, and major differences in resourcing across departments. Rural Livelihoods, for instance, has approximately twenty times the research budget of Education. It is important also to note that the vision of knowledge is primarily about its operational worth, both for DFID and its partners. Across the research programmes there has been a growing emphasis on the relationship between knowledge and action. This has led to a shift in some departments away from a strong focus on the quality of research hypotheses and methodologies to focus on outcomes and dissemination. The growth of ICTs has encouraged far greater attention to the multiple ways in which findings can be presented, and many of DFID's research findings are now summarised on various websites, for instance. (See below for how this has grown into support for external knowledge sharing in a largely serendipitous way.)

There has also been a shift in the language and practice of research partnership with the South. To varying degrees, departments have begun to put far more emphasis on Southern involvement in the identification of researchable problems and in knowledge generation. However, this partnership remains variable. Some research managers argue that partnerships remain unequal, with the British universities still largely in the lead role and with too much decision-making power resting in London rather than in the field.[16] The notion of partnership inherent within these programmes is also interconnected with the emphasis on outcomes. In some programmes, there appears to be a rigid focus on how potential research projects should align with existing priorities, defined very narrowly. Others, however, note that there is a role for research in helping to revise those priorities.

This tension relates to the partnership issue through the question of capacity building. Capacity building appears to be legitimate only as a by-product of the process of researching DFID priorities, and there is apparently no place for a broader vision of capacity development, as there is in Sida, that would have as its primary goal the development of capacities to address broader national concerns, including for pure research. Thus, the vision of what knowledge production should be supported in the South appears to be at variance with the accounts of a number of Southern commentators who call for Southern not Northern, democratic not technocratic, control of these decisions (e.g. Singh 2000; Coraggio 2001; Torres 2001; Tilak 2002). Arguments about national ownership of development, good governance and the knowledge economy have led to a stronger emphasis in other agencies, such as our other three case study agencies, on the importance of broader conceptions of and renewed support for Southern knowledge capacity development. However, it appears that the DFID research agenda is not intended to be a major source of support for this, although there appears to be a growing undercurrent of support, as we show below.

In a number of sectors, resource centres have been set up. Although the approach varies, these have in common a practical concern with knowledge brokerage services. Through a range of modalities, they link advisory staff to external knowledge sources and UK-based staff to field-based staff. Although primarily focused on DFID's own needs, there is some sense within some of these centres of their potential role in broader processes of knowledge sharing. Whether such external orientation will develop is unclear. The official argument in the World Bank (see chapter 4) is that such services will inevitably become more externally oriented over time. However, this inevitability seems questionable, not least because of the uncertainty caused at present by the reviews of, and on-going changes in, advisory and research work.

There are elements of a more external orientation already in existence, however. Four of the former advisory groups[17] are supporting the work of one high-visibility research dissemination service: id21.[18] This hosts summaries of research, both DFID-commissioned and other, on its website and provides electronic and hard-copy briefings about new research. The website is being accessed from many parts of the world, numbering more than 30,000 page views a month. For those with lower levels of connectivity, the regular e-mail and hard-copy mailings are important.[19] Each of these services has approximately 10,000 subscribers.[20] The biggest research programme in DFID, that for Rural Livelihoods, also supports its own parallel service, Livelihoods Connect, with the same partner as id21, the Institute of Development Studies, at the University of Sussex.

It is useful to consider these initiatives together with the projects supported by the KPU. What is positive about these is that they are not seeking to spread the 'gospel according to DFID' in the same way as the influencing agenda, but seem to be genuinely engaged in providing a series of clearing houses for the sharing of research findings between whoever wishes to become involved. Moreover, in some projects at least, there is a genuine concern about accessibility, in terms of both bandwidth and the style in which research findings are presented. However, two major questions arise about the impact of these projects. First, is supporting such dissemination services a cheap but far inferior substitute for supporting knowledge institutions and systems in the South? Second, and more seriously, what actual development impact can these sites show?

This is the current picture of knowledge and research in DFID. However, the appointment of a new Permanent Secretary in late 2001 makes significant change likely. One of his first statements questioned the existing system of sectoral departments controlling their own research budgets. Instead, he raised the possibility of a single research unit, something the KPU had been envisaged to be but had never become. As a Central Research Unit has now emerged, as recommended by the DFID Research Policy Paper, it may take a very different tack on the role of the South in DFID's knowledge generation activities. In the review process, there did seem to be a growing concern with Southern knowledge capacity, but what this would amount to in practice has remained unclear in the near-to-final draft of the Research Policy Paper (DFID 2002d).

DFID as a smarter knowledge user

We have already noted some of the documents that have come out of the Information and Civil Society Department's project for internal knowledge management. We now will take a brief look at the work of the Knowledge and Information Services (KIS) group, which has been charged with this knowledge brief.

The Knowledge and Information Systems project

The initiative that led to the establishment of the KIS team was started by the Information and Civil Society Department in early 2001, as a result of the internal paper '"Getting the knowledge" in DFID' (DFID 2000c), which we discussed above. It has now merged with some of the activities of the Information Systems and Services Department, the unit responsible for internal information technology issues, but remains organisationally under the management structures of the Information and Civil Society Department. The new Knowledge and Information Systems, which will probably be renamed the Knowledge Support Team, has three main areas of activity.

The promotion of knowledge sharing First, it is pursuing a focus on knowledge sharing. This started with some exploration of corporate experiences in knowledge management, such as electronic yellow pages. The case of British Petroleum (BP) in particular was studied quite closely. In mid-2001, the initial work plan for what became the knowledge sharing initiative included the introduction of a yellow pages project, following on from the examination of BP's model in 'Doing the knowledge' (DFID 2000m). However, further exploration of the evidence led to the rejection of this as a useful model for DFID.[21] An interest in storytelling,[22] another strand of knowledge management practice, was also mentioned in the mid-2001 plan but subsequently dropped. Four more elements of the original work plan were as follows:

- a plan for how to use spaces for informal knowledge sharing in the new offices DFID was scheduled to move into in late 2001
- a reduction in information overload
- a cultural shift in attitudes of both managers and staff towards knowledge sharing
- an exploration of a system of incentives for knowledge sharing[23]

Any visitor to the new DFID headquarters in Palace Street, London, who had also visited the previous building, a few minutes' walk away in Victoria Street, would not fail to notice the difference in surroundings. Behind the far more spacious reception[24] is a pleasant atrium with a coffee bar, frequented both by groups of staff and staff with visitors.[25] Throughout the building are a range of small and large meeting rooms. Several staff commented on the far superior working environment and, specifically, its promotion of knowledge sharing. Whilst the relatively junior staff on the knowledge project at the time cannot have been expected to have had a major input into architects' plans, the new building layout does clearly show more concern with the built environment's effect on staff interactions.

The problem of information overload has been noted in a number of consultancy and internal reports of DFID in the last few years. This is linked directly to the growth of electronic communications. There have been attempts to address this problem through training and awareness-raising about the ways in which information should be disseminated. A February 2002 review suggested that the problem was being reduced as electronic working became more commonplace to staff (DFID 2002a, 2002b). This issue also relates to the two other main elements of the KIS team's work, as we shall see.

The knowledge-sharing focus has also shifted somewhat between 2001 and 2002. In particular, the notion of thematic groups, which we saw in operation in the World Bank, has received greater attention in DFID. Thus, an important new element in the work of the staff member responsible for knowledge sharing is the promotion of thematic groups. There are thought to be about fifty such groups. As in the World Bank, these vary hugely in their levels of activity. These are primarily for DFID staff, although some interviewees did point to communities of practice in which they were participating with staff from other agencies and some Southern colleagues. There is senior encouragement for some of the groups, but, even more than in the case of the Bank, they are heavily dependent on the good will of staff who receive little or no credit for the leadership roles they take in such communities. The intention in the latest version of 'Doing the Knowledge', however, is to mainstream knowledge sharing by recognising and rewarding good practice (DFID 2002c: 6–7).

inSight This focus on the day-to-day knowledge sharing of DFID staff is combined with a focus on the development and maintenance of inSight, the new intranet. In June 2001, a second version of DFID's intranet was launched. Whilst the first version largely replicated the paper-based information of the existing DFID structures, the new version is an attempt to encourage new cross-departmental virtual teams and a topic-oriented structure. From interviews since the move to new premises, this new intranet is seen as an important advance in DFID's internal knowledge sharing. As with several other agencies, it is now the case that DFID staff need to go through the intranet homepage to access other sites.

The homepage includes an events calendar and links to different parts of DFID. More importantly, however, it includes a 'Spotlight' section designed to allow senior management to inform staff of major priorities and to encourage discussion on important issues for the organisation. Early indications suggest that this is becoming a useful tool for bottom-up as well as top-down communication.

Using inSight, the Permanent Secretary has personally launched a new concept of 'how to's'. These are intended to be a synthesis of DFID's knowledge on key issues pertinent to its work. Their focus will be on 'know who' and 'know how' more than 'know what'. The intention is in part to be able to direct staff to the relevant person or unit that should be contacted on a particular issue. This sense of bureaucratic correctness is also evident in the objective that each 'how to' should reflect the official DFID position and practice on the issue in question and should be approved by the high-level Knowledge and Communications Committee, and also the Development Committee where they are seen as policy-sensitive. This seems to be a very clear example of an attempt to validate knowledge that goes against much of what is considered to be good knowledge practice. [26]

The first 'how to', on working with the European Commission, has been developed. Others are expected on topics such as PRSPs, but it seems that the careful construction and management of these notes means that they will be relatively few in number.

The first internal survey of knowledge and communications since the introduction of inSight reports that many staff are using it as an important tool for their work (DFID 2002a and b).[27] However, from the external website, such significant development is invisible.

The electronic agency The third current initiative of Knowledge and Information Services is the major attempt to digitise both DFID's library and its internal documentation. DFID is seeking to move rapidly towards both a 'paperless office' and an 'e-library' (DFID 2002a, 2002b). In early 2002, the head of the main library in East Kilbride[28] took charge of a new electronic documentation and records management project, QUEST. This project seeks to shift as much of the basic administration of DFID as possible to electronic documentation. This is in keeping with the broader 'modernising government' initiative and also links to DFID's requirements to meet new freedom of information legislation. At the same time, the library is reducing its book holdings dramatically and is seeking to become primarily a service for e-journals and other digitised material. This requires that the current staff of librarians shift to a new way of working.

It is unclear as yet what this new way of working will be. In the World Bank, the advisory desks have emerged as one route for the work of former documentalists. Box (2001) has argued that the coming of digitised resources can transform documentalists into the key knowledge brokers of organisations. However, the possibility of either of these paths emerging in DFID is limited by the existence of a model of knowledge brokerage already within the advisory groups, as we have noted previously. Nevertheless, there is evidence in the latest plans for 'corporate knowledge sharing' that there may emerge joint working between the KIS and whatever proves to be the final knowledge architecture of the new Policy Division (DFID 2002c).

Other related projects on data, information and learning

It will become clearer after the next two chapters that there are a lot of projects across agencies that are knowledge-related but which are not thought of in these terms. In DFID's case, several of these are related to earlier notions of data and information management.

With its information interests, DFID has been quite heavily involved in database creation and sharing activities. Much emphasis within DFID has been placed on the development of the Project Reporting and Information System Management (PRISM) database of the Evaluation Department. This system seeks to standardise reporting mechanisms of the various departments and provide a single reference point for those seeking to monitor DFID's portfolio of projects. It will be able to show a range of data including collaborators, lessons learned, local contacts and future plans. This is seen as vital to the audit trail on DFID's effectiveness in meeting its stated targets. DFID has also been part of OECD and Development Gateway (see chapter 4) initiatives for inter-agency information sharing, although these remain in the development phase. As noted earlier, DFID is also part of the wider 'modernising government' initiative, which seeks to look into ways of developing electronic government, both in terms of internal operations and relations with citizens.

Internal knowledge management and sharing initiatives are an important element of a number of agencies' concerns with improving staff competences. This is the case in DFID, as some of the earlier discussion makes clear. However, DFID has also been involved in other projects that are more explicitly about staff development in a human resources tradition. As DFID's way of working has changed, so have its staff development programmes. There are basically three levels to these programmes. First, there is awareness building as part of the two-day induction (for example, there is now a half day on poverty). Second, there is a series of two- to three-day courses for middle level administrators on core technical issues such as sector programmes, budgetary support and PRSPs. Finally, there are modules of similar duration on specialist themes for advisory staff. 'Staff appointed in country' get the same induction package plus country-specific orientation but have not yet been on the further training courses. Such programmes reflect a similar concern as in the World Bank with responding to new development challenges. However, unlike the Bank, there appears to be no articulation as yet between the work of the knowledge and training elements of DFID.

An overview of DFID's knowledge projects

What conclusions can be drawn about DFID's knowledge projects? Those under the new KIS unit are very new and developing quite quickly. However, as with the trends at the level of discourse, concerns can be raised about the tendency to focus on the internal (including intra- and inter-government), the technological and the informational. These are clearly seen in some of the projects, such as PRISM, that emerge out of other departments – in that case, Evaluation.

However, there is a more positive story to be told about the work of the advisory groups. Although still at an early stage, they are seeking to encourage a greater Southern role in knowledge generation. Nonetheless, DFID's official hesitations about higher education appear to act as an obstacle to this agenda. It is in the area of sharing existing research findings, and in a user-friendly manner, that the knowledge and research wing of DFID has been more successful. Though modestly funded, the KPU has proved a catalyst to international developments in this field. Building on the international profile of the Institute for Development Studies in digital research dissemination, both the KPU and a set of advisory groups have been strong supporters of initiatives that share research knowledge globally. Importantly, these initiatives do take account of differing degrees of interconnectivity and do seek to link researchers as well as simply present their synthesised findings. However, they are much weaker on the enabling institutional environment that Southern researchers, policy-makers and practitioners need to take a lead role in such networks.

The focus on this particular type of external knowledge sharing has happened not because it is a major priority of DFID but because some staff have taken a particular interest in this area and have committed relatively modest sums of money to supporting initiatives in which elements of their national civil society have developed some comparative advantage.[29] In this sense, the feel of these knowledge projects is much more that of old-style, projectised bilateral aid rather than the program-matic, cross-agency approach that DFID is increasingly emphasising in its mainstream development work.

Before leaving this domain of external knowledge sharing, it should be noted that, in a way that partly parallels trends seen in the World Bank (see chapter 4), there is clear evidence of a shift in the knowledge management strategy towards more 'outward-facing knowledge sharing'. 'Doing the Knowledge II', which is the latest KM strategy of the Infor-mation and Civil Society Department, does quite explicitly underline the importance of 'capacity building' and 'widening and deepening partner-ships'. Nor is this just a matter of ensuring that the Southern partners get improved access to DFID's knowledge, though that is evident; but there is also talk of providing 'electronic space to learn and collaborate with partners'. This would make it possible for DFID staff 'to communicate, consult and work with key partners on shared projects and products' (DFID 2002c: 18–19).

DFID's knowledge practices

The concern of the New Labour government in the UK since 1997 to present its message powerfully has combined with the rapid expansion of web-based publishing to bring about an unprecedented publication of DFID materials, as we have already noted. All of these, in some sense, are knowledge products. However, we will focus here on the White Papers and TSPs as the core presentation of DFID's knowledge to the world. Earlier we considered what the overall messages of these documents were about knowledge in DFID. Now, we shall consider more about how they were produced and from where they sourced knowledge.

The White Papers

According to those closely involved with its production, the first White Paper was an exercise in quickly meeting the manifesto pledge of a new government to make a statement on development. Although there was little time for research or consultation, the White Paper did powerfully articulate a new vision for British development co-operation that drew heavily on international trends towards pro-poor and pro-partnership approaches.

The second White Paper was a somewhat lengthier exercise. It was seen internally as not so much a DFID White Paper as a government paper on globalisation. This meant that a lot of DFID's knowledge ac-quisition in the writing process was from other UK departments of state, particularly those with economic portfolios. A series of rapidly researched and written papers were commissioned and published on the White Paper website. Given the topic of the White Paper, it is perhaps not surprising that these commissioned pieces and the White Paper as a whole had a strong bias towards sources of economic rather than social, political or cultural knowledge.[30] Indeed, interviews with members of the writing team suggest a view of policy that was exclusively economic. Although some consultation took place, it was rather limited in both North and South, and it is difficult to find any sense in the text of influences from Southern points of view. No Green Paper or draft White Paper was ever released for general comment. Indeed, it is easy to get the impression that the principal aim was to illustrate the benefits of globalisation to a sceptical British civil society rather than to engage in a genuine dialogue about how to develop a pro-poor response to globalisation.

The Target Strategy Papers

It is clear that the TSP process was an important source of learning and knowledge acquisition in DFID. All nine TSPs represent considerable synthesis work. Moreover, each process allowed new opportunities for cross-departmental learning, although this inevitably varied in quality and extent. Judging from the Powerpoint slides of an internal presentation on the TSPs (DFID 2000b), there was an intention to make the process genuinely consultative and an opportunity for external as well as internal learning. Each TSP sought to present a synthesis of current evidence as a basis for future DFID activities, including advocacy work and further knowledge generation.

However, a number of concerns can be raised about the effectiveness of the process. Some staff noted that the emphasis on a common format and simple messages reduced the scope for contextualisation of arguments, although some TSPs managed this tension better than others. The way that the TSPs draw on existing knowledge may also be criticised. The knowledge used by the TSPs is noteworthy in its narrowness. A quick calculation of citations in footnotes and bibliographies suggests that less than 4 per cent of sources cited come from the South; whilst over 84 per cent were produced by or for bilateral or multinational agencies or international NGOs.[31] Moreover, much of the agency literature is regional or global in its focus. Whilst the TSPs of course need to be usable by staff, they can be argued to be over-simplistic and convergent in their thinking, leaving little or no room for alternatives. For instance, the Economics TSP fails to cite any of the voluminous Southern critical literature on structural adjustment, and also ignores the criticisms of neoliberal thinking that were made by Stiglitz when he was the World

Bank's chief economist. The Governance TSP takes a highly controversial line on the East Asian miracle and meltdown, which places all the success on neoliberal economic policies and all the failure on cronyism and lack of democracy. This account flies in the face of a large amount of readily available research from both Asia and the West, and ignores the controversy that similar findings produced when they emerged from the World Bank some years earlier (Wade 1996).

Although some papers (for example, Environment, Water and Urban) were written in partnership with UK universities and NGOs, there is little clear evidence of consultation in others. This major synthesis work appears to have largely been conducted by staff within DFID's head office.[32] This seems particularly curious at a time when DFID was also moving strongly to a more decentralised mode of operation, with far greater autonomy for country and regional offices. Indeed, there appears to be some degree of tension around the relative roles of different parts of the organisation at present.

Overall trends across DFID's knowledge products

These documents represent just the tip of the iceberg in terms of what DFID has produced publicly in the last five years. This productivity must be seen positively for its opening up of the Department to greater scrutiny. However, one cannot help wondering whether there has also been an excessive diversion of time and resources into producing documents rather than getting on with development. Moreover, some interviewees noted that the greater visibility of documents meant that more attention was given to making them non-controversial, resulting in a blandness that negatively affected their practical value. These are not criticisms that apply solely to DFID, of course. Rather, it is a symptom of a British government culture of information management.

Taken as a whole, these major DFID documents do reflect the synthesis of a large amount of knowledge. They represent a massive commitment of staff and resources to using that knowledge as the basis for future activities. However, the sources of knowledge used were rather narrow in terms of disciplines, ideology and geography.

It is important to remember that academic literature on how policy is made rejects the simple assumption that policy is based on the best available knowledge (for example, Kingdon 1995; McGrath 2001a). Instead, it suggests that knowledge is typically used to support existing policy views rather than to revise them. The former does appear to be the way that knowledge is used in most of these policy documents. There is a strong sense that DFID already had a vision: on poverty, on globalisation, on basic education, and so on, and that evidence was then marshalled to support this vision. The frequent references to advocacy and influencing in interviews and documents should lead us to expect that knowledge is being deployed to add power to an argument rather than to establish what priorities should be.

DFID's knowledge practices

It is at the level of practices that it becomes most clear how knowledge use in DFID has been transformed in the past five years. There has been a clear growth in knowledge capacity within DFID through its staff recruitment. More staff are comfortable with policy analysis. New sectoral expertise has emerged.[33] Whilst the huge policy effort may have reinforced existing positions at the level of the texts, it appears to have had a more positive learning impact at the level of individual staff, and has encouraged new cross-departmental collaborations. This process of cross-sectoral interaction has been furthered by the informal growth of communities of practice. Improved communications infrastructure has led to weekly teleconferencing meetings between the DFID offices in Africa, and the beginning of a growth of regional communities of practice. Resource centres and their staff provide a valuable new knowledge resource and play an important knowledge brokerage role. The new Regional Economics and Policy Units have the potential to play a similar brokerage role between the centre and the field offices. E-mail and the digitisation of documents have clearly revolutionised work practices, as elsewhere, and there is far more information available than ever before (DFID 2002a, 2002b). Retreats for professional groups and regional teams are increasing. Open attendance seminars over lunchtime have increased significantly in both frequency and attendance. At country and global levels, sharing with other agencies has increased, and PRSPs and sector programmes should support further sharing with Southern partners. In early 2001, the chief economic adviser encouraged his staff to spend one day a week in 'knowledge activities', and there are plans for a knowledge dimension to a new staff appraisal tool. A number of staff have commented to us on the positive impact of the new atrium on informal knowledge sharing.

However, this is an incomplete transformation. There are internal concerns about the extent to which a culture of internal knowledge sharing has been achieved; information overload is a common theme of internal documents and staff comments. Departmental 'empires' still act as barriers to horizontal communication, whilst there remains a perception that vertical communication is still too top-down and centre-to-periphery. Country offices and administrators are perceived to be less involved in many of these new activities than London-based advisers, and the improvements in global connectivity are still being implemented. Whilst recruitment has brought new knowledge and skills into DFID at the country office level, as we noted earlier, there has been insufficient recruitment of local nationals into advisory positions (India has a far better record than Africa in this regard). This is seen as part of a bias within DFID to global knowledge over local.

The review of the advisory groups illustrates senior management concerns about attitudes to knowledge sharing. Moreover, our interviews point to similar limitations in this regard to those in the World Bank. First, there is still a strong sense that knowledge activities are additional to other commitments and not central to effective operational work. Second, there appears still to be a strong perception that knowledge sharing is not likely to be a major factor in promotions. This highlights the failure as yet to resolve the issue of an incentive system for knowledge sharing. Whilst an element covering knowledge sharing is being introduced into annual appraisals, DFID appears to be struggling with this issue in ways similar to those of other agencies, such as the World Bank and Sida.

There are concerns that knowledge activities remain under-resourced and inadequately co-ordinated. There are also tensions over DFID's attitude towards knowledge sharing with external partners. Some staff are very bullish about DFID's role as a leader of development thinking and practice; one interviewee, for instance, spoke of the second White Paper as a 'statement to the world'. Others, however, were concerned about external perceptions of DFID as arrogant, and were worried that DFID appeared too certain about what worked in development. This sense of DFID arrogance is something that emerges relatively often when talking to staff of other agencies.

It is important to contextualise these criticisms, many of which emerged from DFID staff through interviews. Any transformation to becoming a knowledge agency will necessarily be long-term. At the World Bank, James Wolfensohn's declaration that the Bank would be 'the knowledge bank' in four years proved to be wildly over-optimistic, although it did serve to push the transformation process very strongly, as we saw in chapter 4. Many of the tensions outlined in the previous paragraph are evident in the Bank too. Indeed, cultural barriers to learning within organisations are widespread, both in the agency world (we shall explore this in detail in the case of Sida in the next chapter) and beyond (Argyris and Schön 1978).

How should we judge DFID's approach to knowledge and development?

DFID continues to undergo rapid changes in its thinking and practice regarding knowledge and development. Indeed, this rapidity makes drawing conclusions at one particular point in time especially challenging. Nonetheless, a series of points about achievements and challenges can be made. In so doing, it is important to note that such an analysis can work on a number of levels.

First, if we accept that DFID is genuinely attempting to move to a more knowledge-based approach to aid, then we can ask how successful this attempt is, within this paradigm. Significant progress has been made since 2001 in DFID's evolution from information management to knowledge sharing. Perhaps most importantly, there are signs that the argument about the importance of this work has begun to take off. There is a rapidly growing sense that this agenda has high-level support and that the language is beginning to infuse a wider range of discourses and practices. The symbolic importance of the appearance of knowledge sharing in the title of one of the director-generals' posts since February 2002 should not be undererestimated, although the real work of re-visioning has not yet really taken root.[34]

Research agendas have begun to shift from a bias towards problems identified and projects led by UK-based academics to notions of partnership with, and even leadership from, the South. Moreover, the emphasis has shifted from traditional academic approaches to proposal design, project delivery and findings dissemination to more fluid and outcomes-focused approaches that stress the application of the knowledge and the multiple possibilities for knowledge sharing. Concerns with the notion of knowledge as a global public good and awareness of the possibilities of ICT-based knowledge sharing have led DFID to support some knowledge networks that are primarily about sharing between and within research communities North and South. Indeed, DFID has successfully built on the comparative advantage of Britain in this regard, albeit in a rather unstructured way. However, it is currently unclear about whether these developments will survive the current review of DFID's knowledge and research activities.

One of the important lessons from knowledge theory is that most learning is relatively informal (Nonaka and Takeuchi 1995; Davenport and Prusak 1998). This is inscribed in the architecture of the new DFID headquarters, with its atrium and numerous meeting rooms. It is reflected in a strong ICT-fuelled growth in DFID staff participation in knowledge sharing. It is reflected too in the support to learning through mechanisms such as newsletters and seminars both within and outwith the organisation.

Given DFID's major emphasis on information systems, it is not surprising to see major advances in the infrastructure for information sharing within the organisation. It appears that the revised intranet is becoming a genuine tool for knowledge sharing and not just a repository of information. Probably less importantly, there has also been a major expansion in the sharing of information with other agencies.

However, even within these areas of progress there are grounds for concern. DFID appears to have gone further with internally oriented knowledge management to date than with other, less introspective, areas of knowledge and development. Whilst it may be that DFID needs to get its own knowledge 'house' in order before looking outside, this does represent an area of current weakness. As we noted earlier, DFID continues to conflate knowledge and information quite regularly. This appears to have resulted in what the available literature would suggest is an over emphasis on databases and the technology of information and knowledge management at the expense of the human side (McGinn 2001), although there are the beginnings of new, more human-centred trends in the various options for refashioning DFID into a learning organisation (DFID 2000c).

Second, it is possible to raise concerns about how a greater knowledge focus can impact upon the broader process of development co-operation without for the moment seeking to question the desirability of aid or development. As with trends more generally across agencies, it is important to locate DFID's shift towards a more knowledge-based approach in its context. As with the World Bank, DFID did not start with dramatic Southern knowledge deficits or the key question of how knowledge-based aid could assist knowledge development in the South, but has focused on its own knowledge needs. King (2000) has raised the concern that agencies are likely to become more certain of what they themselves have learnt and more enthusiastic that others should share these insights. Again, DFID seems to be a good example of this, as a number of staff noted with concern. There is a need to ask how joint involvement in agency knowledge projects could better build knowledge in the South. DFID's research programmes are becoming more partnership focused and the KPU's two pilots, some resource centre activities, and support to id21 do involve the sharing of knowledge from both North and South. However, an apparent suspicion of higher education seems to result in there being no place in DFID's vision for a broader, longer-term strategy to support national knowledge capacities in the South (a strong theme of our next chapter, when we turn to Sweden). Equally, DFID appears to have had less of an explicit interest in capacity development, until very recently, than a number of other agencies, such as Sida and JICA, and even, since late 2001, the World Bank. In these areas, DFID seems to lag behind the other agencies surveyed in this book, as well as its predecessor agency, the Overseas Development Administration.[35]

Third, there are also more fundamental questions about co-operation and development that this chapter has not sought to address directly so far. The focus on knowledge-based aid does allow questions to be raised about the language of partnership/ownership that is at the heart of current aid discourse, not just in DFID. We have foregrounded some of these questions in chapters 1 and 3, and addressed them in the case of the World Bank. Nothing in our exploration of DFID suggests that asymmetries of knowledge and power are being seriously addressed. There is a danger that DFID illustrates the thesis that the more knowledge based aid is about greater donor certainty and a 'telling' modality, then the more implausible the language of partnership/ownership becomes.

The interplay of partnership and knowledge also points to a fundamental tension in the way that development is understood. Part of the certainty that knowledge-based aid can engender is about the detail of what constitutes development. Thus, DFID appears not only to know that the IDTs constitute an unquestionable core of development but also has a set of other strong beliefs in further elements of development. This vision privileges a body of global knowledge over partnership or ownership.

Fourth, it is possible to question the epistemological basis of the knowledge–development relationship within DFID policy and practice. Throughout these there is a clear sense of an implicit model of 'developmentally useful knowledge' operating. This is typical across agencies (McGrath 2001a). The bulk of the TSPs and the two White Papers demonstrate a tendency towards objective, scientific, acontextual knowledge. Across these documents, the power of economistic thinking is still evident. However, such a reading masks a divergence in epistemologies. Within the research and policy practices of DFID, especially at the country and regional levels, there is a growing sense of the importance of the contextual, political and contested nature of knowledge.

This book argues that one of the benefits of the emergence of knowledge-based aid is that it foregrounds questions at all these levels. In looking at the case of DFID, we have raised concerns at each of them. However, DFID is in a process of rapid change and its responses to knowledge do contain potential for a more partnership- and learning-centred approach to development. Whether the new and positive opportunities for synergy between the knowledge strategies from the information domain and the policy advisory domain are grasped remains to be seen.[36] However, the next chapter, on Sida, does highlight what can emerge when an agency more explicitly stresses learning in its approach to development co-operation.

Notes

1. A similar emphasis on the telecommunications regulatory framework as central to the overcoming of the digital divide is a major strand of the analysis in the *WDR* 1998–99. The powerful effect of this sub-branch of the economics of development thinking is also seen clearly in elements of Sida's work, as we shall see in the next chapter.

2. Underneath the umbrella of two White Papers, the TSPs form the apex of a triangular structure of strategy papers. The two other corners are provided by Institutional Strategy Papers (ISPs), which focus on how DFID can better collaborate with and better influence other agencies, and the Country Strategy Papers (CSPs), which focus on DFID's specific policy and programme priorities in particular Southern countries.

3. However, this World Bank higher education report does not have the status of an official policy document, even though this was the initial intention. As we noted, this highlights the degree of contestation of the move away from primary education fundamentalism that still exists within the World Bank.

4. The notion of influencing others has been a major theme for the former Minister and senior staff. It can be found as a theme in the White Papers and the ministerial introduction to each of the TSPs. In 2000, an internal paper called 'The Influencing Agenda' was commissioned. It was also a recurrent notion in our interviews.

5. The Knowledge Policy Unit is not referred to in the latest internal documents about knowledge in policy division; perhaps it is to be replaced by what is termed a 'knowledge hub'.

6. In this light, it is interesting to note that the Foreign and Commonwealth Office had already agreed on a 'knowledge management programme' in June 2000. Would DFID have been party to this if the Cabinet restructuring of 1997 had not taken place?

7. We shall see subsequently some of the impacts of the 'modernising government' initiative on the work of DFID, as well as government-wide commitments to respond to new freedom of information legislation.

8. The second paper refers particularly to Nokia and BP, but also cites Larry Prusak, co-author of the influential *Working Knowledge* (Davenport and Prusak 1998).

9. 'Joined-up government' was one of the most recurrent slogans of the New Labour government's first term in office, 1997–2001.

10. Information (and knowledge), ICT infrastructure and evaluation are elements of the third directorate; staff learning is covered under the fourth. It

is important to note that the KPU does not fall under knowledge but under policy in this structure.

11. The first two advisory services are multi-departmental and described as divisions; the others are classed as departments.

12. The most recent internal text on the subject, titled 'Doing the Knowledge II', is much more at home with the lexicon of knowledge management and knowledge sharing, tacit and explicit.

13. DFID's 'Research Policy Paper' had gone through its consultation phase by November 2002.

14. This was the third in a series of workshops on knowledge management and development organised by Bellanet, a Canadian NGO with strong links to the International Development Research Centre, Canada's official agency for research co-operation. Both the first workshop in Washington and the second in Brighton had been very much dominated by agency and corporate representatives. The KPU were instrumental in pushing for a third meeting to take place in the South with a more representative group of participants. It had also supported the Brighton meeting.

15. The KPU did not fall under the Deputy-Director General for Knowledge Sharing and Special Initiatives even before the restructuring of Advisory Services. KPU's functions have been absorbed by the new Central Research Unit.

16. DFID's new Research Policy Paper may alter much of this, and not least in the formal 'untying' of research moneys from British research institutions.

17. Economics (through the Committee for Social Science Research, formerly the Economic and Social Committee on Research – ESCOR); Education; Health and Population, and Infrastructure and Urban Development (e-mail from Alistair Scott, id21 Manager, 3 May 2002). These are reflected in the organisation of id21's material into general, health, education and urban sections, each with a separate e-newsletter.

18. Along with ELDIS and the GDNet, this is a project based at the Institute for Development Studies, University of Sussex.

19. The general 'id21News' is e-mailed monthly, whilst the sectoral e-newsletters and the hard-copy *Insights* are quarterly.

20. These statistics come from an electronic communication with Alistair Scott, referred to above. They refer to 2001. A more detailed analysis of user demographics can be found at http://www.id21.org/analysis/index.html. As Alistair Scott notes, web statistics are necessarily very inaccurate owing to caching and other elements of internet architecture.

21. There is another possibility that a change in staffing simply led to the end of an interest in the yellow pages approach, which BP have considered so worthwhile that they have licensed the software behind it for use by other corporations. The European Bank for Reconstruction and Development is one development agency that has purchased this software for its own internal knowledge management activities. An electronic yellow pages seeks to develop a set of tools through which staff can search for those within the organisation with expertise in a particular topic. Rather than just contact details, there are typically facilities for viewing documents, homepages and video clips of those individuals being browsed.

22. Steve Denning, who we met in earlier chapters, has written a book on storytelling, and has left the World Bank to pursue a consultancy and speaking career in this field. He was one of the two authors cited in the 'Doing the knowledge' paper, along with Larry Prusak. The notion of storytelling seems to have been directly imported into DFID from a reading of some of Denning's work.

23. The list of six themes – yellow pages, storytelling and the four listed – comes from interview data from Information Department staff.

24. Next to the reception area is a new information kiosk, reflecting quite closely the layout of the reception area of Sida's headquarters.

25. In this case, the franchised atrium coffee bar is more reminiscent of the main building at the World Bank. However, 'Doing the knowledge' does make explicit mention of Sida's tradition of staff meeting informally over coffee.

26. 'Doing the Knowledge II' acknowledges that 'inSight is currently exploited more as a "top down, centre out" corporate communications tool than a knowledge-sharing system' but argues for ways to increase its knowledge sharing potential (DFID 2002c: 13).

27. A note of methodological caution is necessary here. The 'snapshot' study had a very small sample and modest response rate. Moreover, sample and respondent biases cannot be ruled out. Nonetheless, the study provides a useful corollary to data we have gathered through our own research, and seems broadly accurate.

28. DFID officially has two headquarters. As well as the main building in London, there is a secondary headquarters in the Scottish new town of East Kilbride, near Glasgow. This is where a number of the administrative support departments in the Human Resources directorate, plus other units such as statistical services and civil society liaison, are based. It has been home for several years to DFID's main library, and its principal information point for the public.

29. Indeed, it is worth noting that one of the key players in this regard, Charles Clift at the KPU, has since left this knowledge position.

30. Twenty-three background papers were published on the White Paper website. These were not put out to tender and were largely written by established DFID consultants from the field of economics.

31. This is necessarily a rather crude exercise but its results do seem to be indicative of trends in knowledge use. Only one TSP (Economics) has a bibliography. In the others, references in footnotes were counted. There is likely to be some double counting of sources as a result of this, and we have not attempted to check whether a particular source has been used in more than one TSP. Attribution to agency or South is imprecise, though broadly accurate. There are some cases where we know that a particular journal article is written by agency staff. However, the further away we get from our own professional areas, the less easy it is for us to discern that an apparently non-agency source actually has been written by agency staff. Thus, there may be a tendency to underestimate rather than overestimate the bias towards insiders' knowledge.

32. Some TSPs include a note of the team responsible for putting it together. Our evidence is based on these and on interviews both with participants and

with non-participants in the process. A number of field-based staff were strongly critical of the process and their perceived exclusion from it.

33. However, it is of course likely that there is considerable inertia in the advisory system, with disciplines that have had large numbers of staff historically being reluctant to reduce their numbers even if their relative importance has declined in terms of the overall priorities of DFID.

34. A great deal may depend on how the new vision in 'Doing the Knowledge II' gets taken forward by the new director of the Information and Civil Society Department.

35. Paradoxically, the new DFID Research Policy Paper deals very much more with the reorganisation of centrally funded research in headquarters than with research in DFID's country programmes, whose policies and priorities remain relatively inaccessible.

36. Although the physical and intellectual upheaval in the reorganisation of Policy Division has been very challenging to traditional ways of working, there is already evidence that there are new possibilities for synergy between the strengthened Information Division and the new Policy Division. Thus, while some of the detailed architecture described in this chapter has already changed since the summer of 2002, it is argued by informed insiders that knowledge has actually moved up DFID's overall agenda.

SIX

Knowledge, learning and capacity in the Swedish approach to development co-operation

A number of trends have led development co-operation agencies to embrace the idea of becoming 'knowledge agencies', more efficient and effective users of knowledge both internally and in their work with their Southern partners. At the same time, agencies have become fascinated with the role that knowledge can play in national development strategies in the South.

This chapter seeks to examine the discourses and practices of the Swedish International Development Co-operation Agency (Sida) in terms of our broader concerns with knowledge-based aid. However, what is perhaps most important in the case of Sida is the way that accounts of learning and capacity are often of higher importance than those of knowledge. The main focus here, therefore, will be on the nature of the interplay amongst these three concepts in Sida's discourses and practices. This will contribute to a better understanding of the concept of knowledge-based aid as applied to development co-operation agencies more generally, and the extent to which it is an inevitable trend.

The chapter is based on the analysis of a series of interviews we have conducted with Sida staff, policy documents, research reports and other official texts from Sida and the Swedish Ministry for Foreign Affairs, and, significantly, written accounts by Sida staff about their work and the operation and vision of the organisation as a whole.[1] As will become clear subsequently, these accounts by senior Sida staff past and present provide an invaluable insight into the workings of the organisation, and are generally characterised by a highly reflective approach. Participation in a one-day seminar in March 2002 with more than 30 Sida staff on knowledge, learning and capacity also greatly informed this analysis.

Historical overview

A number of texts and interviews point to the perceived importance of Sida's history for understanding its current way of working and its attitudes towards issues such as learning, knowledge and capacity. It is worth, therefore, briefly outlining this history.

Although Sweden's first treaty with an African state can be dated to 1650, and there is a long tradition of scientific, trade and missionary encounter (Widstrand 1986; Wohlgemuth 2001), Swedish aid to Africa (and to Asia) began formally in the 1950s with major programmes of support to Ethiopia and Pakistan (Heppling 1986; Ministry for Foreign Affairs 1998).[2] In 1962 the Agency for International Assistance (NIB) was set up (Heppling 1986). Its overall goal was determined by the Swedish Parliament: 'To improve the quality of life of poor peoples' (quoted in Sida 1996a: 1). Significantly, this pledge was backed by a major financial commitment. The NIB became SIDA[3] in 1965, and in 1968 Sweden committed itself to putting 1 per cent of GDP into its aid budget (Wohlgemuth 2001: 51).[4] In 1977 four sub-goals were added to the overall goal of Swedish development policy:

- economic growth
- socio-economic equality
- economic and political independence
- democratic development (Ljunggren 1986; Sida 1996a)

In 1988 'sustainable use of natural resources and protection of the environment' was added, followed in 1996 by 'fostering equal rights for women and men' (Sida 1996a). In this way, Sida was ahead of the current trend of a number of donors to establish a poverty super-goal as well as a set of sub-goals on gender, democracy, environment, and so on (Working Group for International Cooperation in Skills Development 2002).

SIDA also anticipated another key element of the new way of working with its strong emphasis during the 1960s on sectoral programmes (Wohlgemuth 1998).[5] Such programmes gave countries considerable flexibility over how Swedish money could be spent within a broad, agreed framework. In the 1970s this evolved into a position where Sweden became less proactive in such relationships, leaving most of the decision making to the Southern partner (Edgren 1986, 1997; Ministry for Foreign Affairs 1998). This approach was to be radically revised in the 1980s as Sweden moved closer to the new neoliberal orthodoxy and became a supporter of structural adjustment and ever heavier conditionalities (Edgren 1997; Olukoshi 1997a, 1997b; Wohlgemuth 1998). At the same time, the downward pressure on the Swedish development budget from growing conservatism at home led to increased attention to efficiency and a search for performance criteria for SIDA's work (Edgren 1997).

The second half of the 1990s saw a further shift in Sida's approach to development co operation. On the one hand, this should be located in broader agency trends, linked to the International Development Targets (IDTs), sector programmes, and so on. However, the change must also be situated in the emergence of the 'new' Sida in 1995. That year saw the merger of the Swedish International Development Agency with three smaller organisations. The oldest of these was the Swedish Agency for Research Co-operation with Developing Countries (SAREC), established in 1975. The other parties to the merger were the Swedish Agency for Technical Co-operation (established 1980) and SwedeCorp (established 1992). The new organisation retained the name Sida, although with a new full title of the Swedish International Development Co-operation Agency. SAREC is now a distinct department within the 'new' Sida, and important elements of its historical perspective appear to have continued. As we shall explore in greater detail below, SAREC has brought into the merged organisation an important emphasis on knowledge generation and on capacity development.

One of the first priorities of the merged Sida was to develop a new strategy; one that responded to the new agency trends. To this end, four 'Action Programmes' were developed by 1997 that sought to develop Sida-wide responses to cross-cutting issues. Linked to Sida's stated goals, these four programmes were on:

- equality between women and men
- sustainable livelihoods and poverty reduction
- peace, democracy and human rights
- environmentally sustainable development

The late 1990s also saw the rethinking of Sweden's relationship with its two major partner regions: Africa and Asia. As Sida is an agency of the Ministry for Foreign Affairs, this macro-level reformulation of Swedish development co-operation was not strictly a Sida responsibility. Nonetheless, it makes sense to see a very close relationship between the roles of Sida and the Ministry, and to talk of a Swedish development co-operation vision.

In parallel with processes in other countries and agencies, the development of a new Swedish Africa policy saw a strong emphasis on the notion of partnership. Importantly, this was reflected in the process of policy formulation, with a serious attempt being made to canvass and incorporate the views of Africans living in Sweden or in Africa (Kifle, Olukoshi and Wohlgemuth 1997). The vision that emerged was one that put solidarity back at the centre of Sweden's development co-operation philosophy (Ministry for Foreign Affairs 1998). There was considerable talk about ethics and attitudes, as well as an emphasis on capacity development in Africa, including in research.

The Asia policy was less focused on the challenges of developing genuine partnership but more reflective of a belief that Asian countries were better positioned to be equal partners in a relationship that was more about co-operation than aid (Ministry for Foreign Affairs 1999). As we shall see, this differentiated approach to Africa and Asia is at the heart of bifurcated strategies for, and assumptions about, knowledge, learning, capacity and partnership.

Sida's discourses of knowledge, learning and capacity

In this first main part of the chapter we shall examine the way that knowledge and learning are talked about in important Sida documents. This will take us from a discussion of knowledge and development, through knowledge and research, and Sida as a learning organisation, on to capacity development. Finally, a dissonant note will be added through a consideration of Sida's information technology policy.

Sida's account of the relationship between knowledge and development

Although it is by no means the sole or dominant theme in Sida discourse, an account of the importance of knowledge for development can be clearly found in the core statement of Sida's vision: *Sida Looks Forward* (Sida 1997c). This vision can be seen in the following quotations:

> Knowledge is our most important resource. During the next five years we shall implement an investment programme for the long-term regeneration of the knowledge and skills of our partner countries, of our Swedish partners and at Sida. (Sida 1997c: 9)

> In all operational programmes the development of knowledge, in the widest sense of the term, is the most important working method. (Sida 1997c: 19)

> The central issue of all development co-operation is to contribute to developing knowledge – in the partner country, in Sweden, and internationally. (Sida 1997c: 28)

These quotations indicate a multi-focused concern with knowledge. First, 'Knowledge is *our* most important resource' (emphasis added): knowledge is what Sida comes to the development co-operation relationship with. However, the following sentence immediately makes clear that Sida is not in the business of simply transferring Swedish knowledge to Southern partners who have a knowledge deficit. Rather, the sentence highlights one of the core elements of current Sida thinking in stating that knowledge development must also take place within Sida and in its Swedish partners. As we shall show, this tripartite formulation is of considerable significance to the way that Sida thinks and works. Indeed, this quotation illustrates the thinking behind our choice of title for this chapter. Although the quotation is explicitly about knowledge, it is also, implicitly, very much about the need for learning. Indeed, we will suggest that Sida regularly privileges learning over knowledge, as a more active and collaborative concept. As we shall argue in more detail later, this quotation also points to the importance of building capacity within the three constituencies for them to be effective development actors. Thus, although the first quotation begins with knowledge, it leads on to stress the importance of learning and capacity development. Such a reading can also be gleaned from the second and third quotations.

From our interviews, it appears that the former director-general of Sida, Bo Göransson, had been interested in the range of arguments about knowledge and development, including the knowledge economy, since his appointment in 1995. This was reflected in his commissioning of a think-piece on the knowledge debates even before the notion of 'the knowledge bank' captured James Wolfensohn's attention at the World Bank in September 1996. This is of potentially great significance for our study as a whole. It may suggest that Sida has to some extent read the same economic trends as the World Bank, but has seen these as leading to strikingly different conclusions. Certainly, we shall attempt to show that Sida appears to be taking a very distinct path regarding knowledge and development.

High-level concern with knowledge and development can be seen in the existence since early 2001 of a 'knowledge group', including several senior Sida staff, but it has not been possible for Sida to find the right mechanism or moment to bring a number of these knowledge initiatives together into a policy-oriented discussion and conclusion. Although the knowledge group is largely concerned with the relationship between Sida's work in basic and higher education, its main output to date has been a paper (only in Swedish as yet) that revisits the broader range of debates about knowledge (Gustafsson et al. 2001).

The importance of debates about knowledge (and learning and capacity) was also illustrated by the whole-day seminar on 'Knowledge, Learning and Capacity Development' for which we served as resource persons in March 2002. Much more than a dissemination seminar for a piece of potentially interesting external research, this was a meeting of staff from across Sida to explore issues of importance to their work.

Sida, knowledge and research

Sida's knowledge discourse is very much shaped by the existence of SAREC. The head of SAREC, Berit Olsson, has been at the heart of the previous director-general's processes of examining the knowledge debates, and is chairing the 'knowledge group'. SAREC's most recent policy also makes clear the understanding within that department of the salience of knowledge for development:

> Ultimately, development depends on the capacity of a country to steer its development in the desired direction, including the capacity to participate in international cooperation on equal terms. A vital part of this capacity is the ability of society to absorb, develop and apply knowledge. (Sida 2000b: 9)

> It is increasingly being recognised that knowledge is as crucial a determinant of development as investment capital, skilled labour and appropriate and accountable institutions. (Sida 2000c: 28)

It is not surprising that this vision should contain a strong sense of the relationship between knowledge and research. However, it is also in line with the emphasis on knowledge as something to be produced rather than simply transferred.

This has been fundamental to SAREC's identity since its establishment in 1975. From its inception, capacity development has been an integral part of its thinking. However, the emphasis has been primarily on the capacity of the Southern partner rather than the Northern.[6] This is understandable given that the core of SAREC's mission has been to work in a field where the resource disparities between Northern and Southern universities have been large, and often growing.

We shall now consider SAREC's account of knowledge in some further detail. SAREC's goal since 1975 has been to support research of development relevance for partner countries (Widstrand 1986; Kihlberg 1987). However, it is important to note that this relevance has always been conceived of broadly:

> It was not only a question of supporting applied research or research that could be directly implemented in development plans. Equally important was support to fundamental theoretical and descriptive research that contributed to improving basic knowledge and created a deeper understanding of the processes and problems of change. (Kihlberg 1987: 9)

Research was to be guided wherever possible by the expressed priorities of partners, rather than being driven by Swedish conceptions of important themes (SAREC and SIDA 1992). SAREC also emphasised the need to address research capacity at the national level. Whereas other agencies tended to support single institutions, SAREC was concerned from the start with systemic and policy issues.

In its current policy SAREC makes a distinction between 'general' (Sida 2000b) or 'modern' (Sida 2000c) knowledge and 'local' (Sida 2000b) or 'traditional' (Sida 2000c) knowledge. Although these two sets of opposites are not necessarily identical, they lead to similar conclusions. First, that globalisation is encouraging a greater gap between knowledge production in the North (here meaning primarily through industrial research and development) and the contexts of the South. Second, that there is a need to mediate between the two sets of knowledge. Third, that research co-operation can play this bridging role. There is little sense here of the current interest of some other agencies in indigenous knowledge. Instead, SAREC seems to have a rather more scientific and technical conception of knowledge. It is possible that it also leads to a greater sense of deficit and transfer than in other elements of Sida's discourse.

However, this notion of Sweden having the knowledge does need to be tempered by SAREC's strong emphasis on national ownership of the research agenda, in partnership with Sweden:

> Until recent years, with a few exceptions, research cooperation was char-acterised by research by industrialised countries 'for' rather than 'with' developing countries. From the early 1990s, however, there seems to be a growing trend towards greater 'partnership'. Large international research programmes now invite decision-makers from developing countries to participate in the formulation and implementation of research agenda that address the interests of the South. International and regional forums have been, and are being, created to this end. One talks more often now of partnership in, and dialogue for, identifying research problems that take account of local conditions in the developing world. The 'partner-ship' approach implies that the 'recipe' is not pre-determined but grows out of an interactive process. (Sida 2000c: 27)

In spite of the growing inter-agency orthodoxy on the IDTs, on poverty and on primary education during the second half of the 1990s, Sida significantly expanded rather than contracted its support for higher education and research. Whilst arguments about globalisation and the knowledge economy are part of the justification for this, an attempt has also been made to claim broader development impacts for research co-operation:

> Positive and sustainable development, including the eradication of pov-erty, requires the development and use of new knowledge:
>
> Knowledge, which can provide farmers on marginal soils with the op-portunity to obtain a greater yield without destroying soil and water

resources; knowledge, which makes it possible to combat HIV/AIDS with educational and health care resources that are a fraction of those available in wealthier countries; or knowledge, which promotes conflict resolution, a democratic culture and democratic institutions in societies in order to prevent wars, dictatorships and ethnic conflicts. (Sida 2000b: 8)

Sida as a learning organisation

There are two principal routes through which the notion of Sida as a learning organisation diffuses across the agency. First, the work programme of the Expert Group for Development Issues (EGDI) has placed a major emphasis on learning. Second, and more centrally to Sida's work, the existence of a Unit for Organisational Learning within Sida clearly has an impact on the theories, policies and practices of the agency as a whole.

EGDI was established in 1995 'to initiate studies that have a potential to make contributions to development thinking and policy making' (EGDI 2001). It is chaired by the Secretary of State for Development Co-operation in the Ministry for Foreign Affairs but it has Sida representation, as well as participation from Swedish and foreign academics. It has made learning central to its mandate and this has resulted in two large products: 'Organisational learning in development cooperation' (Forss, Cracknell and Stromquist 1997) and *Learning in Development Cooperation* (Carlsson and Wohlgemuth 2000a).

However, as a chapter in the Carlsson and Wohlgemuth book makes clear, the concern with Sida's learning capabilities has a longer provenance. Back in 1988 the Swedish National Audit Office conducted an extensive examination of SIDA's practices, based on a large number of interviews with SIDA staff and staff from other development co-operation agencies. The report, 'Lär sig SIDA?' ('Does SIDA learn?'), emphasised issues of policy consistency, leadership and personnel policy as blocks to SIDA's effectiveness as a learning organisation (cited in Edgren 2000).

The Forss *et al.* report is an exploration of agencies as learning organisations that reflects the very real challenges that exist in achieving this aspiration. Much of this is reminiscent of the discussion about the limits to knowledge-based approaches that are illustrated, for instance, in the case of the World Bank (see chapter 4).

The Carlsson and Wohlgemuth anthology is more focused on the experiences of researchers, policy-makers and practitioners, and their reflections on how these relate to the broader issue of learning in development co-operation.

What emerges from both accounts is a belief in the importance of learning for development co-operation. This is in a number of ways a more dynamic and satisfying account than one based on knowledge. It stresses both the personal and organisational and contains a notion of development at each level. It is not simply about the mechanics of capturing, managing or sharing what is already known, but contains a sense of new creation. Moreover, it is a strongly nuanced account. Whilst the more academic Argyris and Schön (1978) and the more celebratory and populist Senge (1990) provide accounts of the power of organisational learning, the story is ultimately one of struggle and of obstacles to change. This view is clear in the Swedish accounts too. The sense is that there are important benefits to be gained from Sida embracing a learning approach, but that there are major barriers to this. Moreover, these are a mixture of structural, cultural and political elements that cannot easily be overcome.

Although a number of Sida staff are aware of the work of EGDI, there appear to be quite serious limits to the extent to which Sida has learned from these attempts to investigate its learning. However, a more concrete impact on the working of Sida has come from the Unit for Organisational Learning, whose activities have reached a significant number of Sida staff.

Established in 1997, the Unit can be seen as a conduit for spreading Senge's theory of the learning organisation throughout Sida. It stresses the importance of changing the organisational culture through addressing systems, incentives and resources. We shall return to look at the Unit as a 'knowledge project' subsequently. However, for the moment we shall seek to outline the key elements of its philosophy.

As its name indicates, the Unit is very much about learning. Its philosophy stresses the importance of inculcating a learning culture and providing opportunities for learning for all staff. This notion of learning includes a language of competence, skills and knowledge. In her presentation to the March 2002 'Knowledge, Learning and Capacity Development' seminar, the Unit's Director, Gisela Wasmouth, made clear the importance of tacit knowledge to organisational learning.

The language of tacit knowledge use appears superficially to be reminiscent of a major thrust of the knowledge management literature as it emerged in the management literature and corporate sector. For instance, one of the most cited books on knowledge management is called *If Only We Knew What We Know* (O'Dell et al., 1998). This concern with 'capturing' tacit knowledge is also in evidence in corporate attempts to develop databases and 'electronic yellow pages' detailing the knowledge within the organisation. The agency interest in knowledge management is also closely linked to this issue of capturing tacit knowledge. However, both the Unit and Sida more generally seem very resistant to the technological approaches to tacit knowledge that have emerged through the knowledge management trend.[7] Instead, the Sida discourse appears to be far more concerned with ways that staff can work together to share tacit knowledge and build explicit knowledge.

Sida's narratives of capacity building and institutional development

Capacity is perhaps even more important a notion in current Sida philosophy than learning, although the two notions are closely intertwined. Over its forty years of existence, Sida has operated with a series of approaches to capacity building that reflect shifting positions on knowledge and learning, and on the role of the South with respect to these. Beginning in the 1960s, SIDA had a model of capacity building and technical assistance that was based in 'a traditional concept of transfer of knowledge from those in agencies and in the rich countries who have knowledge to those who have not' (Gustafsson 2000: 1). Learning was to follow a linear path with the South learning from the existing knowledge of the North. Issues of context and adaptation were of limited importance.

In the late 1970s, a second notion began to take hold: that of organisational development. Here the emphasis shifted from the strengthening of individual competences in partner countries to developing the capacity of the organisations in which they worked. However, the notion was still primarily one of a Southern deficit. The emphasis on the organisational level was also mirrored in the approach of SAREC, established in 1975.

By the late 1980s there had been 25 years' worth of experience in technical cooperation-based capacity development. The value of this was to be seriously questioned by a cross-Nordic study of projects in East Africa (Forss et al. 1988). This found that technical co-operation often weakened rather than strengthened partner country capacity. Too many decisions were taken by donors and too little attention was paid to existing national capacity. Crucially, the report also concluded that technical co-operation required far more than just technical skills on the part of the Nordic actors.

This criticism led SIDA to reconsider what the purpose of capacity development was. The following year, a SIDA response argued that:

Twenty-five years of experience convincingly shows that if a programme is to result in lasting improvements, knowledge and skills must be developed and structures and institutions built up within the recipient countries. ... Competence development is essentially a question of individual learning. (SIDA 1989: 1)

This report stressed the need to focus more on learning processes. In keeping with the Forss Report, it also recommended that Swedish personnel should be used only when it was clear that there was no relevant capacity already present in the country.

In 1992, a more formal statement of SIDA policy on capacity was made: *Development is People* (SIDA 1992). This suggested that technical co-operation had largely failed to achieve its objective of developing capacity. It argued that the capital dimension of co-operation had been privileged over the knowledge dimension. Indeed, an account of knowledge was central to this policy paper:

> The theory behind the transfer of knowledge was that knowledge is a resource that exists in industrial countries, which can be exported to developing countries. The supposition could be supported in that there is an international data base of knowledge which is at present concentrated in the industrialised countries and which all countries want and need access to. However experience has shown that the transfer of knowledge can only happen under certain very specific circumstances. Even in the future there will of course be a certain need for occasional 'transferers' of knowledge within Swedish development assistance, but the main emphasis in the future must use a different basic theory on development and learning, i.e., the competence that must be developed in recipient countries is that which will function as a dynamic and creative force. This idea presupposes that knowledge must be actively acquired rather that [*sic*] passively accepted. ... The technical solutions created by the western world may be of value, but they must be modified or perhaps rediscovered when they are woven together with local experience and cultural patterns. ... Knowledge is not a ready made package, ready for delivery from the industrial world to transplant into the developing country environment. Useful knowledge is acquired during the work process. (SIDA 1992: 2–3)

Thus, we can see that SIDA policy in 1992 was already strongly emphasising the importance of knowledge in context, of adaptation and of local discovery. These were to be issues that would move closer to the development co-operation centre-stage at the end of the 1990s, as the 'knowledge bank' was given a stronger intellectual underpinning during Stiglitz's brief period as World Bank chief economist (see chapter 4).

In 1995, the 'Mission statement' of the new Sida stated that 'Our principal method is capacity and institution development' (Sida 1995). This led to the formation of a working group on capacity development and to a new policy (Sida 2000a). This account is influenced by the new institutional economics, and by the work of Douglass North (1990) in particular.[8] This has led to a new emphasis on institutional development. In such a vision, the building of a critical mass of researchers and educators in partner countries is not enough to ensure that capacity remains in place. Rather, attention must also be paid to systemic issues.

The new policy is closely in line with the 1992 policy's concerns with a more symmetrical view of knowledge and learning, as its lead author makes clear:

> Solutions to complex social and political problems are always 'local'. Solutions can be stimulated by but not solved through transfer of knowledge of analytical frameworks, foreign experts or in other ways.
>
> This conclusion is more than playing with words if seen against the background of the so called knowledge gap and the wide-spread belief in the potential of transfer of information and hence of solution that is opened through the new information technology. Unless there is capacity in countries to analyse their own situation and experience and relate it to what exists elsewhere this is not likely to be the case. Therefore it is absolutely essential that priority is given to strengthening of national systems of education and research. That is a cornerstone in any strategy that aims at building Policy Research Capacity. This is emphasised in the new Sida policy on capacity development. (Gustafsson 2000: 2)

This makes clear the contextual nature of knowledge and the importance of exchange and joint creation of knowledge rather than its transfer. This also implies a nuanced model of knowledge creation in which political and cultural factors matter more than simple technical issues. In this model, the role of outside agencies such as Sida changes from being a provider of knowledge to acting as a partner in learning (Gustafsson 2001).

However, it is apparent that there are two tendencies at work in Sida's conception of partnership and capacity development. This is described internally as the tension between being a 'dialogue partner' and a 'facilitator'.

In the first case, Sida is being driven by the implications of its strong support for sectoral programmes, budgetary support and Poverty Reduction Strategy Papers. This leads to a dual focus on developing policy and ensuring financial probity. There is concern within Sida that the notion of dialogue partnership has seen too much of an emphasis on what Sida already knows (or believes). Part of the concern of the capacity development focus is with what Sida staff need to learn in order to be good dialogue partners. On the other hand, there is also a sense of the importance of Southern partners learning how better to choose from alternative strategies and how to resist agencies' pressures, where this is necessary.

In the second case, the emphasis is much more on twinning. This is based on the notion that the partners already have the requisite knowledge and that Sida can simply facilitate. Twinning is based on a philosophy of mutual learning, rather than knowledge transfer:

> A key word in twinning cooperation is *learning*. The twinned organisations work together with the aid of a combination of long-term advisors and commuting short-term experts, of training in the form of courses and on-the-job training, study visits to Sweden etc. The aspiration is to make learning possible, not merely for individuals but for the entire organisation, in order to create sustainable effects. One way to achieve these effects is to ensure that contacts between the organisations take place at different levels in the hierarchy, in parallel and simultaneously. (Sida 2000d: 2) [emphasis in original]

However, there is a growing sense that Swedish partners in particular should also understand Sida's philosophy of co-operation[9] and the importance of its model of capacity development.

As with other elements of Swedish development co-operation strategy, this dual approach is largely seen as being regionally differentiated. Thus, Eastern Europe and Asia are seen, more commonly, as natural twinning partners, Africa and Latin America as more suitable for dialogue partnerships.

Across the elements of Sida's capacity development approach, the tripartite focus of *Sida Looks Forward* (Sida 1997c) is made apparent. Capacity development is about learning and knowledge development within Sida, its Swedish partners and its Southern partners.

Sida and information

We have shown in this chapter how discourses about knowledge and learning intersect in Sida. We have shown elsewhere how there is a similar intersection between accounts of knowledge and information in DFID (chapter 5) and the World Bank (chapter 4). This can also be seen to some extent in Sida.

In 1999, Sida produced a *Strategy for IT in Development Cooperation* (Sida 1999c). This stresses the importance of information technologies for development. It is mainly focused on infrastructure for bridging the digital divide, an area where it considers that Sweden has comparative advantage.

The language that it uses is very close to that used elsewhere for knowledge. This is even clearer in the background report for the strategy (Sida 1999d). This draws heavily on the network economy ideas of Manuel Castells (1996), which are closely related to knowledge economy arguments. It contains a strong information management focus that emphasises the need for a database that appears very similar to elements of the Development Gateway (see chapter 4). There is also a strong call for support for the International Development Markup Language (IDML) initiative, itself also related to the Gateway during its early discussions. This seeks to develop a common computer language through which development data can be tagged, collected and analysed. The report also points to agreements that Sida has made to collaborate with infoDev, the Global Knowledge Partnership (GKP) and Bellanet. InfoDev is a World Bank programme to support ICT innovation and infrastructural development. The GKP also had its home in the World Bank till the middle of 2001, and is a network for sharing information about knowledge for development. Bellanet is a project of the Canadian International Development Research Centre. It has been a major force in the spread of knowledge management ideas across the development community and in the IDML initiative.

These initiatives with which Sida is working, and the whole emphasis of this policy, are at the informational and technological end of the spectrum of knowledge activities. This is in stark contrast to the learning focus of much of what we have examined so far in this paper. Of course, there is room for diversity within an agency's strategy. However, the IT strategy is not positioned explicitly as complementary to other elements of Sida's work and reads very much as an independent approach that potentially conflicts with a broader philosophical approach to learning and knowledge.

Sida as a generator of development knowledge

Our attention thus far has been on Sida's multi-layered discourse about knowledge and learning. Now we shall turn our attention to the ways in which these discourses appear embedded (or not) in Sida's main documents – what can be termed its 'knowledge products'.

Sida's Action Programmes

The most significant policy documents of Sida are the Action Programmes. These were finalised in 1996 and 1997. They seek to provide an overall policy vision for four cross-cutting themes, drawing on the statutory goals of the agency laid down by Parliament:

- equality between women and men (Sida 1997a)
- sustainable livelihoods and poverty reduction (Sida 1996a)
- peace, democracy and human rights (Sida 1997b)
- environmentally sustainable development (Sida 1996b)

These are then the basis for specific commitments and activities within all of the sectoral departments.

What is striking about the Action Programmes when compared to documents of similar importance from the World Bank or DFID (for example, the Target Strategy Papers) is that they are rather modest in their presentation and visibility. Although they are the core of Sida's work, they are not immediately apparent on Sida's website.[10] Instead of glossy covers and smart layouts, they come in traditional A4 with no pictures and little in the way of text formatting. There is nothing in the presentation that suggests the marketing that is present in many World Bank or DFID documents. This may have something to do with their age, although other agencies were paying more attention to presentation by 1996–97.

The reliance of the DFID Target Strategy Papers on a relatively narrow set of Northern sources has been noted (see chapter 5). Similar criticisms have been advanced about a range of World Bank documents. There is relatively little referencing evident across the four Action Programmes. This makes it difficult to judge the extent to which there was engagement with external academic or development communities. The Action Programmes make a clearly significant step forward where they are explicitly about intra-agency learning. Each of them includes a section in which specific actions by each Sida department are listed.

Given the timing of the Action Programmes in 1996 and 1997, it is problematic to examine them in terms of their knowledge focus. The *World Development Report: Knowledge for Development* (World Bank 1998a) was still another one or two years away, and the notion of 'the knowledge bank' was little known outside Bank headquarters. Whilst Göransson had raised the importance of knowledge rhetorically, it had not become a core concern of Sida at the operational level. However, given Sida's language of partnership and learning, there seem to be valid criticisms of the way that these documents put this language into practice.

Sida's other knowledge products

Sida continues to produce a significant number of documents based on its research. More than seventy reports on educational research have been published over the past twenty years in the widely known Education Division Documents series. The Department for Evaluation and Internal Audit publishes two series: Sida Studies in Evaluation and Sida Evaluation. A range of other, more occasional, reports are produced by other departments. The importance of research in Sida is illustrated by the major Project 2015 initiative that was initiated during the process of forming the new Sida. This led to nine volumes that looked at Sida, general issues of aid and development, and the contexts of partner countries and regions (Sida 1996c–f; 1997d–h).

Two other pieces of Swedish research are worth noting, both for their policy significance and for their processes. One of the activities that the new Sida inherited was a Task Force on Poverty Reduction (Sida 1996g). This task force is important for its development of a detailed reading of poverty research and its policy implications that is contemporary to the World Summit on Social Development and the emergence of the IDTs from the OECD. It is also significant for being based on considerable new commissioned research from a wide variety of authors, including a number of Southern and non-Swedish Northern researchers. Widespread commentary was also sought from Sida and ministry staff.

This participatory approach, with its links to the external research community, was taken further in the process leading to the Swedish Africa policy of 1998. As we noted above, this included extensive consultations with Africans resident in Sweden and a meeting with African commentators in Abidjan. The latter produced a very visible and articulate challenging of Sweden's development co-operation record and its future vision (Kifle, Olukoshi and Wohlgemuth 1997).

Thus, the rather limited evidence from the Action Programmes of external consultation and a research base is somewhat balanced by these examples of far-reaching attempts to engage with external perspectives in constructing Sida's own knowledge.

Sida's initiatives to support knowledge, learning and capacity development

We have discussed at some length a number of the key knowledge projects from the perspective of how they contribute to Sida's overall discourses of knowledge, learning and capacity. However, it is also important to lay out some of the key activities that have resulted from these foci. We shall briefly highlight just three of these: research co-operation, capacity development and organisational learning.

Research co-operation

The twenty years of SAREC's work before the merger has largely continued in the new Sida. Indeed, its budget has more than doubled since the merger. SAREC continues to provide support to Southern systems of higher education and to partnerships between Southern and Swedish institutions. It seeks to support higher education whilst remaining mindful of broader systems of knowledge generation. SAREC provides funds to research councils and universities, which then run research competitions to decide how to use the funds. It is also increasingly supporting ICT use in Southern universities. Through its partnership work, SAREC has traditionally provided funding to joint research programmes between Swedish and Southern universities. Sida is concerned to avoid dependency on Swedish funding for meeting the recurrent costs of partner institutions. Therefore, it is increasingly likely that SAREC's contribution will only be for specific costs incurred in the partnership, for example the costs of meetings for joint fieldwork. This is more feasible in Asia than Africa. SAREC is also the Swedish conduit for supporting multilateral research activities such as those of the World Health Organisation, the Consultative Group for International Agriculture Research and the Africa Economic Research Consortium.

Capacity development

Capacity development work is organised by the Methods Unit, a small group with responsibility for looking at how Sida's work practices need to change to respond to shifts in development co-operation. This unit is also responsible for related work on Sida's approach to Sector-wide Approaches (SWAPs) and for revising the booklet *Sida at Work* (Sida 1998), which lays out the principles under which staff carry out their various activities. All three programmes are supported by cross-Sida working groups. The development of policy is intended to be the first step, subsequent phases being operationalisation of policy documents and development and delivery of training materials. This can lead to a sense of an insular focus on Sida staff's own learning needs. For instance, the booklet *Sida's Policy for Sector Programme Support and Provisional Guidelines* (Sida 2002) states that it is written 'primarily for Sida staff, but can be used by consultants and others who work, on behalf of Sida, with the assessment, implementation and follow-up of sector programme support' (Sida 2002: 4). There is no mention of developing countries being the recipients of these guidelines. However, it is clear that the philosophy of the Methods Unit has a keen sense of the tripartite nature of the learning challenge. Through its collaboration with the training staff in

Sida, one can see a stronger emphasis on the other elements of the capacity development approach. For Swedish partners, the new Centre for Civil Society will attempt to develop their capacity as key players in the Swedish vision of expanded bilateralism. For Southern partners, there has been a shift in the focus of training programmes from areas where Sweden thought it had expertise (forestry, hydroelectricity, and so on) to areas that are priorities of partners. Moreover, the emphasis has also shifted towards greater awareness of the knowledge that the partners bring to the course and towards facilitation of networking between the Southern participants after courses have finished.

Organisational learning

Since its inception in 1997, the Unit for Organisational Learning has developed a range of programmes and activities designed to make Sida more of a learning organisation. Departments are encouraged to analyse their competence needs and to plan accordingly. All managers are required to participate in a programme in which their role as facilitators of learning is particularly emphasised. The Unit encourages working in teams and in projects, as well as mentorship arrangements, as ways of effectively sharing knowledge. Increasingly, the possibilities of e-learning are also being investigated. As a way of mapping the learning activities of Sida, the Unit produces an annual *Human Resources Report*, presenting the wide range of attempts to support learning that are being made. Although there is a perception outside the Unit that it is focused predominantly on generic programmes, it should be noted that it runs a series of introductory modules on the Action Programmes, and has recently started programmes for National Programme Officers.[11]

Knowledge and learning in practice

What difference have these new discourses and activities made to everyday work in Sida? One positive example of new practices comes from the focus on sector-wide programmes. Here it appears that the knowledge challenges inherent in working on sector programmes have made sectoral staff more dependent on collaboration with colleagues from other disciplines. One example from an education programme is particularly instructive. Whilst both education and public administration staff are in the Department for Democracy and Social Development, it was only because of the requirement to know about finance and management in order to implement a sector programme that educationalists actually started collaborating with their public administration colleagues.

One direction that interest in learning-organisation theory has taken in

Sida is into reflection on the limits to good learning practice within the organisation. Two of the chapters in Carlsson and Wohlgemuth 2000a exemplify this approach and will be quoted at some length.

Gus Edgren worked in aid administration for thirty years in different parts of the world, for Sida and the Ministry for Foreign Affairs as well as for UN organisations. As some of our earlier citations of Edgren show, he is a strong advocate of the learning organisation approach. However, he points to a range of blockages to learning within Sida. He notes staff complaints about time pressure and poor attention to detail from senior managers. He argues that concerns expressed in the Audit Office Report of 1988 about incentives and grounds for promotion still hold true. Here there is a parallel to our interviews in the World Bank: whereas the rhetoric is of team work (or 'knowledge sharing' in the Bank), the perception of staff is that individualism, competitiveness and disbursement of funds are what get promotion. He also argues that the preponderance of staff nearing retirement has had the effect of depressing the quantity and quality of learning, as many experienced staff see little need for conscious acquisition of new knowledge and skills. This issue has been acknowledged by Sida's Human Resources Department (Sida 2000e). The relatively small numbers of female staff reaching senior positions, he speculates, must also have a negative impact on motivation and learning. Notwithstanding our example above of cross-disciplinary team working on a sector programme, he points to the tendency for team working not to lead to team learning.

Decentralisation is a practice of all the agencies under consideration, as well as a number of others (for example, the German Agency for Technical Co-operation (GTZ) [Bergmann 2001]). Edgren identifies two issues here that also have wider resonance for other agencies.

First, decentralisation directly engages with current discourses about knowledge, even though this does not appear to have been an important motivation for decentralisation. Decentralisation of authority to the field opens up an opportunity for a more effective translation of knowledge into practice, as field staff are more able to identify development activities that reflect local contexts. Thus, decentralisation can meet the concern that knowledge is more contextual than universal. However, decentralisation requires a more networked model of knowledge sharing/management (Bergmann 2001). Edgren is concerned that learning is reduced as the mechanisms for knowledge sharing are limited.

Second, he notes that the decentralisation process and learning organisation focus point to the need to reconsider the role of national staff from partner countries working in Swedish development co-operation.

He recalls that this was an issue raised in the 1988 Audit Office Report, yet it is still a concern of his more than a decade later:

Field offices are typically staffed with expatriate programme officers who will stay three or four years before they are transferred to another country or to headquarters. As RRV [the Audit Office] points out, the only institutional memory in such a situation will be the donor's consultants, who normally have a much longer shelf life than programme officers. The multilateral agencies have tried to solve this problem by establishing a separate scheme of service for 'national programme officers' (NPOs), a cadre of professionals whose career is based mainly in their home countries. In agencies like UNICEF and UNDP, national programme officers provide a good deal of the agencies' continuity and institutional memory in the country and take part in the organisation's staff training and policy discussion together with international staff.

Sida is also trying to make use of NPOs to provide a continuity platform for decentralisation, but there is still a long way to go before its NPOs can regard themselves as regular staff members of the agency. Changes must be undertaken in the work process at the level of the embassies, to give NPOs more responsible tasks. Sida's internal staff training programmes will have to be opened to NPOs and working material must be produced in other languages than Swedish. And the staff rules applying to local embassy staff regarding, for instance, access to information sources will have to be eased in order to integrate the NPOs in the working team. (Edgren 2000: 48)

Overall he paints a picture of major learning failures:

In some cases, conditions and vested interests are very heavily stacked against absorbing new knowledge. One particularly complex case is the malfunctioning of the aid industry as a system, seen from the point of view of the recipient. The learning blocks may also be caused by a combination of unrealistic political targets, strong commercial interests among consultants or other enterprises and bureaucratic inertia on either side of the partnership, which join forces to resist a proposed innovation. Such resistance is often rationalised by means of an official myth, which is supposed to explain why changes would be impossible or undesirable. Exploding these myths is a key precondition for organisational learning. (Edgren 2000: 65–6)

Edgren makes clear that many of these comments apply to the other agencies he has worked for, and to agencies as a whole. Certainly this accords with our learning from our other case studies. Perhaps the most distinctive feature of Sida in this regard is the level of engagement with the theory of learning organisations. Whether this can lead to a more effective response to these learning failures is an important question, yet to be resolved.

Anna Wieslander has now retired from Sida but was Director of its training centre, as well as holding other posts at headquarters and in the field. From her experience in the training of staff and consultants, she raises concerns about the adequacy of preparation for work in the field. Like Edgren, she also points to the negative effect that overwork has on learning. However, she suggests that there are problems of attitude and organisational culture operating here as well.

> As a writer I also asked myself why colleagues at Sida normally did not read books, nor Sida's own magazine, describing the reality of aid relations. Their reading, as in fact often my own, was many times restricted to 'urgent matters', and did not normally include contextual or background material. It is of course a question of priorities; their reality was day to day relations with colleagues and bosses and an overwhelming amount of bureaucratic procedures. There was no time, I think, to search for content in their work, or to learn about the needs of their 'target groups'. (Wieslander 2000: 261)

This quotation highlights something that emerges also from our case studies in DFID and the World Bank. It places a very important question mark against much of the language of knowledge and learning within agencies. Significantly, it suggests that the problem lies both at the organisational and individual level. Part of the significance of this lies in the emphasis from Sida and the Ministry for Foreign Affairs on the attitudinal dimension of co-operation. Both Karlsson (1997 – when he was Minister for Development Co-operation) and Gustafsson (1999) talk of a new 'code of conduct' for partnership based in values such as humility and openness. Wieslander, however, talks of the historic inadequacies of Swedish development professionals in these areas.

Of course, these are the reflections of experienced Swedish development professionals looking back on a career in this area. It is quite challenging to tease out of these accounts what is a critique of a past that has now been superseded and what still holds true. Nonetheless, there is much in these accounts that coincides with our interviews from Sida and other agencies. Similar findings also emerge from the Forss, Cracknell and Stromquist (1997) study for EGDI. Carlsson and Wohlgemuth's introduction to *Learning in Development Cooperation*, written by a former senior staff member and current Board member (Wohlgemuth), and an experienced consultant for and commentator on Sida (Carlsson), also adds to the picture of the learning challenge that Sida faces. In particular, they raise concerns about how certain important elements of the new aid paradigm impact upon learning within Sida. They argue that sector programmes should be about a long-term focus, but that the new knowledge and learning accounts often emphasise short-term learning. Moreover, they argue that the ever-increasing range of themes that development co-operation is expected to address places severe burdens on the capacity to learn. Overall, whilst there are large amounts of information available, often the quality is poor (Carlsson and Wohlgemuth 2000b).

Concern was also raised in some interviews that there should be more learning from other agencies. Whilst professional knowledge networking with the outside has been common, this has not been so obviously linked to a transfer of knowledge into institutional memory, policy or practice. Another question that emerges from some interviews is whether the notion of the learning organisation and business school thinking fits very well with the conventional Swedish way of working.

In common with other agencies, Sida is active in evaluating its work. This is an obvious potential source of learning. Indeed, it is clear that learning is as much part of Sida's evaluation philosophy as is audit. Nonetheless, the quality and effectiveness of this learning has been inadequate. This concern is captured for instance in the title of a Sida paper: 'Are evaluations useful?' (Carlsson et al. 1999). This paper, co-authored by the head of the evaluation department (Anne-Marie Fallenius), is impressively open about the weakness of evaluation in terms of learning and knowledge. It argues that evaluation is weak in generating new knowledge. Moreover, there is also inadequate knowledge sharing. In spite of the rhetoric, there is not enough participation by partners, thus limiting their, and Sida's, learning opportunities. Dissemination mechanisms do not ensure that the knowledge gets to the full range of relevant people. Those at the implementation level have their knowledge extracted for the purpose of evaluation but little is ever returned in terms of an outside perspective on or synthesis of their experiences. Carlsson concludes in another paper that there is little evidence of evaluation leading to significant changes in policies or practices (Carlsson 2000). Sida has recently put into place a mechanism through which departments are required to respond to evaluation reports. However, our interviews suggest that the impact of this remains limited. Departments do not have to learn from evaluations if they do not want to. There has also been some increased attention to partnership in evaluation, but this too remains more aspirational than actual.

Conclusion

The case of Sida contributes important insights into analysis of the development co-operation agencies' fascination with knowledge. It is striking that there is a range of Sida texts, stretching back for more than a decade, that highlight the importance of knowledge, yet Sida has not followed the knowledge management trends of other agencies.

Sida generally appears deeply suspicious of the technological and deficit assumptions of much knowledge-based aid. Although knowledge is a concept that is used in Sida, the strong preference is for language about learning. This is an important point that appears to reflect the Swedish democratic tradition of adult learning. This concern with learning opens up the possibility of a practice based more on the construction of knowledge than on its dissemination. Moreover, taken together with Sida's discourse of partnership and of capacity development, a positive focus emerges on mutual learning that is led by the South and facilitated by Sida, and other Swedish partners. This notion is far removed from the banking form of knowledge, in Freire's (1972) sense of the depositing of knowledge into passive objects from above (in this case the Northern agency).

This view of a mutual construction of knowledge is reflected also in Sida's research co-operation strategy. Since the incorporation of SAREC, Sida is in a unique position in the bilateral community for the scale of support given to higher education and Southern knowledge generation directly from the agency.

It would be unreasonable, however, to expect a single account of knowledge and learning from an agency as large and diverse as Sida. Thus, it is important to note the far more technological and informational emphasis that comes out of the IT policy. Through a dual focus on better systems for managing inter-agency information and its exchange and on infrastructural development in the South, the policy suggests a reading that is radically different from the bulk of Sida's discourse on knowledge. Here the emphasis appears to be far more on the imperative of better capturing what agencies already know and transmitting it to Southern recipients.

A more agency-centred reading may also be constructed regarding the work of the Methods Unit and the Unit for Organisational Learning. Both units' primary audiences to date have been Sida staff. However, in so far as the organisational learning focus is combined in the current capacity development approach with emphases on development of Swedish and Southern partners, Sida may have developed an approach that is less internally focused than typical agency knowledge strategies.

Our reading of Sida's discourses about knowledge, learning and capacity are relatively positive. But it is important to consider whether they are matched by its practices. It should be noted in this context that much of what we conclude that is critical here is based in the written analyses of Sida staff or writers of commissioned papers. We say this not so much to justify what we write as to note that this is indicative of a degree of openness and reflectiveness that is uncommon amongst agencies. We conclude that the language of partnership and mutual knowledge construction is not as evident as could have been expected when the Action Programmes, Sida's main policy documents, are examined. A similar weakness in engagement with partners appears from accounts of the evaluation process.

Sida's language about internal learning also appears to have a considerable aspirational element. This is reflected in the large number of points of learning blockage that are identified in the work commissioned by EGDI. On the other hand, the attention given to these problems by EGDI, and the existence of the Unit for Organisational Learning, can be seen as very real indicators of a genuine concern to overcome such blockages.

Learning failures are not caused simply by structural and cultural factors within Sida (or other agencies). There also appears to be an attitudinal dimension. There is considerable emphasis within Sida and the Ministry for Foreign Affairs on appropriate attitudes for development co-operation, such as humility and openness. Wieslander's account in particular, however, raises the question of whether this is matched in practice by the attitudes of staff.

The case of Sida points to strengths of vision and challenges of building it into the full range of practices. Its greatest significance, however, lies in illustrating that convergence across agencies is not inevitable in the area of knowledge-based aid. By taking up elements of the knowledge discourse, and in emphasising learning over knowledge at crucial points, the Swedish case also provides a space in which to better understand and critique the discourses and practices of other agencies.

Notes

1. It also is influenced by earlier work on Sida/Ministry for Foreign Affairs by one of the present authors (King 1988; King and Caddell 1998).

2. Building on Sweden's special missionary relationship with Ethiopia, the country was given US$2 million in loans in 1945. This was used to hire Swedes to help in post-war reconstruction (Heppling 1986: 16).

3. SIDA refers to the pre- and Sida to the post-merger agency: see below.

4. This target was not reached until 1975. Since then, Sida's official development assistance budget has always been above the Pearson target of 0.7 per cent of GNP. Sweden is one of four countries to have met the target consistently (the others are Denmark, the Netherlands and Norway).

5. Although one can easily get the sense that sectoral programmes were a new discovery of the late 1990s, Sida was not alone in thinking in terms of such programmes back in the 1960s. A very interesting chapter in this regard is one by Hirschman (1971: ch. 10) where he critiques the USAID sectoral approach of the 1960s in a manner that has considerable resonance for current debates.

6. In the case of knowledge about Africa, it could be argued that Sweden's own capacity development was taken care of at the same time as the establishment of NIB through the establishment of the Institute of African Studies at Uppsala, later to become the Nordic Africa Institute (Widstrand 1986).

7. Although Gisela Wasmouth did attend the July 2000 Brighton workshop on 'Knowledge Management for International Development Organisations', neither she nor her Sida colleagues could be described as believers in the knowledge management approach. This scepticism about broader agency trends regarding knowledge was also evident in a number of interview comments about other initiatives, such as the Global Development Network and the Development Gateway. Sida has declined to be a major funder of either of these initiatives. It is a matter for speculation whether or not such scepticism about these World Bank-led projects owes something to the Swedish tradition of distancing itself from the Bank (Andréen 1986). Note, however, that Sida has become a partner in the GDLN; see chapter 4.

8. The influence of North's thinking can also be seen in the Sida-funded collection, *Institution Building and Leadership in Africa* (Wohlgemuth, Carlsson and Kifle 1998).

9. It is important to remember, though, that many Swedish civil society organisations have had Southern links for far longer than Sida. Indeed, much of the pressure for the establishment of a national development co-operation agency came from the Central Committee for Technical Assistance to Less Developed Countries, founded in 1952 by NGOs representing churches, trade unions, employers and many others (Heppling 1986; Lewin 1986).

10. Perhaps appropriately, they are far more visible in Sida's own resource centre in Stockholm.

11. These are nationals of Southern partner countries employed by Sida within their own countries.

SEVEN

Experience, experts and knowledge in Japanese aid policy and practice

This chapter further confirms what we have learned from Swedish and British aid, and from the World Bank – that the new discourse on knowledge management (KM) and knowledge sharing (KS) is powerfully affected by the particular context and tradition of these agencies. Like the others, this study will also be conducted against the background of wider policy interests in knowledge-based aid (King 2001). Whilst a primary focus of the chapter will be on sketching the development of what we have termed knowledge projects and policies in very recent Japanese aid thinking, we will also examine some of the deeper attitudes in Japan towards both Japanese and Western expert knowledge on international development. The attitudes are very much embedded in the culture and bureaucracy of Japan, and, it will be argued, these older traditions of thinking about expertise and professional knowledge are likely to impact upon and influence in some measure the newer mechanisms for knowledge sharing. We shall especially underline the role of personal expertise as one of the major sites of knowledge. The belief in person-to-person transfer of skills, technologies and attitudes seems to be the Japanese parallel to learning and capacity development which we noted in the Sida tradition.

In particular it might even be argued that one element in the current predominantly Western discourse about knowledge sharing was originally derived from an analysis of what made for success in Japanese firms – including the ways that workers shared their insights about improving the quality and effectiveness of their specific operations. The knowledge discourse is by no means, therefore, a discussion that has been restricted to the West (McGinn 2001); one of the better-known management texts is by Nonaka and Takeuchi (1995), *The Knowledge-creating Company: how Japanese companies create the dynamics of innovation*. Interestingly, there has been little evidence of the Japanese public sector learning from the corporate sector in the way that seems to have happened in Sweden and Britain, and with the World Bank. Indeed, we shall suggest that the adoption of knowledge management in the case of the Japanese International Co-operation Agency (JICA) – Japan's lead implementing agency for ODA – appears to have been derived from the example of the World Bank (itself directly influenced by corporate America, which in turn had in part learnt from Japan) rather than sourced from the Japanese private sector.[1]

As in the other case studies, we shall explore the salience of the knowledge discourse in Japanese co-operation, and see to what extent it is becoming expressed in different products, policies and practices. But right at the outset we must note that the explicit discussion of knowledge management and knowledge sharing began only in 2000 in JICA, and it was not until mid-2002 that it was impacting at all visibly on a selected number of JICA staff.

Thus, by contrast with the World Bank's visibility as the pioneer of knowledge-for-development – in its 1998–99 *World Development Report* and in its many other knowledge initiatives, which are very accessible on the World Bank's website – JICA gives very much less salience to a knowledge strategy in its formal mission statements and in its leading discourse, whether on paper or on its website. Indeed, knowledge activities are not at all currently foregrounded on its website,[2] nor have members of JICA or associated analysts of Japanese aid played any part in the on-line network discussions of 'Knowledge management for international development organisations'. Neither the lack of a strong web presence nor the absence from relevant KM debates on-line are reliable pointers to whether Japan considers knowledge to be central to development. Rather they suggest that the current and explicit discourse about 'knowledge agencies' does not sit easily with those responsible for the public face of JICA. Though change is afoot, as we shall see, much of JICA's public documentation and its website continue to illustrate the separate time-honoured schemes through which its assistance has been traditionally provided.[3] These, taken in their entirety, suggest that a different lens is needed to focus on Japanese development priorities.

Japan's own experience for development

Instead of knowledge, or capacity development, one of the key concepts in Japanese aid philosophy appears to be 'experience'. A strong concern with Japan's own historical experience may be seen in this chapter to be in some creative tension with the newer knowledge activities associated with knowledge management. This Japanese experience is manifested in many different ways, which it may be useful to tease out here. But it is worth considering, at the outset, that on a spectrum from global universal knowledge at one end to very context-specific knowledge at the other, clearly an experience-based approach will be much closer to the contextual and local.

First of all, there is a very clear sense in much official aid discussion of how important Japan's own direct historical experience of development may be to its ability to offer insights to others. At one level, it frequently rehearses its own post-Second World War history of transformation to make a number of fundamental points about this experience. For example, Japan can claim fifty years of being an aid donor, if the reparations to East and South-East Asia are counted as an early form of economic co-operation, from 1953, along with the formal start of economic assistance through Japan's participation in the Colombo Plan in 1954. This makes Japan one of the earliest bilateral donor countries.

But this very lengthy experience of being an aid donor is often discussed in parallel with the experience of being an aid recipient. Although it has become commonplace for Japan to refer to the responsibilities associated with its being the largest bilateral aid donor since 1991, it is also intriguing to note how much significance as a donor it attaches to having been an aid recipient: 'Japan has the experience of being the world's largest recipient country of humanitarian aid, from 1946 for six years after World War II, receiving aid in forms of food, clothing, medicine, and medical supplies' (Kato 2001a: 205). Nor was this only short-term humanitarian aid: Japan is very conscious of having had direct experience of receiving loans from the World Bank for the construction of its transport network, roads, power stations, automobile industry, shipbuilding and steel. It remained a recipient of such loans until 1966. Nor is this something that might be hidden away, or even regarded as a matter of shame. Rather there are stories senior aid officials tell about how Japan experienced early attempts at what would later be called 'conditionality' in the negotiation of these loans, but how it managed to get its own way, because it was convinced of its own priorities, for example, for high-speed trains over air transport. In other words, there was an early emphasis on the ownership of the development process whatever the challenges from the donors or lenders of the time.[4]

This extended historical episode has had a powerful symbolic value in Japanese thinking and official writing about its development experience.[5] Arguably, its own record has contributed to its thinking about the crucial importance of self-help. It has also justified the appropriateness of loans to a country really sure of its development priorities. But as politically significant as any of these is the sense that this special history has conferred a measure of solidarity between Japan and its own current aid recipients, particularly in East and South-East Asia. Again note the key term 'experience' in the following quotation: 'Such a rare position in the donor community, experience as an aid recipient country, has enabled Japan to understand all the more the importance of extending co-operation with due respect for the partner's situation' (Kato 2001a: 205).[6]

It could be argued, therefore, that many of the central elements in Japanese thinking about aid had been acquired early on in the period of being a donor-cum-recipient: the crucial importance of self-help; the priority of country ownership; the recognition of the role of loans; South–South co-operation (including when Japan itself was part of the South); and a focus on the relevance of its own experience in some measure of solidarity with other nations.[7] It should be underlined that this cluster of approaches which we term experience is also shot through with an awareness of the key role of attitude. In other words Japan's approach to aid is not just in the cognitive domain, but, like much in East Asian economies, draws on convictions about the role of effort, achievement and determination, whether in individual development and schooling or in development and transformation at the national level (Cheng 1994).

There is another historical element that has almost certainly played a salient role in fashioning some of the principles behind Japanese aid approaches, and that lies a good deal earlier, in the period of the Meiji Restoration from 1868. This was one of the most planned examples of rapid 'modernisation' in the nineteenth century, and involved a very deliberate selection by Japan from Western knowledge, Western technology and Western institutions. Interestingly, it involved a form of technical co-operation but, again, on Japanese terms. Foreign nationals from several different nations were invited, from both public and private sectors, and reached a maximum of some 850 personnel at the height of this process (Kato 2001a: 206). The precise manner in which Westerners were incorporated into Japanese institutions might be worth pursuing further, but what is already clear is that this whole episode was symbolic of successful borrowing and adaptation, or of what would later be called technology transfer. What is also intriguing is that this experience is even today quite explicitly thought of as being relevant to an understanding of Japanese aid.[8]

According to Sawamura, the Japanese axiom that sums up this kind of deliberate borrowing of knowledge and technology from elsewhere, which is potentially so relevant to current development thinking, is *wakon yosai* – Japanese spirit, Western knowledge. He argues that 'The Japanese have been sensitive and selective in adopting foreign institutions and systems, because they believe that no knowledge is completely free of the culture from which it came, and that seldom is knowledge globally applicable' (Sawamura 2002: 343). But just as the lesson for Japan had been that their own spirit (and priorities) must determine what was borrowed in the 1870s or in the 1950s, so in their role as modern donor it would follow that Japan might expect today's recipients to be as clear about what they wanted to borrow Japanese funds for as they themselves had sought to be. Japan had been very selective about Western knowledge; hence borrowers would need, in turn, to be critical of the wholesale borrowing of both Western and Japanese knowledge. The emphasis on 'Japanese spirit' may be taken to stand for the cluster of attitudinal concerns that are so central to ownership and self-reliance.

If this principle might help to explain a Japanese diffidence about promoting wholesale their own knowledge-for-development, two other dimensions are worth noting briefly. One is that Japan is the only major donor country that has not been associated with some form of extended missionary promotion of Christianity in the developing world (See Orr, quoted in Sawamura 2002); indeed it had itself been the object of missionary attention both before its extended period of deliberate isolation and after the Meiji Restoration.[9] The conviction and the certainties associated with Western evangelism were often found in parallel with a 'civilising mission'. Second, this record and potential advantage of its official aid not being seen as in some sense a continuation of missionary aid – which would distinguish Japan from other donors such as the USA, UK, Germany, Sweden, Switzerland, and so on – could have been compromised by the period of Japanese colonialism, especially in the inter-war years. However, the experience of having been a colonial power would appear to have made the Japanese determined no longer to be involved with the sort of interventions in education and the social sectors with which they had been associated in Korea and elsewhere. In other words, the colonial episode and the consequent sensitivities in Asia seem to have confirmed a Japanese preference for their aid to support technical and infrastructural areas and not the so-called softer fields, such as human resource planning and governance.

Cross-ministerial vs. specialist agency experience of development

We have emphasised that there were some unique features of Japanese aid history which were influenced by aspects of its own transformation, both in the nineteenth century and in the period after the Second World War. These have entered the canon of aid philosophy in Japan and continue to provide a rationale for certain forms of co-operation.

Arguably, the Japanese emphasis on the relevance of their own experience for their development assistance to others is only a version of what was historically a very widespread bilateral aid tendency – to focus on the comparative advantage of what particular industrial countries felt they had to offer to developing countries. We shall suggest shortly that one of the key differences with Japan is that it has been less ready than other bilaterals to shift from this focus on its own comparative advantage and its own experience – expressed in project aid – to a focus on policy, expressed in policy-based lending and sector grants carefully co-ordinated with many other donors.

However, even the delivery of this traditional bilateral project aid has been powerfully influenced by the ODA system in Japan. Unlike the other principal OECD bilateral donors, Japan does not rely on a single ministry or single executing agency for the delivery of its aid. Even though four bodies – Foreign Affairs (MOFA), Finance (MOF), Economy Trade and Industry (METI) and Economic Planning (EPA) – are the main players in economic co-operation, in principle all ministries have access to the aid envelope.[10] In practice, this does not mean that all have such access to anything like the same extent, but it does mean – unlike almost all other Western donors – that there is a substantial international co-operation agenda within such ministries as health, education, agriculture, forestry and fisheries, labour, and construction. This tradition of as many as seventeen different ministries being involved in development co-operation has been changing in the most recent period, as the government has sought to restructure and rationalise the number of ministries and public corporations. Nevertheless there remains a much wider basis of official involvement in ODA than in any other OECD country, with the possible exception of Portugal.

What this means for Japan's knowledge or experience of international development is worth exploring briefly, as it is directly related to our overall topic. Where regular bilateral implementing agencies such as Sida, Canada's CIDA, Germany's GTZ, Denmark's Danida and ODA/DFID have traditionally sought to maintain smaller or larger in-house bodies of sectoral competence (for example, on education or small-scale industry, or agriculture), JICA historically did not need to have its own advisers on these or many other sectors since the responsible line ministry would have taken this role through secondments of its own experts to JICA or to JICA's project development activities overseas.[11] The result of this dispersed ODA involvement could mean that the knowledge base on international co-operation within the Japanese government is very much more diffuse than elsewhere; it may also have meant that the emergence in a single agency of a cadre of people with specialist expertise on the developing world has been less of a priority for Japan than the utilisation of personnel in temporary development roles whose primary knowledge has been of developments in agriculture, health, education or industry in Japan itself.

It is worth remarking here that this particular pattern of dispersed personnel use for development tasks is much more likely to reinforce the notion of the relevance – in all the different sectors – of Japanese experience than the more common bilateral model of a single agency with responsibility for all development assistance. The Japanese model could well make for a more symmetrical discussion about agriculture, forestry, health or education, involving expertise from Japan's line ministries and their counterparts in Indonesia, China or elsewhere, than in the more common bilateral model, which always runs the risk of there being seen to be some specialist knowledge about development priorities on which it is the responsibility of a single development agency to dispense its convictions. JICA could never have rapidly drawn from its own ranks the expertise that could produce some equivalent of DFID's nine sectoral target strategy papers (TSPs) (see chapter 5). Rather JICA has traditionally been a synthesiser of other ministries' expertise, and this has primarily been expertise on Japan and not on 'development'. It makes it, then, a fundamentally different kind of agency from the World Bank, with its claim to be a 'unique reservoir of development experience across sectors and countries' (see chapter 4).

Experts and generalists in development co-operation

If the range of ministries (not to mention other corporations and private sector bodies) involved in Japanese aid were not already sufficiently complex, the challenge of identifying the special character and features of Japanese development aid is made more demanding by the two very distinct categories of personnel involved. Both in JICA and throughout government, there is a major difference between staff on permanent (lifetime) employment, who are termed 'staff' or 'generalists' (*shokuin*), and those who are 'development specialists' or 'senior advisors' (*senmonin*), who may sometimes have higher salaries but have less security of employment.

The great majority of the 1,200 professional employees in JICA, for instance, are generalists, while a significant number of JICA's development specialists (of whom there are just under 90) are associated with JICA's Institute for International Co-operation (IFIC) in Tokyo, and are seen as 'life-work technical experts' – that is, dedicated for life to a particular technical field such as education or industry.[12] This cadre of senior advisers are the closest in character to the DFID advisers we were examining in chapter 5. But unlike their DFID counterparts, JICA's numbers in any field are so small that they routinely need to draw in expertise from outside for most of their regular reports and studies.[13] By contrast, the generalists move every 2–3 years, following a pattern that obtains across all ministries, and, with almost no exception, they hold all the senior positions, including the directorships of JICA departments and divisions.

This differentiation between generalists and specialists obviously has some bearing on the precise nature of JICA's expert knowledge, since the organisation is essentially run by generalists, and even those coming on secondment from other line ministries will usually be generalists, though with a technical bent in some cases. But it is possible to exaggerate this dichotomy between types of staff, because, over the last decade and longer, generalists have been encouraged to develop a degree of specialisation, and in some departments of JICA (for example, mining and industrial development, or health) a good number of the 'generalists' will have had common engineering or medical backgrounds. However, it remains the case that with the regular rotation system none of the generalists can focus throughout their careers on what may have been their primary disciplinary interest.[14]

Nevertheless, the formal situation seems to be that those with the deepest sectoral expertise in a particular field such as education are seldom in a position where they can affect policy directly. But then even this must be qualified, for in JICA as a whole, it must be remembered that overall policy making lies with the Ministry of Foreign Affairs; so neither generalists nor development specialists in JICA are in policy-making roles *per se*, though it is widely accepted that JICA does have a substantial measure of policy autonomy under the overall umbrella of MOFA.[15]

The status of Japanese experience and expert knowledge is thus becoming more complex than where we had reached at the end of the previous section. We had noted that responsibility for development aid is distributed much more widely in government within Japan than in most other OECD countries, and that the major development agency, JICA, has traditionally drawn on the expertise of many different ministries, thus pulling into the development field a potentially rich vein of experience of Japanese development from as many as seventeen (now thirteen) ministries.[16] However, it then appears that these secondees are normally not themselves experts but are generalists with administrative experience of a number of sectors, like the majority of their hosts in JICA.

Consequently, at many different stages of the different project development processes, these regular staff, whether from JICA or from other ministries, need to have recourse to other specialist expertise.[17] Our provisional conclusion is that JICA, like other government agencies and ministries, has a wealth of administrative and procedural expertise, but depends on other sources of expertise for a great deal of its technical and scientific input. We can thus anticipate that the challenge of knowledge sharing within JICA or other Japanese agencies concerned with development aid may be rather different from the kind of knowledge sharing that we have examined, for example, in the thematic groups of the World Bank, among staff with similar professional concerns about a sector or a cross-cutting issue. But just as we have seen sectoral staff in Sida and DFID now dealing with much more complex tasks, so it is possible that JICA staff will increasingly need to face both the sectoral challenge and the larger changes to their roles that shifts in development co-operation itself are producing.

Japan's multiple external sources of development expertise

In a situation where the core, generalist staff in JICA are relatively few in number for one of the largest technical co-operation programmes in the world,[18] it should not be surprising that there are many modalities for JICA to access technical expertise through a variety of routes, to ensure careful project design, implementation and evaluation. The sheer scale of the specialised knowledge and expertise upon which JICA depends must be underlined if we are to understand the sense in which JICA is a knowledge agency. This is not to argue that some other bilateral agencies do not also have large numbers of experts; they clearly do. What seems different is that Japan publicly presents these sources of their own expertise as being at the very core of its development co-operation.[19] The main categories of this diverse expertise are the following.[20]

Despatch of project-type technical co-operation (PTTC) experts[21]

In this project modality, which usually lasts five years but is often renewed, the despatch of experts is one important element of an integrated package, along with counterpart training and equipment. The source of the experts is normally the other line ministries which duly second staff to JICA. Traditionally this opportunity for placing experts in projects overseas had been restricted to these other ministries, but in 2001 there was the beginning of competitive bidding for these openings on a trial basis. The procedures for identifying the almost two thousand such experts in any one year are quite complex, involving partner governments, JICA, MOFA and then the line ministries. Almost 50 per cent of experts in 2001 were drawn from the regular employees of these ministries and associated organisations. It would seem that ministries differ considerably in their capacity to provide experts, with Agriculture, Forestry and Fisheries having a surplus of experts, and others, such as Education and Science, drawing on national universities for their secondees.

Despatch of individual experts[22]

This category is different from the above, since it involves a response to a whole series of different requests by partner governments for individual expertise outside the project framework. The numbers here in any one recent year are rather large, running at 1,750 in fiscal 1999. The actual identification of these experts is carried out with the involvement of JICA's regional departments, but also by MOFA consulting the line ministries who will be the source of these experts. Again, it must be assumed that the scale is such that the line ministries will in turn identify many of these experts from outside their own ranks but, unlike other bilateral agencies, these will tend not to be from the consulting or the private and for-profit sectors.[23]

It should be noted that the recruitment of experts is actually expanding (JICA 2000a: 122), and the two categories so far discussed have, since January 2000, been handled by a new Human Resources Assignment Department. It is interesting to note that this new department is described as a 'personnel bank for the recruitment of experts by JICA' – perhaps an unconscious resonance with the 'knowledge bank' of the World Bank, but one which underlines that it is personnel, experience and expertise that is at the heart of Japanese ODA and not its own codified knowledge in policy papers.

Senior overseas volunteer programme (SOVP)[24] and JOCV

Though not strictly regarded as an expert dispatch programme, there is little doubt that this senior version of the longrunning Japanese overseas co-operation volunteer (JOCV) programme for younger people is drawing very directly on 'the skills and knowledge' needed by developing countries, but also on those attributes that had supported Japan itself during its period of high-level growth. The description of this cadre, which has grown rapidly in the few years since it started, and measured 758 in 2002, underlines their 'outstanding skills and plentiful professional experience' (JICA 2000a: 14). This certainly suggests that a proportion of these senior volunteers would be regarded as similar to the senior advisers or development specialists if they were working in the ministries. The SOVP, if added to the 2,500 JOCV in the field at any one time, produces a significant number of volunteers.[25]

These three categories alone, in fiscal 2000, involved a substantial number of Japanese experts and volunteers (about 7,000) being requested, recruited, trained and marshalled for overseas work. Beyond these, there are significant numbers of Japanese consultants working directly on the different studies which underpin most Japanese development assistance. The main categories of these are also worth noting because of their sheer scale.

Development studies[26]

In its Japanese usage this term describes a wide range of studies carried out as an integral part of project identification, design, support and follow-up. They include master plans, which are comprehensive, long-term sectoral development documents for a country or a region, as well as feasibility studies. In fiscal 1999 alone, they numbered over 250, and routinely they would have used Japanese consulting firms which in turn could have drawn in 'international' consultants for up to half of the team members. The number of expert personnel working on these was no less than 2,974 in this single year. Though not formally termed 'experts', these consultants are recruited through competitions organised by JICA's development study department. The JICA staff involved in this selection process are likely to be generalists, and yet they will have to carry out this process as well as receive up to five reports for each development study project. This is probably one of several procedures where generalists have to turn to external expertise for assistance – just another reason why in-house sector expertise is becoming more compelling.

Basic design studies for general project grant aid

This category of grant aid is for infrastructure and facilities – from school buildings to bridges and roads. But for our current concern with expert knowledge, it should be noted that basic design studies are critical to this category of grant aid. These are handled by Japanese consultant firms, as are the development studies, but on completion they are reviewed and recommended to MOFA by JICA's grant aid management department. Again, there is likely to be a review process by generalist staff of design studies which are of a technical nature. This too is a very major activity, with no less than 240 projects and their associated basic design studies being completed within fiscal 2000.

These are only two of the no less than fifteen categories of study teams that routinely go out from Japan to all the regions where there are possible projects to be developed. The sheer scale of this analytical work can be judged by the fact that in fiscal 1999 alone there were almost 9,000 individuals associated with this series of more than 1,500 study activities.

Thematic and country evaluations

This is a third major area of consultant use. Again, in some of these, the competitive bids amongst Japanese firms can include international consultants for up to 50 per cent of the proposed team. For other mid-term and end-of-project reviews, Japanese firms can be requested to assist in implementation. In the regular evaluations carried out by the evaluation division, there are substantial numbers in any one year; in 1999, for instance, there were two hundred evaluations done, and this includes just the completion, post-project, and post-project status evaluations (JICA 2000a: 154–8; JICA 2000b). Taken together, these will have involved very considerable amounts of development expertise, and again a good deal of the review of the results will have been undertaken by staff inside JICA.[27]

As in other bilateral agencies, it will have been commonplace for evaluations to have been carried out by consultants, but in Japan this exercise seems likely to have involved more varied expertise than other OECD countries because of the multiple sponsorship of evaluations by JICA, MOFA and JBIC. All in all, it would not be surprising if some 4,000 consultants were occupied across all three evaluation categories in any one fiscal year.

The scale of the Japanese expert, study team and evaluation presence

Putting this together with our estimate of formal expert personnel being recruited for work overseas, we reach a figure of around 7,000 for short- and long-term experts (along with senior and regular Japanese volunteers), and study-team personnel in all the different categories of almost 9,000, and a significant number of further personnel involved in the JICA evaluations. It would appear that as recently as fiscal 1999, there may have been between 16,000 and 20,000 Japanese engaged in these overseas expert, analytical and evaluative activities.

Japanese expertise in international perspective

The continuing – and perhaps growing – presence of all these very visible sources of Japanese expertise in their bilateral development co-operation activity comes at a time when, as we have noted, there is a major UNDP-led rethinking – yet again – of technical assistance and technical co-operation (Fukuda-Parr *et al.* 2002). There is clearly still a great deal of questioning of the old paradigm of North–South transfer of expertise, and a concern to explore new and more symmetrical ways of building and networking knowledge and capacity in the North and the South.

It would appear that perhaps unlike some other donors, where there has been a sharp criticism of technical assistance personnel, Japan has has seen a rise in the use of these, and an expansion to include new categories of civil society and local government expertise, even, possibly, during the recent years of cuts to the overall aid budget. It would be intriguing to explore further whether the new paradigm for capacity development, as articulated by UNDP, which highlights notions such as 'scan globally, re-invent locally', may not already be accepted in the *wakon yosai* (Western knowledge, Japanese spirit) conception of expertise we have analysed above.

Indeed, for the World Summit for Social Development (WSSD) in South Africa in September 2002, Japan, significantly enough, chose to highlight and confirm its faith in technical co-operation in spite of the criticisms; and, again, it is interesting to see the reference in Johannesburg to Japan's own development experiences:

> Japan International Co-operation Agency (JICA) places importance on the following aspects in providing technical co-operation to developing countries and supporting their capacity development.

> * respecting ownership of the developing countries
> * sharing knowledge and technology through working together with developing countries
> * establishing human and institutional relationship between Japan and developing countries
> * utilising Japanese experiences in her development process (JICA Programme for WSSD, 30 August 2002, 2 September 2002).[28]

Direct exposure to Japanese experience through overseas training

At the same time, the other key dimension of technical co-operation – participant training in Japan or overseas – has also been growing over the last decade, whilst the training programmes of several other OECD donors have been drastically cut since the end of the Cold War, as was noted earlier.[29] The specifically JICA component of this involved some 7,700 participants coming to Japan in fiscal 1999 for short-term training, while a further 8,000 received training in developing countries, including a very significant number in third countries. In this single year, when all the different training categories are compounded, almost 18,000 trainees were involved, in Japan or overseas. Added to this is a new component of long-term degree-level training to be provided by JICA.

JICA's is of course only one part of the Government's response to international student mobility; a much larger programme is the one designed to bring 100,000 to Japan in any one year. This is the responsibility of the Ministry of Education and Science, and although there has been some slippage from the overall goal of 100,000 by the end of the twentieth century, this is still the target of the ministry for implementation as soon as possible (Shibata 2001).

Behind this powerful emphasis on increased overseas training is the same concern with the direct exchange of expert knowledge *in situ* that is evident in the dispatch of experts to developing countries. This is why the technical training of overseas participants is judged to be 'the most fundamental "human development" programme implemented by JICA' (JICA 2000a: 111). Running through the justification is the crucial exposure, once again, to Japanese experience:

> From the standpoint of technical co-operation there are several advantages in implementing this programme in Japan. These include the following: i) participants are motivated by seeing how new technology and ideas not yet available in their own countries are used; ii) Japan's experience is transmitted to the world at large; and iii) participants have the chance to exchange ideas and experience with colleagues from other countries facing similar issues as themselves. (JICA 2000a: 111)

In case it is concluded that face-to-face contact exclusively with Japanese expertise is the foundation of its aid policy, it should be recalled that JICA is probably the foremost agency protagonist of South–South co-operation, whereby a group of 'pivotal countries', such as Thailand, Brazil, Chile and Singapore, are encouraged to make the transition to donor status by engaging their own experts in technical co-operation to developing countries, through funding from Japan. At the moment, this modality is increasing and is changing its shape, but it certainly can be thought of as a mechanism for transferring Japanese experience and technology through a third party (Miyoshi 2001). It could be argued that both the use of third-country experts rather than Japanese, and the use of third-country training rather than in-Japan or in-country, are aspects of South–South co-operation that Japan takes very seriously.[30]

Conclusions on the expert experience

Given the great importance, nevertheless, that is attached to Japanese expert knowledge in development assistance, there is not a great deal of analysis – at least not in English – that seeks to capture the nature of this learning transaction.[31] The salience of this modality, as a key form of knowledge sharing, needs to be pieced together from different sources. On the one hand, there are clear references in the discussion of experts to the way they represent the best in the Japanese on-the-job training system. In other words, in a small way, experts illustrate some of the facets of the Japanese traditions of learning within the firm for the aid project or programme. For instance, they are clearly seen to be in the business of sharing both knowledge and attitudes, and these attitudes are frequently illustrated by the fact that the Japanese experts are actually to be found in the paddy field or on the project site itself. Unlike British or German expatriates, who may have often been attached to key policy advisory positions in particular ministries, the Japanese experts have typically been middle-level practitioners rather than high-level policy people. The joke about the Japanese expert being called 'Mister Like This' points out the frequency with which Japanese experts might not be able to explain in excellent English but could show how something should be done by actually doing it, 'Like this!'

The emphasis has been on practitioner knowledge rather than on policy knowledge, on people-to-people transfer of skills and technology. Some pride is taken in the difference between many Japanese experts, who are there in the developing world for this particular task, and the number of much longer-term expatriates who work as experts for some of the other donor agencies. Just as the Japanese company has less status distinctions between workers and management, so it is possible that Japanese experts do not immediately fall into the expatriate community in developing countries. Former JICA president, Kimio Fujita, now working as a senior overseas volunteer in Samoa, put this Japanese perception of their difference from Western expatriates sharply:

> For most donor countries and organisations outside Japan, the central theme of capacity building is how to reduce dependence on the expatriate policy advisors who have occupied the central positions in the policy-making agencies of developing countries. Their position is the opposite from that of Japan, which has mainly dispatched specialists to the organisations responsible for implementation in developing countries and is only now looking into ways of sending them to policy-making agencies as well. (Fujita 2001)

Japanese commentators, however, are quick to admit that the success with which experts were able to work in Asia has not been secured as easily in Africa, partly because of skill gaps, and partly because of attitudinal differences.

It is clear from the way that experts are discussed in JICA official documents that along with overseas participant training, they constitute 'the core of co-operation in the field of human resources development in developing countries' (JICA 2000a: 120). But Japanese experts also proved politically valuable to the aid constituency in the late 1990s and early 2000s, when politicians, faced with recession in Japan, began to talk up the importance of 'aid having a clearly visible profile' (a translation of *'nihonno kaoga mieru'* – aid with a Japanese face).[32] The political requirement for Japanese aid to be more visible may have the effect of pushing the expert out of the paddy field and into the ministry, as is argued on the JICA website.[33]

These sections on the philosophy and history of Japanese aid, and on the particularity of Japanese approaches to expertise and to experience in relation to development, have been an essential prelude to any discussion of what phrases such as 'knowledge-based aid' might mean for JICA and for the other agencies in Japan involved in development assistance. In a word, it could be said that the Japanese discourse about development has made little explicit use of the language of knowledge for development, preferring to talk of sharing skills, technology, know-how and experience in all the ways that have been analysed above. There are, nevertheless, a small number of knowledge initiatives which we shall turn to shortly; but first it may be worth looking at the ways in which Japanese aid has been associated with particular expressions of policy. It will be seen that though there is a series of lead documents expressing policy on development co-operation, there continues to be a major reliance on an established canon of positions and attitudes towards development.

Sources of policy knowledge in Japanese development assistance

What we are arguing is that although there is some documentation on development policy, which we shall briefly review, the core values of development seem to have been already set and are to a considerable extent embedded in a long-standing culture of development assistance. These typically include a concern with aid as a means of helping those who help themselves (Nishigaki and Shimomura 1996: 153). Central issues such as this focus on self-help – and all that flows from this – are also reinforced in the ODA Charter of 30 June 1992. This in turn has been elaborated in the Medium Term Policy for Overseas Development Assistance of 1998 (which runs for five years). The relation of this domestic aid policy development process to the series of new aid approaches that have emerged in DAC, the World Bank and in some other donors over the last ten years is worth noting. In a number of important ways this domestic agenda has come into conflict with the aid paradigm associated with the World Bank.

Clearly there has been a desire within the aid policy community in Japan to achieve greater clarity about their own aid philosophy, especially since it came to be the largest bilateral aid donor in 1991. We have said enough above to suggest that there is a rather widespread set of convictions about what Japanese aid approaches consist of, but these have not been powerfully promoted outside Japan. Nishigaki and Shimomura capture this well in some of their discussion about the 'special features of Japan's ODA': 'It is only natural that societies with different historical and religious backgrounds should have different views on aid. What is needed is an awareness that Japan, too, has its own aid philosophy' (Nishigaki and Shimomura 1996:153).

One of the first instances of the desire for a distinctive Japanese a proach surfaced over continued Western support for structural adjustment policies, especially in Africa. Although Japan had given support for these in earlier years, there has been marked evidence since the early 1990s of concern with the assumptions underlying and the impact of adjustment measures (Stein 1998). Further evidence of a desire to promote a different model of development aid was to be seen in Japanese funding of the *East Asian Miracle* study through the World Bank in 1993. This study, Stein argues, was intended by Japan to move the Bank away from its dogmatic neo-classical position and make it more appreciative of state-led development along Japanese lines. This did not happen: 'The result was somewhat disappointing since the report did little to affirm the Japanese view of policies responsible for their own development' (Stein 1998: 17).[34]

If the *East Asian Miracle* study was one of the first substantial attempts to get Asian (and specifically Japanese) development history acknowledged internationally, a second occasion was provided by the OECD–DAC report *Shaping the 21st century: the contribution of development co-operation* (1996). Arguably, Japan took very seriously the discussions that led to this report. While the targets themselves do not particularly reflect anything that could be called a Japanese approach, the background text provides much evidence of Japan's priorities, not least the frequent emphasis on the need for 'locally owned strategies'. JICA also produced a three-volume study on the OECD–DAC's new development strategy (NDS) (JICA 1998), which underlined even more clearly how closely aligned they felt the assumptions of the DAC report were with their own development assumptions.

At the heart of the Japanese belief is self-reliance, and it is interesting to see how powerfully this message from their own experience is confirmed in their commentary on the DAC report:

> Drawing general conclusions from progress that has been made in the development arena, the NDS declares that development assistance can do no more than complement the efforts made by the citizens, organisations, institutions, and governments of developing countries, and that ownership by developing countries will accordingly be of the utmost importance to the achievement of sustainable development. This emphasis on ownership effectively reaffirms the assistance philosophy that Japan has cultivated through years of experience. (JICA 1998: 79)

The role of Japan in shaping key aspects of the DAC report is further confirmed by Fumiaki Takahashi, deputy director-general of the economic co-operation bureau of MOFA in November 1997. He argues that one of the three key principles of the DAC report is the ownership of their development by developing countries: 'One example is the dramatic economic growth in East Asian countries. This example has made clear that first comes the ownership of developing countries and donor countries should act to assist their efforts as equal partners' (Takahashi 1997: 13). Japan's influence on and pride in the DAC report's philosophy itself is made very clear: 'Japan played a leading role in shaping this strategy because she wanted to share her own experience with the other partners – the experience of her post-war reconstruction to become a donor country from a recipient' (Takahashi 1997: 13).

A third example of Japan's seeking to emphasise its own approach to development would be evident in its independent sponsorship of the series of Tokyo International Conferences on African Development (TICAD). These took place in 1993, in 1998 and 2003. In Takahashi's words: 'The main theme of the TICAD process is the importance of self-help efforts of African people and the co-operation between Asia and Africa' (Takahashi 1997: 15).

In contrast to these three examples, which illustrate Japanese involvement in getting some of its own development knowledge accommodated in the international discourse about aid, there are other examples of new aid developments, such as the Sector-Wide Approach (SWAP), the Comprehensive Development Framework (CDF) and the Poverty Reduction Strategy Paper (PRSP), where the Japanese have not been convinced that the modality fits with their own aid and accountability traditions. One reason for some hesitation about these new modalities is a Japanese preference in their own aid priorities for the country-specific approach, worked out bilaterally between their own experts and a particular self-reliant government (or in a South–South medium). By contrast, all the new aid approaches imply very considerable degrees of donor co-ordination around a nationally owned programme. Furthermore, there is a worry that new approaches are being tried out in the developing world that, unlike their own tried and tested schemes, have not really yet been validated carefully. An example of this caution comes from MOFA comments on SWAPs, but it might be extended to other new aid paradigms of the late 1990s and early 2000s:

> SWAPS are just being tried out at the moment, and we don't know whether they are going to prove effective or not. We ought to take our time to judge whether their approach is effective. Certainly, using developing countries as 'experimental sites' for new aid methodologies is something we shall need to be cautious about. (Ministry of Foreign Affairs, Japan, Summary, 2000: 11 [original in Japanese])[35]

Knowledge-sharing initiatives in a culture of valuing experience

We mentioned at the outset of this chapter that a number of agencies have in different ways followed the lead of the World Bank in exploring some dimensions of what it might mean to be a 'knowledge agency'. These have taken very diverse routes, whether in DFID, Sida or CIDA, affected by traditions of organisation and aid philosophy as well as wider movements in Northern governments. It might be assumed that Japanese explorations of knowledge-based aid would also be coloured by something of what we have considered in the previous sections.

We shall first examine briefly a number of knowledge-based activities relating to Japanese aid, and then look in somewhat more detail at a project that is explicitly concerned with knowledge management and knowledge sharing. In doing so, we shall note some tensions between what we have been examining – the experience-based knowledge that is embedded in a particular context and history, and is often largely tacit – and the new initiatives deliberately to construct a more explicit sharing of knowledge, including across embryonic sectoral approaches.

Knowledge via sector work and sector studies

Earlier, we mentioned that there were very few explicit discussions about Japan's policy knowledge, but there are a great deal about Japan's experience. One of the reasons for this relative scarcity, despite the few important illustrations given above, is that the organisation of Japanese co-operation by a series of schemes (for example, dispatch of experts, overseas technical training, project-type technical co-operation) means that what would, in other agencies, be sector concerns – with education, small enterprises, and so on – are dealt with by a whole set of different schemes. It is often said, for instance, that the field of education is actually covered by no less than twenty different divisions in JICA. It has accordingly been difficult traditionally to conceive of how an education sector paper could actually be done organisationally within JICA.[36] And it must be remembered, in addition, that education policy is a prerogative not of JICA but of MOFA, where all macro-level policy is determined. Even that is not the end of the story, for the key role of other ministries in aid policy would certainly require that the education ministry be consulted in an education sector initiative.

Thus, producing a JICA-wide account of education or of other key sectoral issues would have been a really major organisational challenge. One illustration of this challenge to the development of policy knowledge on key sectoral issues can be seen in the division concerned with global issues. There are just seven of these and they cover major fields such as environment, education, gender and WID, poverty, population and HIV–AIDS. It is the intention that they should produce guidelines for each of these major topics, but, so far, the useful little pamphlets that have been produced on each global issue merely exemplify how that topic is being dealt with across the various traditional schemes mentioned above.[37] We shall shortly note how the new knowledge management scheme seeks to build on these global issues by its sectoral approach to a whole series of new 'development issues'.

Knowledge via dissemination of evaluation summaries

One of the forms of information disclosure on aid outcomes that has been of apparent interest to the Japanese public is the publication of evaluation results of all projects. This has happened since 1995, and since 2000 the full text of every evaluation has been available on the JICA website. Also since 2000 a very substantial document synthesising all evaluations in the particular year covered has been published in attractive format. The rationale for this degree of dissemination is 'to provide accurate information on JICA projects to the people of Japan', and 'to increase the understanding of the people toward ODA'.[38] It also reinforces the concern that aid should have a clearly visible (Japanese) face, since the evaluation summaries have plentiful photographs illustrating Japanese experts at work, or trainees experiencing Japanese expertise at first hand.

'Intellectual support' as a new element in expert policy

The development of this modality in recent years has signalled an interest in exchange of experience going beyond the technical. It has tended to be used for expertise connected with institutional and organisational development, especially in transition countries, and often in such allegedly 'soft' fields as legal, administrative and parliamentary systems. By its very existence as a separate concept, it affirms that the bulk of support hitherto has been for 'hard' technical and technological areas. There is an intriguing parallel here with Sida's identification of their concerns with capacity building at the individual/professional, institutional and organisational levels (See chapter 6 and Sida 2000a). JICA describes it thus:

> Intellectual support ... aims at establishment of institutional and legal systems, support for policy making, and improvement of operational capability. In this sense, it is different from just simple transfer of existing technology or skills, as has been done so far. More precisely put, it is the form of support that requires high level intellectual supporting activity, while taking fully into account the economic and social conditions of the recipient country. To help personnel of the recipient country think together and come up with optimum solutions is one example. (JICA 2000c: 4)

The term 'intellectual support' signals an important shift in JICA towards a more explicit approach to policy knowledge in those very sectors such as democratisation and trade liberalisation where Japan had traditionally been very diffident about intervening. It leads Japan into sector support and not just project support, and it suggests a new and interesting example of people-to-people co-operation in the more demanding sphere of policy knowledge:

> The 'Medium-Term ODA Policy' ... placed greater emphasis than ever before on intellectual co-operation ... JICA is being required to change over from an approach based on individual projects to one based on programme units covering the whole of a sector. (JICA 2000a: 24)

An early challenge to 'Knowledge for Development in Japan'

We have said how little explicit writing there is about knowledge for development, or knowledge discourse, at least in English, apart from the knowledge management initiative to which we shall turn in a moment. There is, however, a curiously anonymous document on this very topic produced by FASID (Foundation for Advanced Studies on International Development) as early as March 1998 entitled *Realities and issues of Knowledge for Development in Japan*.[39] Thus, it was published several months before the *World Development Report* of 1998–99, *Knowledge for Develop-*

ment, was made public in September 1998, although work on that *WDR* would have been initiated in 1997. What is especially intriguing about the FASID report is that there is no reference to the World Bank's knowledge interests, but reference is made instead to the knowledge for development activities of DFID, NORAD, Sida, USAID and IDRC. Yet clearly these agencies were reviewed before any of them had developed any explicit knowledge sharing or knowledge management initiatives.

The document as a whole – just 24 pages – is a valuable commentary on the way that Japan and other bilaterals use knowledge. It examines the use of knowledge in the different phases of project development and implementation. Amongst a wide range of insights and suggestions, it sees scope for Japan to develop its unique experience of foreign aid into a more knowledge-based theory. This would be a healthy counterweight to the current approaches, which are dominated by North America and Europe.

Its most persuasive analysis relates to how agencies might best construct bodies of knowledge jointly with developing countries. For this, experience is crucial, and so is theory, but the third element that is essential is trust. One of its main conclusions is that establishing mutual trust with the recipient country and taking part in a joint effort to compile a body of knowledge is essential (FASID 1998: 23).

Although there is a good deal more in this paper, this particular emphasis on 'a joint effort to compile a body of knowledge' is very relevant to our purpose and resonates very much with the approaches of SAREC and Sida. Coming a year or two before agencies seriously began to consider how they should become 'knowledge agencies', it is refreshing in its assumption that knowledge development should probably encompass a shift away from the tradition of delivering specialised knowledge and towards the joint development (with the South) of new knowledge.

Knowledge management in JICA: a new approach

With this much background, we turn finally to look at the only explicit knowledge management (KM) project in JICA, which has been actively in the making since 2000. Its origins lie as far back as 1996 when Koichi Miyoshi, later to become a key member of JICA's Planning and Evaluation Department, and then Senior Advisor in IFIC, was posted to the JICA office in Washington.[40] Subsequently, one of the earliest identified publications by JICA on knowledge management was commissioned by the Washington office of JICA. It was a consultancy to examine knowledge management in USAID and the World Bank (Fillip 1999). It argued that JICA should follow its own organisational needs if it went down a KM track, focusing on the need for specialist expertise and a pilot experiment before going to scale. This is close to what was attempted by JICA three years later, in March 2002.

By the time JICA became interested, in 1998, the architecture of the World Bank's knowledge management project – later renamed 'knowledge sharing' – had, as we saw in chapter 4, been put in place by its director, Steve Denning, and colleagues, and eventually some 130 thematic groups had been formed across the World Bank (Denning 2001; King 2000; World Bank 1998e). So there was something which the JICA visitors and their KM consultant could examine and react to.

It is clear that the World Bank model was influential, but there was a very different set of needs and challenges for knowledge sharing in JICA than in the World Bank. For one thing, those who first began thinking of KM for JICA were aware of their own very different structures. At that time, in 1998, there were no regional departments, though these would come into being within the next two years, and, as we have mentioned, the personnel concerned with a particular thematic area might be scattered over a large number of divisions and departments. This suggested that one possible opportunity for information exchange would be in the form of IT-based knowledge management.

A second clear difference from the World Bank was that the Bank did not have any national constituency to think about, whereas JICA was very aware of its several associated constituencies as well as the increasing importance of making aid visible to the public at large. In any thematic area, there would be expertise in the consulting companies, in the different categories of experts, and in universities, as well as in the volunteers, both junior and senior, and in the NGOs. The ex-volunteers who had been associated with education alone, for instance, would amount to 2–3,000. Even though the potential size of such thematic networks could be very large, the original idea was certainly to start relatively small within JICA, and possibly within the JICA intranet before expanding to involve outsiders.

Where it was anticipated that the KM system would be similar to the World Bank would be in its core emphasis on raising the productivity of JICA staff to make greater use of the knowledge that already existed in the organisation but which was not synthesised and accessible. To facilitate this process of making staff more productive, many different ideas had been mentioned over the two years prior to the formal KM launch. These ideas have included 'help desks' – which have played a key role in the World Bank – which staff could access from anywhere in the JICA system, now that HQ and the offices are all connected by intranet.

But there had also been talk of using the KM system to make more easily available to staff some of the crucial documentation they need in their daily work – such as operational guidelines for specific subsector work, best practice examples of operational documents, terms of reference for consultants, and inventories of professional organisations, personnel and reports concerned with the sector.[41]

But it is clear that the main driver in persuading senior staff to back the KM initiative has been its potential to increase staff productivity. It can also be assumed that the intranet and ICT are likely to play a key role in facilitating this productivity. But equally it might be argued that a primary focus on JICA staff productivity could put at risk some of the wider attractions of a knowledge network in a particular field that pulled together the currently dispersed expert constituencies concerned with that field.

Piloting knowledge management through development issue teams

Nevertheless, in the pilot phase, which started in March–April 2002, there were five development issue teams or thematic groups[42] formed, and they included education, ITC, and poverty reduction. The five expanded to nine teams during 2002, including groups on health and population, water, economic policy, private sector development, agriculture and rural development, and environment; and by June 2003 there were a further seven teams covering South–South co-operation, social security, gender, peace building, aid approach and capacity development, evaluation, and Japanese language. This expansion was based on an official inquiry by the Personnel Department to staff about their readiness to be nominated as core members of the new teams.

It is worth noting that these initial groups were formally identified by the lead actors in the KM initiative; they have not emerged informally, as has happened in some other agencies, such as DFID (see chapter 5). It is also worth observing that the sectoral focus of the nine groups does not coincide with any of the existing departments in JICA's organisational chart, with the exception of agriculture. What this suggests, as we have implied earlier, is that KM will operate to link JICA staff who have some degree of common sectoral interest but who are currently widely dispersed across many different departments and divisions.[43] Thus, there is no education department or division in JICA, but the pilot KM network on education is linking key JICA staff who have some substantial interest in education but are now located in different divisions in JICA HQ, in IFIC, and in one of the other JICA offices in Japan. No members are yet included from overseas JICA offices.[44]

In other words, the KM networks look as if they are deliberately being organised to be cross-cutting, and in this sense they certainly overlap to an extent with the seven global issues which were discussed earlier. Amongst those global issues where there is a direct overlap with the areas picked out for KM are: education, poverty, population and HIV–AIDS, and bio-diversity and green issues. Arguably, if the development issues teams succeed and become established across departments and divisions, they are likely to make the work of the small group of global issues redundant.[45]

The membership, even of these nine first groups, has been quite formally arranged between the planning division and Personnel Department, so as to ensure that those selected have the particular development issue as one of their core professional concerns. Numbers in the first instance remain small, with teams of between ten and fifteen being the norm. Beyond this, their status as members of the team is something that has been negotiated and agreed, so as to ensure that there is some time allocation for the development issue team set aside by individual members. Their status as teams is therefore very different from those agencies where groups with common interests in particular development issues have been formed autonomously.

Inevitably, the composition of the teams has had to face the distinction between generalist and specialist staff. What is clear in the pilot phase is that the initiative has emerged from generalist staff who have been concerned with the need to move towards greater specialisation and sectoral expertise. Thus the bulk of the teams' membership is from the generalist staff, but there are normally one or two senior advisers or development specialists included in each team. Quite how the work of the teams will get allocated and executed between generalists and existing specialists is still a moot point. But understandably, IFIC, as the institute housing the bulk of the development specialists or senior advisers, will have a vested interest in seeking to involve its experts in the emerging teams.

The rationale for these first groups has also been quite carefully pre-specified. It is clear from the internal 'Guideline for the Management of the Development Issue Teams' (JICA 2002b) that they are principally concerned to reflect the dramatically changing duties of JICA staff, given the ongoing reform of the organisation and the sheer concentration of knowledge that is now available. There is a marked awareness in the guideline of changes in international development co-operation, with greater donor co-ordination and a sense that other donors are active in knowledge accumulation: 'Each donor agency is strengthening its system focusing on the accumulation and use of knowledge and know-how.' In response to these trends, the knowledge management initiative is seen as a deliberate attempt by JICA to be in step with these wider trends and thus to 'strengthen knowledge of development issues and to increase effectiveness and efficiency of its work'. In other words, there is an explicit desire for JICA to be able to reflect the international move towards being 'a core agency of knowledge'. But at the same time, the development teams are seen as building up JICA's capacity in sectoral specialisation by this knowledge networking. It should be added that this emphasis on sectoral professionalism probably coincides with the interests and desires especially of the younger staff joining JICA.[46] What is certainly a challenge in this new approach is whether the sectoral specialisation, which many staff in JICA see as a distinct possibility for the organisation, can be delivered by teams which continue to be based in their old schematic departments and divisions. In other words, can the new world of greater specialisation really be piloted by staff based in the older world of JICA's traditional schemes? To answer that, we need to examine the scope of what the teams are expected to do.

The activities and duties of the development issue teams

Each of the emerging development issue teams has had to consider how to deal with what is a rather demanding series of duties and activities, some of which will be mentioned here. In the first place, they have been required, like the very much smaller global issues teams a few years earlier, to develop a set of guidelines specific to their particular issue. In effect, this can be seen as the first move towards the generation of an issue policy paper. But even this single objective presents a considerable challenge when it is remembered that the work of the teams has to be combined with their regular duties in their existing departments. Work has certainly started on these guidelines, but in several instances it would appear to have drawn on issue-specific work that was already under way in IFIC.[47] Indeed, IFIC has itself been identified as being responsible for no less than three of the development teams in the next round. The overall ambition of the knowledge management initiative is for the full complement of 23 development issue teams eventually to develop no less than some 60 issue-specific guidelines.[48] The intermediate aim is to have the first 17 issue strategy papers complete by October 2003, when JICA was scheduled to become a new and more autonomous entity. They will be the first official papers which indicate directions for operations from a sectoral or issue-wise viewpoint.

Amongst other tasks with which the development issue teams are charged are the development and management of an issue-specific knowledge base. Again, this is probably easier said than done, since the determination of the contents of such a sectoral knowledge base has had little or no earlier work done on which this could readily be based.[49] One early version of what such a knowledge-based website would encompass underlines just how much new work would be involved:

A knowledge-based website consisting of general information on development issues, guidelines for 61 sectors and issues, a business record on JICA's operations, case studies on JICA and other donor countries, examples for JICA's operation document, a project design matrix, the project instruction document, a directory for related personnel and organisation and a directory for reference materials, books, and reports (Kato 2001a: 215)

By September 2002 a database system (called the JICA Knowledge Site) had already been put into operation. The intention was eventually to ensure that every key document of JICA projects was stored in the system. In addition, consultants and experts are being stipulated to feed good practice examples back to the database. With these arrangements, the database would be expanded into a major knowledge base for Japan's ODA programme.

Even more demanding in the list of more than ten suggested activities of the development issue teams are a whole series of obligations that, arguably, could be effectively carried out only if the team members were to become something much closer to DFID style advisers. Thus, the guidelines for the teams suggest that they should undertake project formulation assessment, participate in project implementation, provide technical advice on projects, and participate in ex-post evaluation research. The terms of reference suggested for each of these tasks are such that they could be done only if the staff were to become full-time specialists. They seem impossibly demanding for what are essentially part–time teams composed principally of generalists.

In addition to these activities, which can be seen as aimed at the use of the new teams internally in JICA, there is another set of tasks aimed much more at JICA's external relations and external networking. But they are almost equally demanding. For instance, one arena mentioned is participation in meetings such as those organised by DAC (OECD). This is an interesting illustration of the aspirations of these new teams, since it has often been said that JICA takes inadequate advantage of DAC and similar meetings because of the absence of sectoral specialists. Equally, it is suggested that the development issue teams could plan research and organise workshops in their thematic areas related to reform and new developments. This, too, along with participation in international working groups, has traditionally been a great challenge to JICA's existing capacity.

A different aspect of the teams' external face is the suggestion that they organise networks of ouside experts, and administer these as part of a wider resource for JICA. In addition, it is mentioned that the teams could identify from outside expertise a support or advisory committee, which the teams would manage as an additional resource for the development of specialist knowledge.

Overall, this set of tasks for the emerging teams would represent a series of major commitments if even just a few of them were to be taken seriously. But it should be emphasised that in agencies where there already are specialist groups of advisers, it is seldom possible for anything like this range of obligations to be covered satisfactorily. Of course, it must be remembered that these were indicative guidelines for the pilot phase, and they may well be reduced in ambition at the evaluation stage. Nevertheless they are instructive for pointing to a desire in JICA to furnish itself with a greater degree of sectoral professional capacity.

Information vs knowledge content

The substantive challenge of the content of these emerging knowledge-sharing networks is that it is relatively easy – if time-consuming – to make available on a knowledge website all the evaluations and other key documents of JICA programmes and projects, or to digitise project and operational documentation that is not already in electronic format. But KM designers in JICA are already aware that the challenge is not to make more information available but to make more readily available the critical synthetic policy-related material on the mass of information that is already present.

Thus there are, for many of the cross-cutting areas that have been selected for the KM networks, substantial quantities of issue-based and thematic studies already generated by IFIC. There are, doubtless, some very suggestive development studies and basic design studies; and there is a whole series of evaluative studies carried out on all the projects in recent years. So, if the KM system is to go beyond listing, for example, sectoral information on education or health projects and look, instead, more into the kind of material needed for the 'intellectual support' of partners wishing, like Vietnam, to rethink the focus of their primary education system, then a much more strategic and demanding kind of analytical task is at hand for these emerging development issue teams.

Critical synthesis of the best available material generated by IFIC and by different consultancies requires very high-order analytical skills. In a small way, we can see that the leadership of these teams faces something of the same order of challenge that we noted the topic advisers in the development gateway face in respect of information accumulation versus synthesis and analysis.

Audiences for the development issue teams

Like KM initiatives in other agencies, it would appear from a close analysis of the issue team guideline that the first audience for the work of the emerging teams is JICA itself, and within JICA the main focus is on the partially specialised generalists who have been selected for the specific teams. A second audience, once the teams have achieved a certain quality of output, would be the JICA field staff, JOCVs, senior volunteers and associate experts. A third very important audience is the external constituency of university and consultancy expertise. It is clear that the issue teams are expected to relate to this large group and to communicate actively with them. Equally they are required to draw from this external group an advisory or support committee.

The one constituency which has become increasingly important politically to JICA, which is not mentioned explicitly in the issue team guideline, is the general public. The focus seems to be much more on the need for a sea change in the character of JICA's in-house expertise. But arguably, if aid is to have a clearly visible (Japanese) face, as the axiom runs, then it might have been expected that a number of the KM products would be available and easily accessible to interested members of the public on line.[50]

Indeed, JICA's concern for aid visibility within Japan suggests that the new KM system should also make provision for constituencies such as NGOs and municipalities that are involved in development assistance. This dimension became more important as Government implemented the requirements of greater public disclosure during 2002. This external demand will naturally encompass many of the expert bodies which have been mentioned in this chapter. This has already been anticipated in some of the early thinking about the outside dimension of knowledge sharing in JICA:

> This network-hub will connect knowledgeable and experienced person-
> nel in universities, think-tanks, NGOs, government organisations and
> related institutes to JICA's training programmes. An overseas network
> will also be developed including JICA experts, senior overseas volunteers,

overseas JICA offices, Japanese embassies, and JBIC overseas offices (Kato 2001a: 215).

Certainly, the ambition of the KM designers in JICA has always been to serve these many outer circles of Japanese interest and expertise. But the larger organisational challenge, which began to be faced in these young pilots in the middle of 2002, is how to reform the existing staffing arrangements in ways that would make this possible. The fundamental question is whether there can be such a radical shift towards greater specialisation and sectoral approaches of the kind the issue teams aspire to unless the larger civil service culture of which the KM initiative is a minute part also begins to shift.

But, intriguingly, the promotion of these KM issue teams comes at a time when the Prime Minister is personally promoting a shift in the organisational culture of many public bodies. Thus JICA itself is in the very process of being 'corporatised' and becoming more autonomous as an independent administrative agency. Whether this will encourage it to espouse global trends towards greater staff specialisation is still very much an open question. KM supporters in JICA would be the first to admit that without this wider shake-up of public sector bodies, it would, frankly speaking, be very hard to change the culture of an organisation which believes, like the rest of government, in generalists. But when JICA is indeed reborn into a new agency in October 2003 in line with the 'Koizumi Initiative' on overall public sector re-engineering, the KM initiative could well be given a more solid backbone and become an effective tool for enhancing the cost performance of the organisation.

Knowledge management and knowledge in practice

The first six months of operation of these new KM issue teams was too short a period to allow a judgement as to whether they are breaking new ground in knowledge sharing. The final framework for full-scale implementation of the issue teams had not yet been seen, and the pilots had only just been evaluated; but what can be said is that the existing teams operated according to a rather uniform preliminary framework and detailed set of procedures.[51] Indeed it might be argued that a remarkable amount was achieved by the individuals concerned, but that this is precisely due to the very specificity of the provisional framework, and the detail of the duties to be undertaken by team members. In other words, it might be argued that there has been the beginning of a new way of working – inter-departmentally on sectoral development issues – but that this has been achieved because of the very strength of the rules and procedures in the Japanese bureaucracy. There is, for example, a great deal of reporting and monitoring to be undertaken on each of the persons involved in each of the teams – even during the trial period. This degree of detail on the duties and performance of the development issue teams puts them well towards the most formal end of the knowledge management spectrum – very far from the informality of DFID groups, and much more formal than even the many groups that sprang up in the World Bank in response to the new knowledge initiative.

We reach therefore a provisional but rather paradoxical position on the KM issue teams. They are operating in one of the most work-intensive cultures in the world, where, routinely, both managers and staff stay on in the office for 3–4 hours after the normal end of the working day. Yet they received for this KM initiative a hugely demanding brief of duties and activities in their present guideline, and a high degree of detailed specification on what should be achieved. Moreover, this is only a part-time assignment. This comes close, perhaps, to what one JICA staff member termed 'knowledge integrated in procedures. When staff think of work procedures, it is knowledge expressed in very detailed guidelines.'

This makes the JICA issue teams potentially one of the most structured examples of KM in the agency world, and one of those most concerned with knowledge as codified in guidelines, databases, knowledge-based websites, directories and lists of resource people.[52] By contrast, the comparative advantage of Japan in fifty years of development co-operation, as we saw in the first half of this chapter, has been in knowledge-as-experience, transferred face-to-face, in the paddy field or engineering site. But this has not been straight technology transfer; for success it has depended on two-way learning, strongly self-reliant recipients, and an awareness of the crucial roles of experience, positive attitudes and effort.

Inseparable, therefore, from the issue of the content and structure of the knowledge management system must be this deeper question of how – in the approach of *wakon yosai* [Western knowledge–Japanese spirit] – a knowledge management concept imported from North America may be best adapted to the local culture and more specifically to the Japanese aid philosophy. Those thinking about KM for Japan are already aware that in the Japanese context it is much more common to talk of sharing experience than of sharing knowledge. Just as the very widespread Japanese expert system in developing countries is not just about sharing knowledge on its own but is bound up with a whole package of knowledge, skills and attitudes, and with sharing a discipline of work, and an insight into the Japanese way of thinking about effort and achievement, so the new knowledge management system might also draw upon this Japanese tradition of knowledge-in-practice.[53]

This particularly rich Japanese history of sharing their own development insights might have suggested that JICA could have founded their KM approach more deliberately on very lengthy field experience. This would have incorporated, for the many different sectors where Japan has sought to pass on its own development experience, the core values of that expertise-in-practice. It would have involved starting quite the other way round from the formal KM project, with an understanding of that 'expert learning' in the field setting, the essence of group learning in a self-reliance context, and the further illustration of these core learning values in South–South co-operation.[54] This expert knowledge derived from both Asian and African experiences could have benefited from then being incorporated into some of the mechanisms for knowledge management and knowledge sharing that JICA's KM project is currently exploring.

Indeed it would still be possible for the emerging development issue teams in their many different sectors to tap into these layers of field experience and expertise. Rather than there being the kind of internal–external knowledge-sharing tension that we have noted in the World Bank and DFID, it would be more a question of the centre or the headquarters seeking to capture and synthesise the different traditions of field-based learning.

But there is another set of players that have often remained the poor cousins in centralised agency knowledge management and knowledge-sharing initiatives, and those are the developing-country partners. If JICA is going to make the transition from the collaborative delivery of specialised skills and experience through its experts to the 'joint development of new knowledge' (FASID 1998), then there will need to be some thought given to ways in which the Southern partners can continue to contribute to and gain from the new knowledge based systems. To an extent, some of their needs may be met through other knowledge initiatives to which we shall briefly turn.

Other mechanisms for sharing development knowledge

Two modalities that are very directly involved in the sharing of policy knowledge for development in very different ways are the Japanese hub of the Global Development Network (GDN), and the emerging J-Net, which is a distance learning network which promises to link Japanese knowledge and experience to an expanding number of centres, initially in South-East Asia, and later more widely.

The Japanese regional hub of the GDN

Japan took a strong interest in the potential of the GDN from its origin in 1998 as a World Bank initiative for developing policy think tanks in the different regions of the world. The purpose of the GDN as a whole was to facilitate the bridging of research and policy, particularly in the South. There are accordingly seven regional hubs in the South, and there are now three in the OECD countries (in Germany, USA and Japan). The Japan Bank for International Co-operation's Research Institute for Development and Finance provides the hub of a GDN regional network in Japan. As such it covers 'all the information related to development studies currently existing in Japan' and provides access to search sites of seven major development-related agencies in Japan, including JICA, JBIC, FASID and the Institute for Developing Economies (IDE) (Global Development Network–Japan 2001). The intention of those behind this initiative is to extend the current number of seven sites to include universities with strong collections on development studies.

The aim of the regional hub in Japan, according to the Director General of the JBIC Research Institute, is 'to provide knowledge and development research of Japan to the developing countries'. Its main modality at the moment is the provision of the expanding database of search sites, and linkage to the other regional hubs, as well as information on the research competitions and research-capacity-building activities of the GDN as a whole.[55]

In other words, the focus is very much at the moment on what Japan can offer the developing world in respect of publications and research expertise. Whether it can move from making this one-way offer of research expertise on Japanese knowledge on development towards being a hub that offers a possible site, as did GDNet (see chapters 4 and 5), where both Japanese and Southern partner research might be located will be worth consideration by its designers.

J-Net: knowledge sharing through distance technical co-operation

This initiative, which derives from the G8 Summit in Okinawa in August 2000, plans eventually to provide distance learning through a series of thirty dedicated centres in the South linked to JICA offices that specialise in IT, located in Tokyo and in Okinawa. Initially, centres have come on stream in Malaysia, Indonesia and the Philippines, and in each country these involve the local JICA office as well as another national site.[56] Further satellite centres were opened in Thailand, Vietnam and Laos during 2003. Those who are planning this ambitious project are based within JICA's J-Net department, but one early view of its potential sees that the currently 'under-utilised knowledge of Japanese society could be systematically researched, compiled, and digitised for international co-operation. The capacity of domestic-sector organisations to share their knowledge with foreign counterparts could also be greatly enhanced through this process.' [57]

The first stage of this scheme was operational by the end of April 2002. More than 500 hours of programming for the first half of the twelve months in 2002–3 were completed. Content development and implementation of the programme started in April 2002. Aside from fixed centre-based distance learning, JICA will also develop a substantial volume of web-based training, possibly in conjunction with Canada's CIDA.

One of the paradoxes of Japan is that for a country at the leading edge of IT products and hardware, there is not a great deal of IT awareness in public-sector bodies such as JICA, nor long traditions of distance rather than face-to-face learning in its institutes of higher education. Indeed there is an estimate that only 10 per cent of JICA staff are IT-literate. Hence, an early purpose of J-Net will be to increase IT awareness in JICA itself. A training programme for this purpose has been contracted to the private sector.

There are of course parallels with the World Bank's GDLN. Indeed, J-Net seems to be working closely to make use of GDLN's open platform, on which either WB or other agencies' distance programmes can be provided, so that it can reach out to some thirty other countries in Africa, Latin America and Europe where JICA does not have its own satellite centres.

As to the content of J-Net, there still seems to be a good deal of flexibility about what audiences will take advantage of J-Net for what purpose. Distance technical co-operation is seen as a way of increasing the effectiveness and efficiency of all JICA's existing schemes – such as the sending of experts or the overseas student training programme in Japan.

Unlike GDLN's WBI courses, which are increasingly being offered in the distance mode (see chapter 4), there are presumably language constraints if the medium of J-Net is to be Japanese or even if it has to be English. Nevertheless, the process of codifying and digitising the existing two hundred face-to-face courses for capacity building is actively going ahead.[58] Naturally at this pilot stage, there are currently many more questions being asked than are being answered about J-Net, and there are few detailed sources available on its potential and scope.[59]

But what is intriguing is that, unlike the KM pilot, there is clearly an aspiration to open J-Net to multiple audiences. Thus NGOs are being asked if they would like to provide content; and there are ideas of using

J-Net for development education between Japanese children and children in developing countries. But it is also seen to be a vehicle for closing the gap between expertise in Japan and in recipient countries. On the knowledge front, it allows JICA to make a very strong statement about the potential symmetry offered by J-Net in knowledge acquisition and development, as compared to older approaches:

Sharing and creation of knowledge with developing countries:

The utilisation of IT enables the sharing and creation of skills and knowledge between researchers from Japan and developing countries through cooperation and exchanges on development issues on even terms rather than the traditional top-down basis. (JICA 2001b: 24)

In their own way, therefore, these latest knowledge-sharing projects (the GDN hub and J-Net) cover some of the external dimension of knowledge management which, we noted, is, for the moment, taking a secondary place to the development of the internal aspect of knowledge sharing teams in JICA. Conceptually, it may be possible eventually to integrate these different dimensions, so that GDN, J-Net and the mainstream knowledge management project all become parts of a larger initiative in knowledge sharing.

Conclusion on sharing expertise for development

There can only be the most tentative conclusion, since this chapter was researched at the same time as two of JICA's most explicit knowledge development projects (KM and J-Net) were being started. But hopefully we have said enough to give some sense of the factors that are likely to influence the shape and up-take of these and other associated knowledge initiatives. How the KM initiative may influence a new way of working in JICA is also too early to say, though it was interesting to see the attempt to spread the example of the KM pilots to other departments in advance of JICA attaining its more independent status in October 2003.

One of likeliest provisional conclusions must be that, although there is evidence that JICA's knowledge management project was originally a borrowing from the World Bank, all that is known about Japan's own development path would suggest that KM will be adapted to JICA's and Japan's own traditions and culture. In which case one of the first things likely to change will be its name. An agency that has been so diffident in the past about its claims to 'development knowledge' is going to be happier with a title that stresses 'sharing expertise for development'.

Second, JICA is an agency that continues to regard people rather than policy to be central to its comparative advantage. There will, accordingly, be pressure to ensure, if it does adopt an expertise-for-development project (or whatever knowledge management finally gets called), that this visibly involves and serves a wide range of its own very large number of development actors – in Japan, in developing countries and in 'graduate' countries.

Finally, if Japan is to be true to its faith in the need for new developments to be re-invented, in turn, by its Southern partners, in the spirit of self-help, then it seems likely that, if there is value in this new knowledge initiative, it will need also to be re-engineered in the South. Sawamura puts this last point succinctly:

> Japan is in a position to build unique development knowledge for developing countries. … Japan needs to critically analyse and evaluate Japanese knowledge, along with global knowledge, in collaboration with local people and their local knowledge. An inter-learning approach is a Japanese tradition in providing aid. It is vital to create knowledge that is owned by the recipient country. … The Japanese aid approach is supposed to be one of collaborative knowledge production, and not simply one which applies globally distributed knowledge, or simply transplants Japanese knowledge to foreign soil. (Sawamura 2002: 346)

Notes

1. There is little tradition of the Japanese public sector learning from its own private sector.

2. Neither the English nor the Japanese version of the website carries information on 'knowledge projects'; nor is there any information readily available on the intranet of JICA. This is certain to change as the knowledge management pilot projects (see below) become more established.

3. The website's home page in English lists the main schemes such as technical training programme, dispatch of experts and provision of equipment, and thus directly parallels accounts of JICA activities in other media. See for example, JICA's *Annual Report 2001*.

4. Nishigaki and Shimomura (1996: 142) make a similar point: 'The second significance is Japan's unique history as a donor country that has experienced for itself the hardship and humiliation of being on the receiving end of aid.'

5. Typical of this tendency in aid thinking would be the following from an Annual Report of Japan's ODA by the Ministry of Foreign Affairs (MOFA): 'Support of self-help efforts: This reflects the belief in Japan that true development, with economic independence, can be achieved only when a recipient country promotes development strategies through its own self-help efforts. This is a line of thinking derived from Japan's own development experience after World War II and from its experience in giving development assistance to East

Asian countries, an idea Japan had advocated before Western donor countries' (MOFA, 1995: 45)

6. The importance of this view of itself as understanding both donor and recipient roles is present in one of the main pages of the JICA website: 'Whilst receiving aid itself in the 1950s from the World Bank for the reconstruction of its own economy, Japan began the process of delivering aid to developing countries' (JICA 2002a). See also Shinsuke Horiuchi, special adviser to the Foreign Minister, at the Johannesburg World Summit on Sustainable Development in 2002: 'Japan entered the aid arena assuming to be an equal partner' quoted in the draft speech for JICA workshop on 'Why South–South co-operation now?' August 2002.

7. Nishigaki and Shimomura (1996: 155) comment: ' ... we believe that ... the spirit of self-help ... can be seen to have been a pervasive element in Japan's subsequent economic development and that it has also had an enormous, if largely unconscious, influence on our aid philosophy. In that sense, Japan's aid philosophy with its emphasis on self-help efforts can be said to be deeply rooted in Japanese history.'

8. The whole episode is discussed by Keiichi Kato, the former Director of the JICA Institute for International Cooperation (IFIC) as recently as 2001 in an article on 'Knowledge perspectives in JICA': 'Together with foreigners, efforts were made for economic development and the modernisation of Japan with the joint co-operation of the public and private sector' (Kato 2001a: 206).

9. The emotions and controversy surrounding the promotion of missions by the Jesuits in the sixteenth century are powerfully captured by Endo Shusaku in *Silence*, 1969, Tuttle Publishing.

10. The involvement of so many players in ODA may have its origins in the fact that no less than eleven ministries were originally involved in war reparations and economic co-operation.

11. A valuable insight into Japan's system of official development assistance, written from outside, is Baudry-Somcynsky and Cook (1999). The practice of line ministries seconding their staff to JICA has been shifting over the years, from a time when as many as 50 per cent of JICA staff (and all directors of JICA departments) were seconded, to a much smaller and decreasing proportion now.

12. A discussion of the work of senior advisors (development specialists) is contained within the published description of IFIC (2001). Interestingly, this talks of 'their expertise and experience regarding development co-operation', not of their knowledge.

13. These study committees, though organised and often led by JICA's sectoral experts, usually publish with a disclaimer that they do not necessarily reflect the views of JICA.

14. For example, the two generalists who were primarily responsible for introducing JICA's knowledge management scheme during their time in planning and evaluation in headquarters were both moved to very different positions in mid-2002.

15. The notion of JICA versus MOFA policy is further complicated by the fact that the thirteen-strong board of JICA was initially composed entirely of

non-JICA secondees; and even now no less than ten of the thirteen members are ex-officials of other ministries.

16. The two ministries most closely involved in sending long-term experts through JICA are economy, trade and industry (METI) and agriculture, forestry and fisheries (MAFF).

17. In addition to the use of senior advisers (development specialists), JICA also draws upon expertise from a significant number of associate experts or specialists – who spend one year in JICA HQ and two years overseas. The number in this category (98) are not very different from the senior advisers, but one of them has suggested that the associate experts are in some sense the 'foot soldiers' of Japan's development assistance, implying that this is an important category.

18. According to the latest OECD DAC report, Japan is second only to the USA in the size of its technical co-operation spending (OCDE 2002: 49). We shall note shortly that the calculation of ODA on technical co-operation is notoriously uncertain across agencies.

19. Under JICA activities, one click from JICA's home page, there are descriptions of Technical Training, Dispatch of Experts, Provision of Equipment, Project-Type Technical Co-operation, Dispatch of JOCVs and Development Studies, all of which emphasise Japanese expertise and experience (JICA.go.jp/english/about/index.html downloaded on 27 June 2002).

20. For further discussions see Ruggles 2001.

21. For more detail, see JICA Annual Report 2000a (123–38).

22. For more detail, see JICA Annual Report 2000a (20–22).

23. Of the experts recruited and despatched in 2001, only 3 per cent came from the private commercial sector. It would be interesting to know whether the fact that a very substantial number of Japanese experts come from the public sector and are already on salary may result in the reported budget for Japan's technical assistance appearing to be much smaller than countries where experts are primarily recruited from consulting companies and the private sector.

24. For more detail, see JICA 2000a: 14–16.

25. Volunteering remains very popular in Japan, with over 8,000 applying for the 1,250 positions in 2000.

26. For more detail, see JICA 2000a: 129–32.

27. In addition to JICA's evaluations, there are separate evaluations carried out by the economic co-operation bureau in MOFA, and by the Japan Bank for International Co-operation (JBIC). See, for instance, Ministry for Foreign Affairs Japan, 2000.

28. There seems to be little of DFID's current interest in untying aid in JICA's promotion of Japanese comparative advantage: 'One of the features of JICA's operations is that aid with "a clearly visible profile" is positioned through the activities of JICA experts and Japan Overseas Cooperation Volunteers (JOCV), at the centre of its programmes' (JICA 2001b: 39).

29. In the case of several OECD donors, the end of the Cold War led to the end of the East–West competition to offer training places abroad to developing countries.

30. JICA highlighted this modality in its presentation in the WSSD, Johannesburg.

31. JICA's home page has traditionally noted the total numbers of personnel in different expert, trainee and volunteer categories.

32. JICA's Annual Report 2000 is a good illustration of 'aid with a Japanese face', as the very large bulk of the many photographs are of Japanese experts, volunteers and teachers working with partners in the developing world.

33. On the JICA website, under the scheme, 'Dispatch of Technical Co-operation Experts' this visibility of experts is clearly reinforced: 'These experts are sent to virtually every country in the developing world. In particular, "aid with a clearly visible profile" can be provided efficiently by Japanese experts working as advisers at the heart of government in the recipient country. It is stressed by former JICA president, Fujita, however, that Japan must not fall into the bad habits of the Western expatriate advisers who work at the heart of government.'

34. Stein has argued that one of the most important springs to the differentiation over aid approaches was Japan's readiness to take a more critical stand in its bilateral relations with the United States.

35. There is evidence, in JICA's 2001 Annual Report, of JICA exploring sector programming, but this is still being conceptualised as using all the traditional tools of Japanese ODA (JICA 2001b: 30–32).

36. Hence the few attempts at exploring education policy have been executed in the time-honoured manner of IFIC committees largely dependent on external expertise but with one or two senior advisers taking a lead role. See, for example, JICA 1994.

37. Thus for the global issue environment it is noted that in 1997 there were 1,572 overseas trainees in that field, 309 JICA experts dispatched, 80 cases of PTTC, 85 JOCVs dispatched, and 115 development studies. The rest of the fold-out pamphlet is taken up with examples of how environment is handled in various modalities, drawn from case studies.

38. There are apparently very large numbers of hits on the JICA website for some of these reports.

39. In fact, it was commissioned by MOFA to FASID in October 1997 in a desire to explore the latest international thinking about development issues. FASID, an institute supported by MOFA, was already aware of the emerging knowledge interests in the World Bank, but chose to focus the study around developments in selected bilaterals.

40. Koichi Miyoshi was based in Washington from 1995 to 1998. His colleague in Evaluation and Planning, Masaei Matsunaga, visited the World Bank during this period. They have both played key roles in the development of the Knowledge Management project in JICA.

41. Keiichi Kato has suggested the content of a knowledge-based website as follows: 'A Knowledge-based Web site consisting of general information on development issues, guide lines for 61 sectors and issues, business records on JICA operations, case studies of JICA and other donor countries, examples for JICA of operational documents, project design matrix, project instruction document,

directory for related personnel and organisations, and directory for reference materials, books and reports' (Kato 2001: 215). Given the sheer quantity of expert assignments and of development and basic studies, web-based provision of material that would expedite such contracts would clearly be valuable.

42. The informal networks which are at the basis of KM in many different organisations, such as DFID, are severally termed communities of practice, thematic groups, knowledge networks and so on. In JICA, the pilot groups are currently called development issue teams.

43. It should be remembered that, because of the rotation system, almost none of the JICA staff are full-time specialists like the ninety senior advisors in any sector such as health, governance, education and so on.

44. For instance the Education 'Development Issue' team is led by a secondee from the Ministry of Education and Science, has one senior adviser from IFIC, and a small number of other JICA staff based in headquarters, as well as one person from a JICA office elsewhere in Japan.

45. With the benefit of hindsight, global issues can be seen as a precursor of the concept of the cross-cutting issue; there is already evidence of the global issues being in part incorporated by the new series of development issues.

46. One of the core staff in JICA's KM development has reflected on how JICA staff in the field can be at a disadvantage when working in co-ordination with the sector specialists of the other aid agencies, since the JICA staff typically can't bring a strong sector specialism to the table.

47. For example, the education development issue team has taken over the work on basic education that was already well developed in IFIC.

48. The relationship between the number of issue teams and the number of guidelines suggests that teams will develop more than one set of guidelines. Thus already there are some 23 guidelines completed but there are only some 9 teams formed.

49. Some work on synthesising was done in the case of the global issues, but, as was mentioned earlier, this did not constitute much more than illustrating aspects of how that particular theme appeared under the different existing schemes of JICA.

50. There is a suggestion that the KM system may be partly open to the public in 2003.

51. This is not to say that the groups all march in step; some move ahead faster than others. Nor is it the case that the creation of new groups is straightforward. Rather, the initiating department has to struggle to extend the KM idea to new departments.

52. At the moment, however, the principal activities are developing sector-specific guidelines, and conducting a number of seminars.

53. The JICA President , Takao Kawakami (2002), has expressed the essence of Japanese co-operation as follows: 'Particularly important in the area of economic and technical co-operation … is the "people-to-people" aspect of co-operation; in other words, "heart-to-heart" contact between the people involved on both sides.'

54. An example of the attempt to synthesise Japan's experience in a single

sub-sector, science and maths education, is to be found in Nagao (2001) 'Can Japan be a good maths and science teacher for Africa?'. JICA's presentations in the Johannesburg summit 2002 also seek to capture this particular comparative advantage.

55. Interestingly, on the key home pages of GDN, there is no mention of either the regional hub in Japan nor its counterpart for Europe in Bonn (www.gdnet.org/subpages/community.html, downloaded 23 March 2002).

56. In Indonesia, the second site is in the Indonesia Export Training Centre, for instance.

57. Interview with Masaei Matsunaga, Planning and Education Department, JICA, Tokyo, 13 December 2001.

58. Interestingly, Matsunaga, one of the key champions of the knowledge management system in JICA, has been moved to take charge of getting the traditional face-to-face programmes on to J-Net.

59. Even JICA–IFIC's report, *The information revolution in development assistance*, has only two paragraphs on J-Net (JICA 2001a). See, however, JICA's newsletter *Frontier* 2002, which carries an upbeat article on J-Net. Also the range of possibilities outlined by the 2001 Annual Report (JICA 2001b).

EIGHT

Conclusions and implications for knowledge, aid and development

At the start of this book we set out to understand better the nature of knowledge-based aid and its broader significance for agency practices, for knowledge systems globally, and for broader policies, practices and theories of aid and development. In the past four chapters, we have sought to develop our analysis through an exploration of four very different development co-operation agencies. It is time now to see what that analysis amounts to.

Where does knowledge-based aid come from, and is it just a passing fashion?

In chapters 2 and 3, we explored the origins of knowledge-based aid. We argued that knowledge-based aid is only a small element of the broader changes that have taken place in aid since 1990. The 1990s were the decade of the 'world conference', with its attempts to generate global agreements on issues such as social and sustainable development, education for all and women's rights. The resolutions of these conferences were selectively presented anew by the Development Assistance Committee (DAC) of the OECD, to form the six International Development Targets. More generally, the rise of the significance of the DAC was an element in a broader shift of power away from the United Nations and towards organisations more explicitly and effectively dominated by the countries of the North (Mundy 1998). The emergence of the European Union, the World Trade Organisation and the G8 as important players in development were also part of this trend. At the same time, a new architecture of donor co-ordination mechanisms emerged, whilst the end of the Cold War and the abandonment of much of the tradition of social democracy in a number of European countries have furthered a broader ideological convergence of agencies, notwithstanding some of the divergence we have pointed to in previous chapters. Aid has become even more policy oriented. Older fashions of a primary focus on poverty and of sector programmes have been reinvented and revised. The naked use of conditionalities has been replaced (though far from completely) by a greater emphasis on national ownership of development and policy dialogue between donors, governments and civil society. The Poverty Reduction Strategy Paper has become the primary locus for such dialogue. Whilst much of the change may appear highly cosmetic from the standpoint of those on the receiving end, there has been considerable impact on the internal workings of aid.

Importantly, the new overall way of working in aid brings with it new knowledge needs. These are intimately connected to the way that ICTs are shaping working practices in agencies, although they go beyond this. At the same time, the new aid agenda brings with it a new importance for knowledge as a major theme of development and co-operation. Mirroring the existing literature on economic success in the North, a new account of knowledge for development has emerged, most notably connected to the World Bank's *World Development Report 1998–99* (World Bank 1998a). Again led by the World Bank, agencies have also begun to draw upon the experiences of large corporations in pursuing the more efficient and effective management of their knowledge resources. Such an interest from agencies also clearly draws upon their own concerns about effectiveness, the wider critique of the performance of aid, and concerns about aid fatigue amongst Northern electorates. Through the interweaving of these accounts in a literature and practice of knowledge management, agencies have begun to look at internal patterns of knowledge use as a central element of responses to the critique of their effectiveness. At the external level, the notion of knowledge sharing has become attractive as a way of distancing agencies from the widespread critique of conditionalities, whilst at the same time seeking to ensure that agency positions have influence over national policies. For some in agencies, the external sharing agenda promises more, pointing to the possibilities for organisational transformation and a genuine repositioning of the power balance between Northern agencies and Southern partners.

Aid is full of passing fashions and of pendulum swings amongst them. It is possible that knowledge-based aid is simply another such fashion. Certainly, it faces considerable opposition within and outside the aid community. Given that one of its most powerful sources of impetus came from Wolfensohn's strategy for reforming the World Bank, and that Bank presidents have a habit of downplaying their predecessors' big ideas in favour of new ones, it is likely to have less direct championing from the very top of the aid business when Wolfensohn's reign ends in 2005.

Does knowledge-based aid work?

In providing a summary analysis of knowledge-based aid we shall begin by taking it on its own terms. That is to say, we shall examine it whilst assuming that it is a worthwhile and genuine attempt to improve aid. We shall turn later to more fundamental questions about the whole aid project.

We have outlined some of the key factors in the development of knowledge-based aid. A widely understood set of new tools has emerged for both internal and external aspects of knowledge-based aid. Internally, communities of practice, help desks, intranets, and improved spaces for informal knowledge sharing are all elements of the standard agency and corporate repertoires. Externally there is more diversity, although research co-operation, support to networks and portals, improved Southern connectivity, and e-learning are some of the more popular responses.

Different agencies draw upon the internal and external tool kits in different ways. Some of this seems to reflect little more than the personal interests of innovators within the agencies. However, there are also signs that political or ideological factors can make a difference. For Sida, long-term support to higher education systems in the South is seen as an essential element of solidarity; for DFID, an ideological certainty about the need to focus tightly on primary education for poverty reduction has meant reluctance to follow such a path, even as it becomes more fashionable. However, it is also noteworthy that the tools chosen and the ways in which they are interpreted do not always seem to reflect national cultural contexts in a simplistic way.

Variations within agencies in attitudes and approaches to knowledge-based aid are often more pronounced than variations across them. A wide range of departments are typically found to be engaged in the field of knowledge management and sharing. Whilst it is impossible simply to read off their responses from their institutional positions, they do tend towards reflections of their own departmental concerns.

Information Technology departments appear to favour a model of knowledge management that is close to their technology function and which prioritises the role of databases, software and infrastructure. Moreover, in some cases, it appears that the growing sophistication of software leads to a reduced role for technical support staff in the process of sharing knowledge. Thus, it is possible that IT departments can come to feel threatened by certain approaches to knowledge sharing. Libraries are also potentially threatened by the growth of digitised forms of data and information. Indeed, DFID is one example of an agency that has effectively ended its traditional library work in favour of new digital forms. However, digitisation can provide new opportunities for the empowerment of documentalists and their transformation into information (and perhaps knowledge) brokers. This possibility, and its emergence in one non-agency case study, is outlined in a paper by Box, former director of the European Centre for Development Policy Management (Box 2001).

Human Resources staff are also involved through the growing relationship between knowledge and learning activities. In some agencies, such as the World Bank, the role of chief learning officer has been created. In Sida, we have seen how the director of organisational learning stresses the role of her unit in supporting processes of tacit knowledge development and sharing. The articulation between learning and knowledge activities is just beginning to become more evident in DFID and JICA.

Information and Communications departments have seen radical changes in both their internal information management responsibilities and their external communications work. In all of our cases, this work has been further affected by trends towards greater transparency, including compliance with new Freedom of Information legislation, in the cases of DFID and JICA, but also by a strong culture of 'spin' in DFID (reflecting the British government as a whole) and the World Bank.

Evaluation departments are challenged by the new knowledge and learning emphases to reconsider how they conduct evaluations (including how they include partners and their knowledge), how they share their findings and how they maximise the impact of their work.

Externally oriented training programmes are no longer present across all agencies. However, where they do exist, the knowledge and ICT agendas combine, as in JICA, to bring new dynamics. The growing emphasis on context is reflected in programmes that seek to use the existing knowledge of participants far more than was historically the case. However, more visibly, the principal change is towards electronically based distance learning. Perversely, this may in fact contradict the contextual emphasis noted above in favour of the spread of more 'canned knowledge' (Coraggio 2001).

Sectoral professional departments are impacted upon in the way that research comes to be seen as knowledge production. At the same time, professional staff have often relied on their own individual networks of professional contacts for knowledge sharing. With the pressures of the new aid way of working, most especially inter-sectorality, they are increasingly engaging in new communities of practice, and clearly have new knowledge and skill needs.

At the level of country and regional offices, problems of distance from headquarters and limited connectivity are often common. Nonetheless, there appears to be a growth in engagement with the agency-at-large through communities of practice and other elements of electronic working. Sector programmes and PRSPs are encouraging greater cross-agency co-ordination at the national level. However, there are serious questions about whether the maintenance of positions is still more important than the sharing of knowledge.

Different departments have distinct traditions even within groupings such as the sectoral and regional departments. In regional departments, this often relates to the history of working with particular geographical regions and the relationships that have emerged. In the cases of both JICA and Sida, it is possible to see the relationship with Africa as different from that with Asia. The emergence of Eastern Europe as a recipient region has also had significant impacts within agencies, given the range of unique features of this region as compared to more traditional areas of focus. In sectoral departments, attitudes towards knowledge and its sharing can relate strongly to disciplinary traditions (for instance, between economics and anthropology).

Knowledge-based aid can be seen as having an internal and an external dimension. In this analysis of its early performance we shall take each of these in turn.

Internal knowledge-based aid

The overall impact of knowledge-based aid on agency staff is difficult to establish, even in the World Bank, where it formed a central plank of Wolfensohn's professed strategy for reform. Six years on, much of the rhetoric of the knowledge bank is about the need to impact upon the Bank's operational work in a more profound way. In the other agencies under scrutiny, awareness, let alone impact, is often more difficult to find.

Whilst the direct impact of knowledge projects on everyday agency practices needs to be treated with caution, it is apparent that these practices have undergone some major changes since the mid-1990s. The spread of electronic working and networking, the practical implications of the new development co-operation, and the rise of electronic and open government projects have combined to change the way that agency staff operate and co-operate. A series of new structures to support knowledge working have emerged. Although in very different ways and to differing extents, communities of practice have been supported. Agency intranets have improved greatly and are being used more as a result. Connectivity of country offices has begun to improve markedly, although the bilaterals lag behind World Bank offices in this regard. Seminar programmes have increased greatly across agencies in recent years and have become more inter-disciplinary. The new DFID headquarters is a clear reflection of a heightened awareness of the importance of spaces for knowledge sharing, an awareness that was built into the architecture of the Sida and World Bank headquarters before the idea of knowledge-based aid was invented. This of course points to an important health warning about analysing knowledge-based aid. Much of what is positive about it at the practical end already existed within agencies and has simply had a knowledge 'flag' attached after the event. Nonetheless, there is enough evidence to suggest that knowledge use in agencies has become more efficient than previously.

However, it is clear from our interviews that knowledge-based approaches have had a small, though real, impact on the everyday activities of most agency staff. What has taken root is typically the ICT-based new tools of e-mail and intranet, rather than the full range of new approaches, let alone a new philosophy.

Indeed, there appears to be a range of serious problems with the internal dimension of knowledge-based aid that highlights confusions of purpose and operationalisation. We have noted the important role that the ICT revolution has played in the impetus towards knowledge-based aid. However, with this has come a strong technological bias, particularly where, as was common, IT departments became lead units in promoting knowledge strategies. Conversely, it has become clear that much of what is successful in knowledge sharing is dependent on the quality of interactions between people and the knowledge that they bring. There remains a tension in much knowledge sharing between these human and technological elements. Sida has tended to overstress the former and DFID, until recently, the latter. The danger of seduction by technology is also present in agency e-learning strategies. It remains debatable whether increased quantities of learners are also receiving an improved quality of learning experience. Whilst pointing to this technological bias, however, it is important to note that both DFID and the World Bank appear to illustrate a tendency for approaches to become less technologically driven over time. Whether there is any general law of the development of knowledge-based aid operating here is unclear.

Alongside a bias towards technology has often lain a confusion about what is being shared. There has often been too much focus on data and not enough on knowledge. This is significant in a number of ways. First, the economic argument is for knowledge use, not data management, as the critical factor in the success of individuals, firms and economies. Second, a data-based approach tends to assume that facts and figures are what constitute development, and that development is technical and universal in its tools and approaches. Third, the downplaying of knowledge is also a downplaying of the importance of experience and interpretation. Each of these trends is, however, subject to countervailing forces.

Much of the knowledge literature stresses the central importance of tacit knowledge, but it appears that this can lead to two very different conclusions. On the one hand, it can imply the need to support mechanisms that allow staff to share their tacit knowledge with others in ways that stress the human interaction at the heart of the knowledge sharing. This can be illustrated by elements of Sida's organisational learning approach, such as mentoring and the deliberate use of mixed-age mission teams. On the other hand, it can lead to the conclusion that as much tacit knowledge as possible should be captured and codified. This is illustrated in an apparent belief in DFID that all the relevant knowledge about a project can be distilled into short, standardised project data sheets.

Moreover, the expansion of document production, linked as it is to the broader new development co-operation, has seen a shift towards a far greater emphasis on highly aggregated analysis and on policy. It may be argued that agencies are now too policy focused. The emphasis on policy, and on staff with policy capabilities, appears to cut across the language of better understanding of country contexts. Moreover, it is based in a simplistic model of the relationship between policy and practice that seems to have been little influenced by forty years of policy theory (for example, Hirschman and Lindblom 1969 [1962]; Lindblom 1968; Kingdon 1995; Page 2000).

Questions of whose knowledge gets shared are important on a number of levels. Internally within agencies, there are a series of tensions in this regard. This is most sharply drawn in JICA, owing to the different status of specialist contractors and generalist staff. However, there remain serious gaps between headquarters and field offices and between national and local staff across many bilateral agencies. Whose knowledge gets shared within agencies also depends strongly on internal agency views of what constitutes important knowledge. Agencies have tended to privilege quantitative, scientific and economic knowledge over other forms, and these biases have not fully been overcome. Yet, other forms of knowledge are central to the success of development activities. Agency knowledge systems remain poor at dealing with complexity and with conflicting interpretations. Moreover, there is a likelihood that Northern and agency sources of knowledge will be privileged at the expense of alternative accounts. There is a danger too that codification will privilege universal over contextual accounts. This may happen also as agencies move from face-to-face towards distance learning.

This issue of the tension between universal, theory-based accounts and contextual, experientially based ones is significant. During the 1990s, the World Bank often used the notion of 'learning from experience' to justify its policy prescriptions. In reality, this largely amounted to a highly partial presentation of country-level evidence to support an already theoretically or ideologically derived position. This use of country-level data continues in the present. However, there does appear to be a genuine sense in some of the World Bank's communities of practice that there should be a redressing of the balance between universal theory, lessons from comparative experience, and the particular context of the country in question. What headway such a position can make against the bureaucratic tendency towards standardisation and routinisation is not clear. This is a point we shall return to on a number of occasions in this chapter.

Internal knowledge sharing is designed in part to answer the challenges brought to agencies by increased decentralisation. However, it is clear that the bilateral agencies examined in this book are still facing challenges in this area. Even where connectivity is good, there is evidence that staff in country offices often feel remote from decision-making at agency headquarters. Moreover, there are concerns in each of the bilaterals that not enough is being done to draw upon the rich contextual knowledge of their nationally appointed staff.

There are also similar unresolved tensions over the extent to which knowledge sharing should be managed as opposed to facilitated. DFID's approach to communities of practice stresses the informal nature of knowledge sharing and seeks to do little to interfere with its operation. However, JICA's approach is to stress the importance of sharing knowledge well and to seek to achieve this through formal structures and management. It is probable that there are merits in a position in which informal knowledge sharing is encouraged and the quality and quantity of learning significantly enhanced. However, there is no sense from our case study agencies of anything resembling good practice on how to do this.

Incentives for knowledge sharing have not developed very far to date. Many agency staff believe that knowledge sharing will never really be more important than disbursement. This tends to limit the credibility of any appraisal and rewards system that seeks to take account of good practice in knowledge sharing. Moreover, staff appear widely to see knowledge sharing as more work even where they are personally enthusiastic about its potential to be a model for better work.

There is a widespread sense across our agencies and others of a tension between a learning and a lending culture (for example, Bergmann 2001; Denning 2001). Even in Sida we heard comments about the perception that it was disbursement not knowledge sharing that was the route to promotion. Whilst the World Bank is beginning to talk of non-lending activities (see chapter 4), the majority of agency staff need to show their effectiveness by getting projects and programmes approved, moneys disbursed, and successes claimed. All this emphasis on product cuts across issues of process. Working with partners and being aware of the range of opinions on a project often make little sense to overworked and ambitious agency officials.

At the heart of the challenge for internal knowledge sharing in agencies lies the question whether it can successfully support and promote a change in organisational cultures. Whilst it is clear that much of the support for internal knowledge sharing is pragmatic (or even cynical), it is equally apparent that some staff, such as Denning and many of his network of knowledge evangelists in the World Bank, have been attracted to knowledge approaches precisely because they offer the potential of transforming the organisation.

Rather than attempt a futile confrontation with the way that the Bank operates, they have sought to convince managers and staff that knowledge sharing means smarter work rather than more work, assuming that a change in practice will inevitably lead to a change in organisational culture. Our evidence suggests that there are staff (and some managers) who are ready to believe this message, but that they are also often of the opinion that this has not yet come to pass. However, our evidence, and evidence from agencies' own self-appraisal, is that there are considerable organisational barriers to the transformation sought. It is argued, and correctly, that not enough has been done to provide incentives for knowledge sharing. However, the challenges are greater than this and go to the heart of organisational cultures. Bilateral agencies remain parts of government bureaucracies in which internal and external politics are often of far more importance than development or knowledge sharing. The far larger World Bank is probably more bureaucratic than any bilateral agency, notwithstanding its long-established antipathy to national bureaucracies. So the attempt to change organisational cultures by changing knowledge practices may well fail because those organisational cultures are so resistant to change. The potential of knowledge-based aid to transform aid and aid organisations is one to which we shall return at a number of points later in this chapter, as it is central to a critical reading of the merits and demerits of the whole approach.

External knowledge-based aid

There are some positive examples of agency support to external knowledge sharing through on-line communities and websites. DFID in particular appears to have been relatively successful in this field in spite of its apparently having never been explicitly prioritised at senior level.

The projects that DFID has supported have developed considerable levels of knowledge sharing between individuals and organisations in both the North and the South in a multidirectional way. Part of the success of such initiatives may well lie in the way that DFID has remained at arm's length from these projects. They have developed their own governance and ways of working as supported projects without having to brave the politics of being DFID-owned or managed.

In DFID too, research agendas have shifted from a bias towards problems identified and projects led by UK-based academics to notions of partnership with, and even leadership from, the South. Moreover, the emphasis has moved, from traditional academic approaches to proposal design, project delivery and findings dissemination, to more fluid and outcomes-focused approaches that stress the application of the knowledge and the multiple possibilities for knowledge sharing.

However, much of the cross-agency attention to Southern knowledge capacity remains very tightly focused on development issues, often simply on better project implementation. Nonetheless, in the Swedish concern for wider issues of support to Southern knowledge systems, Japan's large-scale commitment to long-term institutional partnerships and freeing up of its own university system, and the World Bank's 're-discovery' of higher education, there are signs of hope for broader and deeper support to Southern knowledge capacity. The strong focus of JICA and Sida on long-term and resource-intensive support to selected Southern knowledge partners raises the question of whether DFID and the World Bank's greater interest in networks can succeed in the longer term without strong institutions or on-going institutional support.

It is apparent that much of what is successful in external knowledge sharing has come about not because of an explicit corporate strategy to promote such sharing. The lack of explicit organisational structures to promote such sharing has not stopped it occurring, as is evident, for instance, in the range of DFID activities to support knowledge networks. Equally, there is much external knowledge sharing that went on long before the term was invented. It is difficult, therefore, to assess the ideal degree of structure that should be given to external knowledge sharing activities. Moreover, it is important to note that part of the success of the external sharing work that DFID has done is that it has allowed editorial freedom to the projects it is supporting. Thus, there is a clear distinction (although an implicit one) between DFID's very strong emphasis on getting its development messages across through its own work and its willingness to support other accounts through its support to projects such as id21. This could be seen as being a serious tension, although it may be one that DFID is wise to live with. Critics have worried that the Development Gateway will lack such freedom, but it may be that these fears are exaggerated in practice as more of the editorial work migrates outside the Bank, albeit largely to orthodox development organisations.

Some general comments on knowledge-based aid

The current internal bias in knowledge-based aid is justified by project managers and some senior champions as being necessary to build a foundation for a new approach that will eventually be more external than internal in orientation. This appears broadly to have been the path followed by the World Bank. However, this argument is open to question. Instead, it can be argued that the internal focus is indicative of an unwillingness in agencies at the broader organisational level to address more fundamental issues about the global knowledge system.

The knowledge revolution in agencies remains largely a series of uncoordinated projects that are being implemented without any real overall vision or strategy. Indeed, it is important to consider what are the alleged benefits of knowledge-based aid. Much of what we point to in this book as positive has been achieved without it being part of an explicit knowledge strategy and without any considerable new knowledge-based expenditure. It is not self-evident that more planning or more expenditure on knowledge sharing would have clear and unambiguous benefits.

At the same time, there is a real tension between incrementalism and mega-projects in the internal and external knowledge-sharing domains of knowledge-based aid. This issue needs to be better linked to an understanding of the nature of organisational change. The review within the World Bank of all knowledge activities most clearly shows the tension that exists between an encouragement of innovation and a fear of duplication. This is also closely related to the overall organisational theory-in-use: whether innovation and complexity or routinisation and bureaucratic structures are the dominant model. Those who claim that knowledge-based aid can revolutionise aid and attune it more to national contexts and ownership are not generally simply 'masters of illusion', as Caufield (1996) dubbed the World Bank, with its penchant for spin. However, there is simply not enough evidence to suggest that any attempt to transform the nature of aid agencies and aid itself is likely to succeed.

Knowledge-based aid is still a very new concept. Denning (2001), as one of its leading architects, has cautioned against the pressure to evaluate too early and about the difficulty of such evaluation. Nonetheless, it is inevitable that knowledge-based aid will be subject to the same forces of evaluation as the rest of aid, as seen in the 2002 World Bank evaluation of its knowledge activities. At present, the evidence for its impact is largely couched in quantitative terms, such as numbers of communities of practice, website hits, and so on. To be meaningful, these will have to be broadened to address the far more challenging and pertinent issues of how far knowledge-based aid has changed the everyday practices of agencies and, most importantly, how it has impacted directly on the lives of the millions of poor people in the South who are the intended beneficiaries of aid. As with many other elements of aid, empirical evidence for such impacts will be difficult to produce.

Adding in learning and capacity

Across our agency chapters, a sense has emerged that the language of knowledge-based aid is increasingly becoming interlinked to notions of learning and capacity. As we suggested in chapter 6, the choice of Sida as one of the case study agencies has been particularly valuable for highlighting the significance of the gap between the ways that knowledge and learning are thought of and acted upon in the development context.

There has been an apparent convergence in language between Sida and the World Bank since late 2001. The same tendency was becoming evident in DFID in 2002. In the case of Sida, we have discussed how there is a growing interaction between the activities of different strands of its work, which have taken the concepts of knowledge, learning and capacity largely in isolation from each other. On that of the World Bank, the presentation to the Board of the Ramphele review of knowledge activities in late 2001 led to a new degree of emphasis on the importance of learning and capacity as part of a broader knowledge strategy.

Whilst there are a range of Sida texts that highlight the importance of knowledge, stretching back for more than a decade, Sida largely has not adopted knowledge management techniques. Instead, there is wide suspicion regarding the assumptions of much of knowledge-based aid, and a strong preference for talking about learning, which points towards a practice that is more about knowledge construction than knowledge dissemination. Moreover, taken together with Sida's discourse of partnership and of capacity development, a positive focus emerges on mutual learning that is led by the South and facilitated by Sida and other Swedish partners. This view of a mutual construction of knowledge is reflected also in Sida's research co-operation strategy since the incorporation of SAREC.

There is a danger in the knowledge-based approach: that it assumes that technology is the principal answer to development problems and thus fails to address the serious organisational blockages to learning that some of the reflections of Sida staff so clearly address. Moreover, as we have noted already, there is a similar possibility that knowledge- and ICT-oriented strategies for supporting networks fail to address the importance of individuals and institutions in building capacity. Here the Swedish emphasis on twinning may serve as an important counterweight to some of the knowledge-based strategies for capacity development. Whilst the Japanese have received considerable criticism within the aid community for their resistance to untying technical assistance, it can be argued that the Japanese insistence on long-term personal relation- ships as the heart of knowledge sharing, mutual learning and capacity development is a sound perspective.

The knowledge-based aid debate can potentially benefit from the heightened attention given to capacity at the moment. We showed in chapter 6 how Sida was powerfully re-emphasising its long-standing com- mitment to capacity development that seeks to build on what countries already have capacity to do, emphasises the role of mutual learning, and highlights the centrality of people, attitudes and relationships. While the World Bank's revisiting of the notion of capacity does talk of enhance- ment of existing capacity, there is little sign of the broader attitudinal imperative suggested by Sida. Instead, the model of the aloof technical expert appears to be alive and well, although questioned by some Bank staff.

The growing emphasis on staff learning, as defined by Human Resources departments, has not yet been adequately articulated with internal knowledge-sharing strategies. Here as elsewhere, it appears that knowledge-based aid approaches have not sufficiently engaged with what has already been going on in agencies. Instead, their promoters often appear to be more mindful of what the corporate sector is doing than what is going on within their own organisations.

Knowledge-based aid or learning-led development?

In chapter 4, we looked at the debate about the transformatory pos- sibilities of knowledge-based aid through the different perspectives of Steve Denning and David Ellerman, two prominent figures in the first six years of the knowledge bank. The World Bank is perhaps different from other agencies as a result of its status and size. However, it is clear that much of the Denning and Ellerman accounts has resonance for the broader discussion here. What they both very valuably do is take us into the heart of the issue about knowledge-based aid. Their disagreement about the likelihood of transformation of aid and aid agencies through knowledge approaches is crucial. Whilst it does seem reasonable to argue that there are tendencies towards some of the positive changes that Denning is highlighting, we find it difficult to share his optimism about the transformatory potential of knowledge-based aid. Instead, we favour Ellerman's argument that the fundamental nature of aid bureaucracies and the aid mentality make radical transformation unlikely.

They also provide useful insights for the more pragmatic debate about how aid can be improved (if it is to continue in something like its current overall form). Denning points to the positive impact that new ways of using knowledge can have within an agency and, hence, in relationships with others. However, Ellerman usefully extends this by further emphasising the importance of learning over knowledge transfer and, more importantly, by making the issue of autonomy enhancement and, hence, capacity development central to the issue.

After revisiting these very valuable perspectives from within the World Bank, we shall now conclude by briefly seeing how this discussion of knowledge-based aid articulates with wider debates about knowledge, aid and development.

Knowledge-based aid and knowledge, aid and development: some concluding thoughts

Does knowledge-based aid have a future? We have noted the optimistic position that it will transform aid organisations but also the improbability of this. On the other hand, there are those, most significantly in the current US Administration, who argue that it is part of a new fuzziness within the World Bank that needs to be stopped. If the knowledge bank did collapse then the impetus towards knowledge-based aid would clearly be reduced. What seems likely is that some elements of the approach will become firmly embedded in most agencies, with some positive impacts. What is possible, but less probable, is that the current revisiting of technical assistance and capacity development, alongside knowledge-based approaches, will support a significant shift in emphasis within development co-operation to a more country-led approach. However, country-led development is not necessarily the same as genuinely participatory and democractic development.

Knowledge-based aid can make positive contributions to understandings and practices of knowledge, aid and development. It is raising awareness within the aid community that knowledge is complex and contextual. There is a new and growing understanding of knowledge as tacit and community-based. There is even a heightened sense of its relationship to power and ideology. Though not unproblematic or un-contested, there is a significant shift towards agency recognition of and even support for indigenous knowledge and national knowledge systems in the South. Agency funding for knowledge networks and sites (even the oft-criticised Development Gateway) has increased multi-directional knowledge flows, and is likely to have facilitated greater questioning of agency orthodoxies.

There is a growing discourse that aid is not simply technical. The language of knowledge-based aid, at its most philosophical, does contain a strong sense of the need for aid to be less donor-dominated. This sense reinforces the wider discourse of ownership–partnership. At its most radical, it is leading to arguments from within agencies that aid should be about mutual learning and autonomy enhancement rather than tell-ing and conditionalities.

These trends also mean, at least at the discursive level, the beginning of a move away from technical and economistic notions of development to a sense that development is what countries and communities define it as, including the cultural and the spiritual.

However, these positive elements do need to be weighed in the balance. There are still powerful tendencies within agencies towards certainty and telling. Knowledge-based aid can mean better internal knowledge management of the kind where the official version is reinforced. Equally, it can mean the use of new tools to get the message out to others, to tell them more effectively what it is right to think.

Questions of whose knowledge gets shared are important on a number of levels. Agency-generated knowledge is more likely to be valued than that from external sources. Headquarters knowledge still tends to dom-inate over field knowledge, even in theoretically decentralised agencies. In bilateral agencies the knowledge of citizens is typically given more weight than that of local staff. Quantitative, scientific and economic knowledge is usually taken more seriously than knowledge of other kinds. Agency knowledge systems remain poor at dealing with context, complexity and conflicting interpretations, preferring routinised and universal responses.

Such trends could result in knowledge-based aid being an even worse form than the previous model. Conditionalities could be extended through the greater certainty amongst the donors that they had the answers to all development problems, and more effective inculcation of these items of development faith to recipients.

The relationships amongst knowledge sharing, the real political eco-nomy of aid and the inner workings of aid agencies needs consideration. The battles of knowledge-sharing projects in agencies highlight the real tensions that exist about management culture. One version of knowledge sharing is really about saving the soul of the agency. However, part of the attraction of knowledge sharing to others within agencies is that it appears to address problems regarding aid effectiveness and the legitimation crisis of conditionalities. Power dynamics would suggest that the latter understanding is likely to triumph, although perhaps not completely.

The benefits to Southern partners are particularly unclear. Although PRSPs, budgetary support and sector programmes are supposed to lead to better Southern ownership of development, it appears that their related knowledge-sharing activities are often more about better co-ordination between agencies. Indeed, better co-ordination between agencies may potentially reduce national ownership, as governments and civil society are faced by a more concerted agency position.

Knowledge sharing in agencies needs to be consistent with the overall agenda of national ownership of development and genuine development partnerships. However, external sharing for all agencies is seriously compromised by the extent that they are perceived, and perceive themselves, still to be in the 'driving seat' of development co-operation. This highlights the important role that attitudes play in development co-operation. Much of the knowledge-sharing literature assumes that it is good to share, that sharing is safe, and that it is done on equal terms. There would be few, however, who would argue that such openness and symmetry are a good description of how either aid or bureaucracies work.

Questions about the broader impact of knowledge-based aid cannot be understood outside the context of development. There is much scepticism North and South about the larger development project, given the paucity of evidence for its success in its first fifty years of existence. Crucially, the performance of knowledge-based aid cannot be fully evaluated without consideration of the interlinked impacts of globalisation, debt and war.

Finally, and perhaps most crucially, it is far from clear what knowledge-based aid is likely to do to improve the lives of those who are ultimately the supposed beneficiaries. Too much knowledge-based aid rests on the questionable assumptions that better knowledge makes for better policies, and that better policies lead to better lives. The worst excesses of knowledge-based aid rhetoric (as seen in parts of the *World Development Report 1998-99*) deny both the agency of such people and the structures that impact upon them, arguing that their ignorance is the key factor in their poverty. Yet there is still very little in knowledge-based aid that suggests how this is to be reversed or that can show positive impacts on their lives.

Knowledge-based aid is like several other recent elements of aid–development discourse (such as ownership and participatory development). At its best, its language and, occasionally, its practices suggest a real move away from much of what has been criticised about aid and development. However, there is at least as much in it to suggest that it is either a limited improvement in practice or, more seriously, both a device that disarms critics and a shift towards greater domination. The most positive future for knowledge-based aid is likely to depend on the extent to which it moves further towards a reconceptualisation that connects it intimately with shared knowledge and capacity development in the South.

Bibliography

AMTEC (2001) 'Report to DFID on an information needs analysis pilot study on staff in overseas offices (DFID Southern Africa)', Farnham: AMTEC.

Andréen, S. (1986) 'The international commitment', in P. Frühling (ed.) *Swedish Development Aid in Perspective*, Stockholm: Almqvist and Wicksell.

Apffel-Marglin, F. (1996) 'Introduction: rationality and the world', in F. Apffel-Marglin and S. Marglin (eds.) *Decolonising Knowledge*, Oxford: Oxford University Press.

Apple, M. (1993) *Official Knowledge*, London: Routledge.

Arce, A. and N. Long (1992) 'The dynamics of knowledge', in N. Long and A. Long (eds.) *The Battlefields of Knowledge*, London: Routledge.

Argyris, C. and D. Schön (1978) *Organisational Learning*, London: Addison-Wesley.

Ball, S. (1990) *Politics and Policy Making in Education*, London: Routledge.

Bandow, D. and I. Vásquez (eds.) (1994) *Perpetuating Poverty*, Washington: Cato Institute.

Baudry-Somcynsky, M. and Chris Cook (1999) *Japan's system of official development assistance*, Profiles in partnership, No.1, Ottawa: IDRC.

Baumann, P. (1999) 'Information and power: implications for process monitoring. A review of the literature', London: Overseas Development Institute, Working Paper 120.

Bayart, J.-F. (1993) *The State in Africa*, Harlow: Longman.

Bellanet (2002) 'Knowledge management profile of the World Bank', interview with Bruno Laporte and Ron Kim, *Knowledge Management for Development Downloads* on www.bellanet.org

Berg, E. (2000) 'Learning in the development debate', in J. Carlsson and L. Wohlgemuth (eds.) *Learning in Development Cooperation*, Stockholm: Expert Group on Development Issues.

Bergmann, H. (2001) 'Knowledge management in a development agency: the case of GTZ', in W. Gmelin, K. King and S. McGrath (eds.) *Development Knowledge, National Research and International Cooperation*, Bonn and Edinburgh: CAS/DSE/NORRAG.

Bernstein, B. (ed.) (1971) *Class, Codes and Control. Volume 1*, London: Routledge and Kegan Paul.

Bissio, R. (2001) 'Knowledge for development: public good or good for the Bank?', *Norrag News*, 29, 9–12.

Bond, P. (2000) *Elite Transition*, London: Pluto.

Box, L. (2001) 'Inside out and upside down: a case study on the harsh realities of going virtual', in W. Gmelin, K. King and S. McGrath (eds.) *Development Knowledge, National Research and International Cooperation*, Bonn and Edinburgh: CAS/DSE/NORRAG.

Boyer, R. (1990) *The Regulation School*, New York: Columbia University Press.

Bretton Woods Project (2001) 'A Tower of Babel on the Internet? The World Bank's Development Gateway', downloaded from http://www.brettonwoodsproject.org/topic/knowledgebank/gateway on 17 October 2001.

Caddell, M. (1999) 'What knowledge for development? Some thoughts on the 1998–1999 World Development Report, Knowledge for Development', *Norrag News*, 24, 7–10.

Caddell, M. (2002) '"Outward looking eyes": Visions of Schooling, Development and the State in Nepal', unpublished PhD dissertation, Department of Sociology, University of Edinburgh.

Carlsson, J. (2000) 'Learning from evaluations', in J. Carlsson and L. Wohlgemuth (eds.) *Learning in Development Cooperation*, Stockholm: Expert Group on Development Issues.

Carlsson, J. and L. Wohlgemuth (eds.) (2000a) *Learning in Development Cooperation*, Stockholm: Expert Group on Development Issues.

Carlsson, J. and L. Wohlgemuth (2000b) 'Learning in the development debate', in J. Carlsson and L. Wohlgemuth (eds.) *Learning in Development Cooperation*, Stockholm: Expert Group on Development Issues.

Carlsson, J., M. Eriksson-Baaz, A.-M. Fallenius and E. Lövgren (1999) 'Are evaluations useful? Cases from Swedish development cooperation', Stockholm: Sida.

Carton, M. (1998) 'Poverty, solidarity and globalisation: a Swiss perspective', in K. King and M. Caddell (eds.) *Partnership and Poverty in Britain and Sweden's New Aid Policies*, Edinburgh: University of Edinburgh, Centre of African Studies, Occasional Paper No. 75.

Castells, M. (1996) *The Rise of the Network Society*, Oxford: Blackwell.

Catterson, J. and C. Lindahl (1999) 'The sustainability enigma', downloaded from http://www.egdi.gov.se/pdf/19991pdf/1999_1.pdf on 1 November 2001.

Caufield, C. (1996) *Masters of Illusion*, New York: Henry Hunt and Co.

Cedergren, J. (1998) 'Partnerships in development: a realistic proposition?', in K. King and M. Caddell (eds.) *Partnership and Poverty in Britain and Sweden's New Aid Policies*, Edinburgh: University of Edinburgh, Centre of African Studies, Occasional Paper No. 75.

Centros de Estudios Internacionales (2000) 'The World Bank: the interplay of rhetoric and reality', downloaded from http://www.bicusa.org on 12 December 2000.

Chabal, P. and J.-P. Daloz (1999) *Africa Works*, Oxford: James Currey.

Chambers, R. (1995) 'Paradigm shifts and the practice of participatory research and development', in N. Nelson and S. Wright (eds.) *Power and Participatory Development*, London: Intermediate Technology Publications.

Chang, H.-S., A. Fell and M. Laird, with J. Seif (1999) 'A comparison of management systems for development co-operation in OECD/DAC members', Paris: Organisation for Economic Cooperation and Development, Development Cooperation Directorate, Report DCD(99)6.

Cheng, Kai-Ming (1994) 'Quality of education as perceived in Chinese culture', in T. Takala (ed.) *Quality of Education in the Context of Culture in Developing Countries*, Tampere: University of Tampere, Department of Education.

Chossudovsky, M. (1997) *The Globalisation of Poverty*, London: Zed.

Clift, C. (2001) 'Knowledge sharing: inside in, inside out, outside in, outside out', in W. Gmelin, K. King and S. McGrath (eds.), *Development Knowledge, National Research and International Cooperation*, Bonn and Edinburgh: CAS/DSE/NORRAG.

Collins, P. (1991) *Black Feminist Thought*, New York: Routledge.

Commission on International Development (1969) *Partners in Development*, London: Pall Mall.

Cooke, B. and U. Kothari (eds.) (2001) *Participation: the New Tyranny?*, London: Zed.

Coraggio, J.L. (2001) 'Universities as sites of local and global knowledge (re)production', in W. Gmelin, K. King and S. McGrath (eds.) *Development Knowledge, National Research and International Cooperation*, Bonn and Edinburgh: CAS/DSE/NORRAG.

Cornia, A., R. Jolly and F. Stewart (1987) *Adjustment with a Human Face*, New York: UNICEF.

Crewe, E. and E. Harrison (1998) *Whose Development?*, London: Zed.

Crossley, M. and K. Holmes (2001) 'Challenges for educational research: international development, partnerships and capacity building in small states', in *Oxford Review of Education*, 27, 3, 395–409.

Dahlman, C. J. (1984) 'Foreign technology and indigenous technological capability in Brazil', in M. Fransman and K. King (eds.) *Technological capability in the Third World*, Basingstoke: Macmillan.

Davenport, T. and L. Prusak (1998) *Working Knowledge*, Boston: Harvard Business School Press.

Denning, S. (2000) *The Springboard*, Boston: Butterworth-Heinemann.

Denning, S. (2001) 'Knowledge sharing in the North and South', in W. Gmelin, K. King and S. McGrath (eds.) *Development Knowledge, National Research and International Cooperation*, Bonn and Edinburgh: CAS/DSE/NORRAG.

Devarajan, S., D. Dollar and T. Holmgren (1999) 'Aid and reform in Africa: lessons from ten case studies', Washington: World Bank.

DFID (1997) *Eliminating World Poverty: A Challenge for the 21st Century. White Paper on International Development*, London: HMSO.

DFID (1999a) *Learning Opportunities for All*, London: DFID.

DFID (1999b) *Renewable Natural Resources Research Strategy*, London: DFID.

DFID (2000a) 'White Paper. Section 2.4. Knowledge We Wills', London: DFID, draft White Paper text.

DFID (2000b) 'DFID's strategic overview', London: DFID, printout of powerpoint presentation.

DFID (2000c) '"Getting the knowledge" in DFID', London: DFID, unpublished paper.

DFID (2000d) 'Information management and DFID', London: DFID, draft strategic framework.

DFID (2000e) *Education for all: the challenge of universal primary education. Strategies for Achieving the International Development Targets (Target Strategy Papers) Consultation Document*, London: DFID.

DFID (2000f) *Poverty Elimination and the Empowerment of Women. Strategies for Achieving the International Development Targets (Target Strategy Papers)*, London: DFID.

DFID (2000g) *Halving World Poverty by 2015. Strategies for Achieving the International Development Targets (Target Strategy Papers)*, London: DFID.

DFID (2000h) *Realising Human Rights for Poor People. Strategies for Achieving the International Development Targets (Target Strategy Papers)*, London: DFID.

DFID (2000i) *Achieving Sustainability. Strategies for Achieving the International Development Targets (Target Strategy Papers)*, London: DFID.

DFID (2000j) *The Challenge of Universal Primary Education. Strategies for Achieving the International Development Targets (Target Strategy Papers)*, London: DFID.

DFID (2000k) *Better Health for Poor People. Strategies for Achieving the International Development Targets (Target Strategy Papers)*, London: DFID.

DFID (2000l) *Eliminating World Poverty: Making Globalisation Work for the Poor*, London: HMSO.

DFID (2000m) 'Doing the knowledge', London: DFID, unpublished paper.

DFID (2001a) *Addressing the Water Crisis. Strategies for Achieving the International Development Targets (Target Strategy Papers)*, London: DFID.

DFID (2001b) *Meeting the Challenge of Poverty in Urban Areas. Strategies for Achieving the International Development Targets (Target Strategy Papers)*, London: DFID.

DFID (2001c) *Making Government Work for Poor People. Strategies for Achieving the International Development Targets (Target Strategy Papers)*, London: DFID.

DFID (2001d) 'Working together more effectively and knowledge management', London: DFID, unpublished paper.

DFID (2001e) *e-business Strategy*, London: DFID.

DFID (2002a) 'Short management report for the Knowledge Sharing and Communications Snap-Shot Study', London: DFID, unpublished paper.

DFID (2002b) 'Report of the Knowledge Sharing and Communications Snapshot Study', London: DFID, unpublished paper.

DFID (2002c) 'Doing the Knowledge II' London: Knowledge and Communications Committee, DFID.

DFID (2002d) 'Research for poverty reduction: DFID Research Policy Paper', Second Draft, 26 September 2002, London: DFID.

DFID (2002e) 'Knowledge sharing consultative group' powerpoint, London: Policy Division, DFID.

Dore, R. (1997) 'The distinctiveness of Japan', in C. Crouch and W. Streeck (eds.) *Political Economy of Modern Capitalism*, London: Sage.

Drucker, P. (1969) *The Age of Discontinuity*, London: Heinemann.

Edgren, G. (1986) 'Changing terms', in P. Frühling (ed.) *Swedish Development Aid in Perspective*, Stockholm: Almqvist and Wicksell.

Edgren, G. (1997) 'Structural adjustment and the foreign aid industry', in Sida (ed.) *Development Cooperation in the 21st Century*, Stockholm: Sida.

Edgren, G. (2000) 'Fashions, myths and delusion: obstacles to organisational learning in aid agencies', in J. Carlsson and L. Wohlgemuth (eds.) *Learning in Development Cooperation*, Stockholm: Expert Group on Development Issues.

Edwards, M. (1998) 'Are NGOs overrated? Why and how to say "no"', *Current Issues in Comparative Education* 1, 1, downloaded from http://www.tc.columbia.edu/cice/vol01nr1/meart2.htm on 12 December 2000.

EGDI (Expert Group on Development Issues) (2001) 'About EGDI', downloaded from http://www.egdi.se/aboutegdi.html on 11 December 2001.

Ellerman, D. (2000a) 'Must the World Bank have official views?', unpublished paper.

Ellerman, D. (2000b) 'Knowledge and aid', unpublished paper.

Ellerman, D. (2001a) 'Notes on control and "ownership" problems', unpublished paper.

Ellerman, D. (2001b) 'Freedom of speech, freedom of conscience and the World Bank', Washington: World Bank, Newsletter of the World Bank Group Staff Association, November to December.

Ellerman, D. (2003) 'Autonomy-respecting assistance: toward new strategies for development assistance', in R. Hayman, K. King and S. McGrath (eds.) *A New Approach to African Development? Internal and External Visions*, Edinburgh: Centre of African Studies, Edinburgh University.

Emmerij, L. (1996) 'The social question and the Inter-American Development Bank', in O. Stokke (ed.) *Foreign Aid towards the Year 2000*, London: Frank Cass.

Escobar, A. (1995) *Encountering Development*, Princeton: Princeton University Press.

FASID (Foundation for Advanced Studies on International Development) (1998) *Realities and Issues of Knowledge for Development in Japan*, Tokyo: FASID.

Ferguson, J. (1994) *The Anti-Politics Machine*, London: University of Minnesota Press.

Fidler, S. (2001) 'Who's Minding the Bank?', *Foreign Policy* 126, 40–51.

Fillip, B. (1999) 'Knowledge Management for Development Agencies: a Comparison of World Bank and USAID Approaches and some Implications for JICA', Washington: JICA.

Forss, K., J. Carlsen, E. Frøyland, T. Sitari and K. Vilby (1988) 'Evaluation of the effectiveness of technical assistance personnel financed by the Nordic countries', unpublished report for DANIDA, SIDA, NORAD, FINNIDA.

Forss, K., B. Cracknell and N. Stromquist (1997) 'Organisational learning in development cooperation: how knowledge is generated and used', Stockholm: Expert Group on Development Issues.

Forster, J. (1998) 'The new boundaries of international development cooperation', in K. King and L. Buchert (eds.) *Changing International Aid to Education*, Paris: UNESCO.

Foucault, M. (1970) *The Order of Things*, London: Tavistock.

Foucault, M. (1972) *The Archaeology of Knowledge*, London: Tavistock.

Fransman, M. and K. King (eds.) (1984) *Technological Capability in the Third World*, Basingstoke: Macmillan.

Freire, P. (1972) *Pedagogy of the Oppressed*, Harmondsworth: Penguin.

Fujita, Kimio (2001) interviewed in November 2001, *Japan Economic Review*, downloaded from JICA website [jica.go.jp] 26 August 2002.

Fukuda-Parr, S., C. Lopes and K. Malik (eds.) (2002) *Capacity for Development*, London: Earthscan/UNDP.

Gadamer, H.-G. (1975) *Truth and Method*, London: Sheed and Ward.

German, A. and J. Randel (1998) *The Reality of Aid 1998-9*, London: Earthscan.

Giddens, A. (1990) *The Consequences of Modernity*, Cambridge: Polity.

Global Development Network – Japan (2001), downloaded from www.gdn-japan.jbic.go.jp on 11 December 2001.

Gmelin, W. (1998) 'The Europeanisation of aid', in K. King and L. Buchert (eds.) *Changing International Aid to Education*, Paris: UNESCO.

Gmelin, W., K. King and S. McGrath (eds.) (2001) *Development Knowledge, National Research and International Cooperation*, Bonn and Edinburgh: CAS/DSE/NORRAG.

Gorjestani, N. (1999) 'Knowledge sharing and innovation', Washington: World Bank, Africa Region, Findings No. 45.

Gorjestani, N. (2002) 'Debriefing for knowledge retention', downloaded from http://www.worldbank.org/ks/presentations.html on 31 May 2002.

Gustafsson, I. (1999) 'New partnership possibilities', *Norrag News* 25, 4–6.

Gustafsson, I. (2000) 'From provider of expertise towards facilitator of contacts and sharing of experience', paper presented at the Global Development Network Conference, Tokyo, December.

Gustafsson, I. (2001) 'Building North–South knowledge capacity', in W. Gmelin, K. King and S. McGrath (eds.) *Development Knowledge, National Research and International Cooperation*, Bonn and Edinburgh: CAS/DSE/NORRAG.

Gustafsson, I., A. Lind, B. Olsson, A. Sandström and M. Söderbäck (2001) 'Att Äga, förmedla och utveckla kunskap', Stockholm: Sida, internal discussion document.

Guttal, S. (2000) 'The end of imagination: the World Bank, the International Monetary Fund and poverty reduction', Bangkok: Focus on the Global South.

HMSO (Her Majesty's Stationery Office) (1970) *Changing Emphasis in British Aid Policies: More Aid to the Poorest*, London: Cmnd 6270, Overseas Development Ministry.

Hall, R. (2002) 'Knowledge management practices in Australian organisations: progressive development or deepening inequality?', conference on 'Development through Knowledge', 21–22 November 2002, Geneva: Graduate Institute of Development Studies.

Hall, S. and M. Jacques (eds.) (1989) *New Times*, London: Lawrence and Wishart.

Hancock, G. (1989) *Lords of Poverty*, New York: Atlantic Monthly.

Hayek, F. (1945) 'The use of knowledge in society', *American Economic Review* 35, 4, 519–30.

Hayman, R., K. King and S. McGrath (eds.) (2003) *A new approach to African development? Internal and external visions*, Edinburgh: Centre of African Studies, Edinburgh University.

Held, D. *et al.* (1999) *Global Transformations*, Cambridge: Polity.

Heppling, S. (1986) 'The very first years', in P. Frühling (ed.) *Swedish Development Aid in Perspective*, Stockholm: Almqvist and Wicksell.

Heyneman, S. (1997) 'Economic growth and international trade in education reform', paper presented at the Oxford International Conference on Education and Development, September.

Hirschman, A. (1958) *The Strategy of Economic Development*, New Haven: Yale University Press.

Hirschman, A. (1971) *A Bias for Hope*, New Haven: Yale University Press.

Hirschman, A. and C. Lindblom (1969) [1962] 'Economic development, research and development, policy making: some converging views', in F. Emery (ed.) *Systems Thinking*, Harmondsworth: Penguin.

Humphries, S., R. Hanig and P. Senge (2000) 'Action review of staff learning: phase one report', Society for Organisational Learning, unpublished report.

JICA (n.d.) Institute for International Co-operation (IFIC), published description of its activities, pp. 15, Tokyo: JICA

JICA (1994) *Study on Development Assistance for Development and Education: the Study Group on Development Assistance for Education and Development*, Tokyo: IFIC, JICA.

JICA (1998) *The OECD/DAC's New Development Strategy: Report of the Issue-wise Study Committee for Japan's Official Development Assistance*, Tokyo: JICA.

JICA (2000a) *Japan International Cooperation Agency Annual Report 2000*, Tokyo: JICA.

JICA (2000b) *Annual Evaluation Report*, Tokyo: JICA.

JICA (2000c) *Report on Intellectual Support for Electric Power Sector Development Committee for the Promotion of Cooperation on Intellectual Support for Electric Power Sector*, Tokyo: JICA.

JICA (2001a) *The Information Revolution in Development Assistance*, Tokyo: JICA (IFIC).

JICA (2001b) *Japan International Co-operation Agency JICA Annual Report 2001*, Tokyo: JICA.

JICA (2002a) 'Japan's Official Development Assistance', downloaded from http://www.jica.go.jp/english/about.0l.html on 23 March 2002.

JICA (2002b) 'Guideline for management of the development issue teams (for the trial introduction period)' Personnel Division and Planning Division, 13 March 2002, Tokyo: JICA (original in Japanese).

JICA (2002c) Programme for the World Summit on Sustainable Development, Johannesburg August 2002, London: attachment from JICA Office, London.

JICA Newsletter *Frontier* (2002) 'Making use of J-Net for International Cooperation' (original in Japanese). Tokyo: JICA.

Johanson, R. (2001) 'Sub-Saharan Africa (SSA) regional response to Bank TVET policy in the 1990s', Washington: World Bank, Africa Region.

Johanson, R. (2002) 'Vocational Skills Development in Sub-Saharan Africa: Synthesis of a World Bank Review', draft of September 2002, Washington: World Bank, Africa Region.

Johnson, P. (2002) 'New technology tools for human development? Towards policy and practice for knowledge societies in southern Africa', *Compare* 32, 3, 381–9.

Jones, P. (1992) *World Bank Financing of Education*, London: Routledge.

Kanbur, R. (2000) 'Aid, conditionality and debt in Africa', paper presented at the Centre for Theology and Public Issues, University of Edinburgh, November.

Kaplan, D. (2000) 'The role of knowledge in a contemporary industrial strategy', Pretoria: Department of Trade and Industry.

Kapur, D., J. Lewis and R. Webb (eds.) (1997) *The World Bank: Its First Half Century*, Washington: Brookings Institution.

Karlsson, M. (1997) 'Foreword', in H. Kifle, A. Olukoshi and L. Wohlgemuth (eds.) *A new Partnership for African Development*, Uppsala: Nordic Africa Institute.

Kato, K. (2001a) 'Knowledge perspectives in JICA', in W. Gmelin, K. King and S. McGrath (eds.) *Development Knowledge, National Research and International Cooperation*, Bonn and Edinburgh: CAS/DSE/NORRAG.

Kato, K. (2001b) 'A brief history of knowledge perspectives in JICA', *Norrag News* 28, 57–58.

Kawakami, Takao (2002) 'JICA Special', in *The Japan Economic Review*, 15 February, p. 4.

Kifle, H., A. Olukoshi and L. Wohlgemuth (eds.) (1997) *A new Partnership for African Development*, Uppsala: Nordic Africa Institute.

Kihlberg, M. (ed.) (1987) *SAREC's First Decade*, Stockholm: SAREC.

King, K. (1986) 'Problem and prospects of aid to education in Sub-Saharan Africa', in H. Hawes and T. Coombe (eds.) *Education priorities and aid responses in Sub-Saharan Africa*, London, Overseas Development Administration, HMSO.

King, K. (1988) 'Donor-aided research and evaluation in education: the case of SIDA and SAREC', Edinburgh: University of Edinburgh, Centre of African Studies, unpublished paper.

King, K. (1991) *Aid and Education in the Developing World*, Harlow: Longman.

King, K. (1997) 'Aid for development or for change? A discussion of education and training policies of development assistance agencies with particular reference to Japan', in K. Watson, C. Modgil and S. Modgil (eds.) *Educational Dilemmas: Debate and Diversity. Power and Responsibility in Education*, London: Cassell.

King, K. (2000) 'Towards knowledge-based aid: a new way of working or a new North–South divide?', *Journal of International Cooperation in Education*, 3, 2, 23–48.

King, K. (2001) 'Knowledge agencies: making knowledge work for the world's poor?', in W. Gmelin, K. King and S. McGrath (eds.) *Development Knowledge, National Research and International Cooperation*, Bonn and Edinburgh: CAS/DSE/NORRAG.

King, K. (2002) 'Knowledge management, knowledge agency, knowledge history: knowledge, technical assistance and capacity building in historical perspective', paper to conference, 'Development through Knowledge?', 21–22 November 2002, Geneva: Graduate Institute of Development Studies.

King, K. and L. Buchert (eds.) (1999) *Changing International Aid to Education: Global Patterns and National Contexts*, Paris: UNESCO Publishing/NORRAG.

King, K. and M. Caddell (eds.) (1998) *Partnership and Poverty in Britain and Sweden's new Aid Policies*, Edinburgh: University of Edinburgh, Centre of African Studies, Occasional Paper No. 75.

King, K. and S. McGrath (2002) *Globalisation, Enterprise and Knowledge*, Oxford: Symposium.

Kingdon, J. (1995) *Agendas, Alternatives and Public Policies. Second Edition*, New York: Harper Collins College.

Klees, S. (1998) 'NGOs: progressive force or neoliberal tool?', *Current Issues in Comparative Education* 1, 1, downloaded from http://www.tc.columbia.edu/cice/vol01nr1/meart2.htm on 12 December 2000.

Kothari, U. (2001) 'Power, knowledge and social control in participatory development', in W. Cooke and U. Kothari (eds.) *Participation: the New Tyranny?*, London: Zed.

Kuhn, T. (1962) *The Structure of Scientific Revolutions*, Chicago: University of Chicago Press.

Lave, J. and E. Wenger (1991) *Situated Learning*, Cambridge: Cambridge University Press.

Leadbeater, C. (2000) *Living on Thin Air*, Harmondsworth: Penguin.

Leijonhufvud, A. (1981) *Information and Coordination*, New York: Oxford University Press.

Lewin, E. (1986) 'The qualities of smallness', in P. Frühling (ed.) *Swedish Development Aid in Perspective*, Stockholm: Almqvist and Wicksell.

Leys, C. (1996) *The Rise and Fall of Development Theory*, London: James Currey.

Lindblom, C. (1968) *The Policymaking Process*, Englewood Cliffs: Prentice-Hall.

Lintonen, K. (2000) 'Learning in development cooperation: the case of Finland', in L. Wohlgemuth and J. Carlsson (eds.) *Learning in Development Cooperation*, Stockholm: Expert Group on Development Issues.

Ljunggren, B. (1986) 'Swedish goals and priorities', in P. Frühling (ed.) *Swedish Development Aid in Perspective*, Stockholm: Almqvist and Wicksell.

Long, N. (1992) 'From paradigm lost to paradigm regained?', in N. Long and A. Long (eds.) *The Battlefields of Knowledge*, London: Routledge.

Lorde, A. (1984) *Sister Outsider*, Trumansburg: The Crossing Press.

Machlup, F. (1962) *Production and Distribution of Knowledge*, Princeton: Princeton University Press.

March, J. and H. Simon (1958) *Organisations*, New York: John Wiley.

Marshall, A. (1891) *Principles of Economics. Second Edition*, London: Macmillan.

Mathias, P. (1969) *The First Industrial Nation*, London: Methuen.

Matsunaga, M. (2001) 'Putting untapped knowledge to use in international cooperation', *Norrag News* 28, 45–46.

Mbembe, A. (2001) *On the Postcolony*, Berkeley: University of California Press.

McGinn, N. (2001) 'Knowledge management in the corporate sector: implications for education', in W. Gmelin, K. King and S. McGrath (eds.) *Development Knowledge, National Research and International Cooperation*, Bonn and Edinburgh: CAS/DSE/NORRAG.

McGrath, S. (1998) 'Education, development and assistance: the challenge of the new millennium', in K. King and L. Buchert (eds.) *Changing International Aid to Education*, Paris: UNESCO.

McGrath, S. (1999) 'Education, Development, Assistance: The Challenge of the New Millennium', in K. King and L. Buchert (eds.) *Changing international aid to education: global patterns and national contexts*, Paris: UNESCO Publishing/NORRAG.

McGrath, S. (2001a) 'The social theory of knowledge and knowledge for development: is mutual understanding possible?', in W. Gmelin, K. King and S. McGrath (eds.) *Development Knowledge, National Research and International Cooperation*, Bonn and Edinburgh: CAS/DSE/NORRAG.

McGrath, S. (2001b) 'Confessions of a long distance runner: reflections from an international and comparative education research project', in K. Watson (ed.) *Doing Comparative Education Research*, Oxford: Symposium.

McNamara, K. (2002) 'Knowledge sharing, qulaity and impact in Bank operations', downloaded from http://www.worldbank.org/ks/km_doc_operations. html on 31 May 2002.

McNamara, R. (1981) *McNamara Years at the World Bank*, Baltimore: Johns Hopkins University Press.

McNeill, D. (2000) 'Power and ideas: the role of multilateral institutions in development policy', paper presented at the GDN 2000 conference 'Beyond Economics', Tokyo, December.

Mearns, R. and M. Leach (eds.) (1996) *The Lie of the Land*, Oxford: James Currey.

Mehta, L. (2000) 'The World Bank and its emerging knowledge empire', *Human Organisation* 60, 2, 189–196.

Meyer-Stamer, J. (1999) 'The World Development Report 1999, annotated outline, Knowledge for development, 7 August 1997', *Norrag News* 24, 10–13.

Ministry for Foreign Affairs, Sweden (1998) *Africa on the Move*, Stockholm: Ministry for Foreign Affairs.

Ministry for Foreign Affairs, Sweden (1999) *Our Future with Asia*, Stockholm: Ministry for Foreign Affairs.

Ministry of Foreign Affairs, Denmark (2002) *Danish Assistance to Vocational Education and Training*, Copenhagen: Danida.

Ministry of Foreign Affairs, Japan (2000) 'Report of Official Development Assistance: Summary', Tokyo: Ministry of Foreign Affairs (Japanese version).

Ministry of Foreign Affairs, Japan (2001) 'Annual evaluation report on Japan's economic cooperation: summary', Tokyo: Ministry of Foreign Affairs, Economic Cooperation Bureau.

Miyoshi, K. (1999) 'Knowledge management in development aid agencies', *Journal of International Development Studies* 8, 2, 29–42 (original in Japanese).

Miyoshi, K. (2001) 'Toward the promotion of support for South–South cooperation, to build an effective framework of international cooperation', Tokyo: JICA, unpublished paper.

Mkandawire, T. (2000) 'Non-organic intellectuals and "learning" in policy-making in Africa', in L. Wohlgemuth and J. Carlsson (eds.) *Learning in Development Cooperation*, Stockholm: Expert Group on Development Issues.

Moran, B. (1999) 'Nigerian identity formations in the Usenet newsgroup soc.culture.nigeria', Edinburgh: University of Edinburgh, Centre of African Studies, unpublished MSc dissertation.

Mosley, P., J. Harrigan and J. Toye (1991) *Aid and Power*, London: Routledge.

Mosse, D. (2001) '"People's knowledge", participation and privilege', in W. Cooke and U. Kothari (eds.) *Participation: the New Tyranny?*, London: Zed.

Muller, J. (2001) *Reclaiming Knowledge*, London: Routledge.

Mundy, K. (1998) 'Educational multilateralism at the crossroads', in K. King and L. Buchert (eds.) *Changing International Aid to Education*, Paris: UNESCO.

Mwiria, K. (2001) 'Education decision-making and knowledge sharing: some lessons from the Eastern and Southern Africa region', in W. Gmelin, K. King and S. McGrath (eds.) *Development Knowledge, National Research and International Cooperation*, Bonn and Edinburgh: CAS/DSE/NORRAG.

Nagao, Masafumi (2001) 'Can Japan be a good math and science teacher for Africa?' paper to CICE International Conference on Education, 7–8 December 2001, Hiroshima University.

Nishigaki, A. and Y. Shimomura (1996) *The Economics of Development Assistance: Japan's ODA in a Symbiotic World*, Tokyo: LTCB International Library Foundation.

Nonaka, I. and H. Takeuchi (1995) *The Knowledge-Creating Company*, Oxford: Oxford University Press.

Norrag News (2001a) 'Special issue on the brave new world of international education and training', Volume 27.

Norrag News (2001b) 'Special issue on knowledge, research and international cooperation', Volume 28.

North, D. (1990) *Institutions, Institutional Change and Economic Performance*, Cambridge: Cambridge University Press.

OCDE (Organisation pour Coopération et Développement Economique) (2002) Les dossiers du CAD. Coopération pour développement. Rapport 2001, 2002, vol. 3 no. 1, Paris: OCDE.

O'Dell, C. and C. Grayson with N. Essaides (1998) *If Only We Knew What We Know*, New York: Free Press.

OECD (Organisation for Economic Cooperation and Development) (1996) *The Knowledge-Based Economy*, Paris: OECD.

OECD–DAC (OECD–Development Assistance Committee) (1996) *Shaping the 21st Century: the contribution of development co-operation*, Paris: OECD.

Olukoshi, A. (1997a) 'The quest for a new paradigm for Swedish development cooperation in Africa: issues, problems and prospects', in H. Kifle, A. Olukoshi and L. Wohlgemuth (eds.) *A New Partnership for African Development*, Uppsala: Nordic Africa Institute.

Olukoshi, A. (1997b) 'Sweden and Africa: some personal reflection', in H. Kifle, A. Olukoshi and L. Wohlgemuth (eds.) *A New Partnership for African Development*, Uppsala: Nordic Africa Institute.

Paccagnella, F. (1997) 'Getting the seats of your pants dirty: strategies for ethnographic research on virtual communities', *Journal of Computer-Mediated Communication [On-line]* 3, 1, downloaded from http://www.usc.edu/dept/annenberg/vol3/issue1/paccagnella.html on 22 November 1999.

Page, E. (2000) 'Future governance and the literature on policy transfer and lesson drawing', paper prepared for the Future Governance Workshop, London, January.

Piore, M. and C. Sabel (1984) *The Second Industrial Divide*, New York: Basic Books.

Polanyi, M. (1958) *Personal Knowledge*, London: Routledge and Kegan Paul.

Polanyi, M. (1967) *The Tacit Dimension*, London: Routledge and Kegan Paul.

Psacharopoulos, G. (1981) 'Returns to education: an updated international comparison', *Comparative Education* 17, 3, 321–41.

Psacharopoulos, G. (1982) 'The economics of higher education in developing countries', *Comparative Education Review* 26, 2, 139–59.

Rahnema, M. with V. Bawtree (eds.) (1997) *The Post-Development Reader*, London: Zed.

Reich, R. (1991) *The Work of Nations*, London: Simon and Schuster.

Rist, G. (1997) *History of Development*, London: Zed.

Rist, G. (ed.) (2002) *Les Mots du Pouvoir*, Geneva, Institute of Development Studies.

Ritzen, J. (2000) 'Where the World Bank stands: issues in knowledge creation and management', paper presented at the meeting on 'Knowledge creation and management in global enterprises', Washington, February.

Roe, E. (1991) 'Development narratives: or, making the best out of blue print development', *World Development* 19, 4, 287–300.

Romer, P. (1986) 'Increasing returns and long-run growth', *Journal of Political Economy* 94, 5, 71–102.

Ruggles, R. (2001) 'Overview of Japanese ODA responsibilities & approaches', Draft paper for CIDA HQ and field staff, 6 September 2001, Tokyo: JICA.

Sachs, W. (1989) 'On the archaeology of the development idea. Six essays', University Park PA: Pennsylvania State University, Science, Technology and Society Program.

Sadler. M. (1979) [1900] 'How far can we learn anything of practical value from the study of foreign systems of education?', in J. Higginson (ed.) *Selections from Michael Sadler*, Liverpool: International Publishers.

Samoff, J. (1995) 'Agitators, incubators, advisers: what roles for the EPUs?', Stockholm: SAREC.

Samoff, J. and N. Stromquist (2001) 'Managing knowledge and storing wisdom?', *Development and Change* 32, 4, 631–56.

SAREC and SIDA (1992) *The Ownership and Cultivation of Knowledge*, Stockholm: SAREC/SIDA.

Sawamura, N. (2002) 'Local spirit, global knowledge: a Japanese approach to knowledge development in international cooperation', *Compare* 32, 3, 339–48.

Schön, D. (1971) *Beyond the Stable State*, London: Temple Smith.

Schumpeter, J. (1934) *Theory of Economic Development*, London: Harvard University Press.

Scott, J. (1998) *Seeing like a State*, London: Yale University Press.

Sen, A. (1999) *Development as Freedom*, Oxford: Oxford University Press.

Senge, P. (1990) *The Fifth Discipline*, London: Century.

Shibata, M. (2001) 'What ever happened to the 100,000 students-to-Japan target?', *Norrag News* 27, 9–10.

Shusaku, Endo (2002) *The Samurai*, London: Peter Owen.

SIDA (1989) 'Competence development strategy for programmes supported by Sida', Stockholm: SIDA.

SIDA (1992) *Development is People*, Stockholm: SIDA.

Sida (1995) 'Mission statement', Stockholm: Sida.

Sida (1996a) *Sida's Poverty Programme*, downloaded from http://www.oida.oe/Sida/articles/6600-6699/6663/PovertyProg.pdf on 20 November 2001.

Sida (1996b) *Sida's Policy: Sustainable Development*, Stockholm: Sida.

Sida (1996c) *Aid Dependency*, Stockholm: Sida.

Sida (1996d) *Asia*, Stockholm: Sida.

Sida (1996e) *Southern Africa*, Stockholm: Sida.

Sida (1996f) *North East Europe*, Stockholm: Sida.

Sida (1996g) *Promoting Sustainable Livelihoods*, Stockholm: Sida.

Sida (1997a) *Sida's Action Programme for Promoting Equality between Men and Women in Partner Countries. Experience Analysis*, downloaded from http://www.sida.se/Sida/articles/7500-7599/7515/analys.pdf on 20 November 2001.

Sida (1997b) *Justice and Peace. Sida's Programme for Peace, Democracy and Human Rights*, Stockholm: Sida.

Sida (1997c) *Sida Looks Forward*, Stockholm: Sida.

Sida (1997d) *Development Cooperation in the 21st Century*, Stockholm: Sida.

Sida (1997e) *Aid Management*, Stockholm: Sida.

Sida (1997f) *Social Development*, Stockholm: Sida.

Sida (1997g) *Latin America*, Stockholm: Sida.

Sida (1997h) *East and West Africa*, Stockholm: Sida.

Sida (1998) *Sida at Work*, Stockholm: Sida.

Sida (1999a) *IT in Swedish Development Cooperation*, downloaded from http:

//www.sida.se/Sida/articles/5400-5499/5490/udreport.pdfon 20 November 2001.

Sida (1999b) *Strategy for IT in Development Cooperation*, downloaded from http://www.sida.se/Sida/articles/5400-5499/5490/strategy.pdf on 20 November 2001.

Sida (1999c) *Sida's Management Policy*, Stockholm: Sida.

Sida (1999d) 'Swedish international development cooperation', downloaded from http://www.sida.se/Sida/articles/2900-2999/2927/index.html on 21 October 1999.

Sida (2000a) *Capacity Development as a Strategic Question on Development Cooperation*, Stockholm: Sida.

Sida (2000b) *Research Cooperation. An Outline of Policy, Programmes and Practice*, downloaded from http://www.sida.se/Sida/articles/5500-5599/5503/policy1.pdf on 20 November 2001.

Sida (2000c) *Research Cooperation. Trends in Development and Research*, downloaded from http://www.sida.se/Sida/articles/5500-5599/5503/policy2.pdf on 20 November 2001.

Sida (2000d) 'Twinning: cooperation between organisations in the public sector', downloaded from http://www.sida.se/Sida/articles/7600-7699/7647/F9185.pdf on 20 November 2001.

Sida (2000e) *Human Resource Report. Annual Report 2000*, Stockholm: Sida, Human Resource Department.

Sida (2002) *Sida's Policy for Sector Programme Support and Provisional Guidelines*, Stockholm: Sida.

Sidibé, M. (1997) 'Capacity building as a measure to lessen aid dependency for Africa', in H. Kifle, A. Olukoshi and L. Wohlgemuth (eds.) *A New Partnership for African Development*, Uppsala: Nordic Africa Institute.

Singh, M. (2000) 'Knowledge management/knowledge sharing for social justice: the South African case', paper presented at the GDN 2000 conference 'Beyond Economics', Tokyo, December.

Smith, A. (1966) [1776] *Inquiry into the Nature and Causes of the Wealth of Nations*, London: Everyman.

Smith, L.T. (1999) *Decolonising Methodologies*, London: Zed.

Song, S. (2001) 'Knowledge management for development organisations', *Norrag News* 28, 49–50.

Stein, H. (1998) 'Japanese aid to Africa: patterns, motivation and the role of structural adjustment', Chicago: Roosevelt University, unpublished paper.

Stiglitz, J. (1998) 'Towards a new paradigm for development: strategies, policies and processes', downloaded from http://www.worldbank.org/html/extdr/extme/js-101998/index.htm on 9 June 1999.

Stiglitz, J. (2000) [1999] 'Scan globally, reinvent locally', in D. Stone (ed.) *Banking on Knowledge: the Genesis of the Global Development Network*, London: Routledge.

Stone, D. (ed.) (2000) *Banking on Knowledge: the Genesis of the Global Development Network*, London: Routledge.

Stone, D. (2002) 'Using knowledge: the dilemmas of "bridging research and policy"', *Compare* 32, 3, 285–96.

Takahashi, F. (1997) 'Japan's ODA and the challenge of development', paper presented at the Financial Times Seminar, 'Japan's Official Development Assistance: the dynamics of development', November, London.

Thurow, L. (1996) *The Future of Capitalism*, London: Nicholas Brealey.

Tilak, J. (2001) 'External aid, development of knowledge bases: national and international experiences', in W. Gmelin, K. King and S. McGrath (eds.) *Development Knowledge, National Research and International Cooperation*, Bonn and Edinburgh: CAS/DSE/NORRAG.

Tilak, J. (2002) 'Knowledge society, education and aid', *Compare* 32, 3, 297–310.

Torres, R.-M. (2001) '"Knowledge-based international aid": do we want it, do we need it?', in W. Gmelin, K. King and S. McGrath (eds.) *Development Knowledge, National Research and International Cooperation*, Bonn and Edinburgh: CAS/DSE/NORRAG.

Tvedt, T. (1999) *Angels of Mercy or Development Diplomats?*, Oxford: James Currey.

United Nations Educational, Scientific and Cultural Organisation (UNESCO) (2002) *EFA Global Monitoring Report 2002. Is the World on Track?* Paris: UNESCO.

Uphoff, N. (1996) *Learning from Gal Oya*, London: Intermediate Technology Publications.

Wade, R. (1996) 'Japan, the World Bank, and the art of paradigm maintenance', *New Left Review* 217, 3–36.

Watson, K. (1998) 'Memories, models and mapping: the impact of geopolitical change on comparative studies in education', *Compare* 28, 1, 5–31.

Wenger, E. (1998) *Communities of Practice*, Cambridge: Cambridge University Press.

Widstrand, C. (1986) 'Creating knowledge', in P. Frühling (ed.) *Swedish Development Aid in Perspective*, Stockholm: Almqvist and Wicksell.

Wieslander, A. (2000) 'When do we ever learn?', in J. Carlsson and L. Wohlgemuth (eds.) *Learning in Development Cooperation*, Stockholm: Expert Group on Development Issues.

Wilks, A. (2002) 'From the Adam Smith Institute to the Zapatistas: an internet gateway to all development knowledge', *Compare* 32, 3, 327–37.

Wilks A. and F. Lefrancois (2002) 'Blinding with science or encouraging debate? How World Bank analysis determines PRSP policies', London: Bretton Woods Project and World Vision.

Wohlgemuth, L. (1998) 'Education and geo-political change in Africa: a case for partnership', in K. King and L. Buchert (eds.) *Changing International Aid to Education*, Paris: UNESCO.

Wohlgemuth, L. (2001) 'Swedish relations and policies towards Africa', *Africa Insight* 31, 4, 48–55.

Wohlgemuth, L., J. Carlsson and H. Kifle (eds.) (1998) *Institution Building and Leadership in Africa*, Uppsala: Nordic Africa Institute.

Wolfensohn, J. (1996) 'People and Development', Washington: World Bank, Annual Meetings Address, October.

Wolfensohn, J. (1997) 'The challenge of inclusion', Washington: World Bank, Annual Meetings Address, September.

Wolfensohn, J. (1998) 'The other crisis', Washington: World Bank, Annual Meetings Address, October.

Wolfensohn, J. (1999) 'A proposal for a Comprehensive Development Framework (A discussion draft)', downloaded from http://www.worldbank.org/cdf/cdf.pdf on 9 June 1999.

Woods, N. (2000) 'The challenge of good governance for the IMF and the World Bank themselves', *World Development* 28, 5, 823–41.

Working Group for International Cooperation in Skills Development (2002) 'Debates in skills development. Paper 6', Bern/Geneva: SDC/ILO/NORRAG.

World Bank (1981) *Accelerated Development in Sub-Saharan Africa*, Washington: World Bank.

World Bank (1992) *Effective Implementation: Key to Development Impact*, Washington: World Bank.

World Bank (1993) *East Asian Miracle*, Washington: World Bank.

World Bank (1995) *Priorities and Strategies for Education*, Washington: World Bank.

World Bank (1996a) *The Knowledge Partnership*, Washington: World Bank.

World Bank (1996b) *The World Bank Participation Sourcebook*, Washington: World Bank.

World Bank (1997) *The Strategic Compact*, Washington: World Bank.

World Bank (1998a) *World Development Report 1998/9. Knowledge for Development*, Oxford: Oxford University Press.

World Bank (1998b) 'Renewal at the World Bank. One-Year progress report', Washington: World Bank.

World Bank (1998c) *Indigenous Knowledge for Development: a Framework for Action*, Washington: World Bank, Africa Region.

World Bank (1998d) *Assessing Aid*, New York: Oxford University Press.

World Bank (1998e) *What is knowledge management? A background document to the World Development Report* (of 1998–9), Washington: World Bank.

World Bank (1999) *Education Sector Strategy*, Washington: World Bank.

World Bank (2000a) *Knowledge for All*, Washington: World Bank.

World Bank (2000b) 'Supporting research, networking, and communities of practice', downloaded from http://www.worldbank.org/knowledgebank/research.html on 17 January 2001.

World Bank (2000c) *Higher education in developing countries: peril and promise*, Washington: The Task Force on Higher Education and Society, World Bank.

World Bank (2001a) *Assessment of the Strategic Compact*, Washington: World Bank.

World Bank (2001b) *Strategic Framework*, Washington: World Bank.

World Bank (2001c) 'Enhancing the use of knowledge for growth and poverty reduction', Washington: World Bank, unpublished paper.

World Bank (2001d) *A Chance to Learn: Knowledge and Finance for Education in Sub-Saharan Africa*, Washington: World Bank.

World Bank (2001e) 'The knowledge bank: issues, current commitments and next steps', Washington: World Bank, unpublished paper.

World Bank (2001f) 'Building staff capacity for development: a new learning framework', Washington: World Bank, Human Resources.

World Bank (2001g) 'Other stories', downloaded from http://www.worldbank.org/ks/k-practice_stories_short.html on 31 May 2002.

World Bank (2001h) 'Technology Framework', hotlink from Gateway home page (http://www.developmentgateway.org) accessed on 21 June 2002.

World Bank (2001i) 'The Development Gateway portal: where worlds of knowledge meet: a concept note', Washington: World Bank.

World Bank (2002a) *Constructing Knowledge Societies: New Challenges for Tertiary Education*, Washington: World Bank.

World Bank (2002b) *Knowledge Bank Vision*, Washington: World Bank.

World Bank (2002c) 'Enhancing the use of knowledge for growth and poverty reduction', Washington: World Bank, unpublished paper.

World Bank (2002d) *Knowledge Sharing*, pamphlet, Washington: World Bank.

World Bank/Harvard (2001) 'World Bank–Harvard team effectiveness study: feedback report', Washington: World Bank, unpublished report.

World Bank Institute (2000) *2000 Annual Report*, Washington: World Bank.

Index

British Petroleum, 113

Zed titles on development, aid and global institutions

Walden Bello, *Deglobalization: New Ideas for Running the World Economy*

Walden Bello, Nicola Bullard and Kamal Malhotra (eds), *Global Finance: New Thinking on Regulating Speculative Capital Markets*

Patrick Bond, *Against Global Apartheid: South Africa Meets the World Bank, IMF and International Finance*

William F. Fisher and Thomas Ponniah (eds), *Another World is Possible: Popular Alternatives to Globalization at the World Social Forum*

Peter Griffiths, *The Economist's Tale: a Consultant Encounters Hunger and the World Bank*

Fatoumata Jawara and Aileen Kwa, *Behind the Scenes at the WTO: the Real World of International Trade Negotiations*

Martin Khor, *Rethinking Globalization: Critical Issues and Policy Choices*

Martin Khor *et al.*, Third World Network, *WTO and the Global Trading System: Development Impacts and Reform Proposals*

John Madeley, *A People's World: Alternatives to Economic Globalization*

Richard Peet, *Unholy Trinity: the IMF, World Bank and WTO*

SAPRIN, *Structural Adjustment: the SAPRI Report*

David Sogge, *Give and Take: What's the Matter with Foreign Aid?*

Bob Sutcliffe, *100 Ways of Seeing an Unequal World*

Teivo Teivainen, *Enter Economism, Exit Politics*

Ian Tellam, *Fuel for Change: World Bank Energy Policy: Rhetoric vs Reality*

Paulo Vizentini and Marianne Wiesebron (eds), *Free Trade for the Americas? The United States' Push for the FTAA Agreement*

David Woodward, *The Next Crisis? Direct and Equity Investment in Developing Countries*

For full details of this list and Zed's general catalogue, please write to: The Marketing Department, Zed Books, 7 Cynthia Street, London N1 9JF, UK or e-mail: sales@zedbooks.demon.co.uk

Visit our website at <http://www.zedbooks.co.uk>